220.6
F22   Farbridge, Maurice.
            Studies in Biblical
       and Semitic symbolism.

220.6
F22   Farbridge, Maurice.
            Studies in Biblical
       and Semitic symbolism.

Temple Israel Library
Minneapolis, Minn.

———

    Please sign your full name on the above card.

    Return books promptly to the Library or Temple Office.

    Fines will be charged for overdue books or for damage or loss of same.

STUDIES IN BIBLICAL AND SEMITIC SYMBOLISM

THE LIBRARY
OF
BIBLICAL STUDIES

Edited by

Harry M. Orlinsky

STUDIES IN BIBLICAL AND SEMITIC SYMBOLISM

BY

MAURICE H. FARBRIDGE, M.A.

Langton Fellow and Faulkner Fellow in Oriental Studies in the Victoria University of Manchester.

PROLEGOMENON BY

HERBERT G. MAY

KTAV PUBLISHING HOUSE, Inc.

NEW YORK

1970

FIRST PUBLISHED 1923

NEW MATTER

© COPYRIGHT 1970

KTAV PUBLISHING HOUSE, INC.

SBN 87068-046-3

LIBRARY OF CONGRESS CATALOG CARD NUMBER: 78-79490

MANUFACTURED IN THE UNITED STATES OF AMERICA

CONTENTS

Need of symbols inwoven with human nature—not
only in the ancient East, but even in Mediaeval
England symbolism permeated the whole life of
the people—various definitions of symbol—the
symbol has often replaced the object it was
originally intended to represent—symbolical
actions preceded human speech—their use by the
Hebrew prophets as a means of attracting
attention or creating an indelible impression on
the mind—Ezekiel's parables—the Hebrew
prophets opposed the making of any visible
representation of the deity because the Semites
identified the god with his image—Goldziher's
method of discovering myths from metaphorical and poetical language—fire as a symbol
in the Old Testament—the modifications of
symbols in the course of their migrations, with
examples.

Reasons for tree-worship and tree-symbolism—
floral symbolism dates back to a time when man
sought to express his love of purity and beauty
through flowers—the flower represented to the
Oriental all the mysterious phenomena connected
with birth reproduction and fecundity—
Hebrews drew inspiration from transient flower
and ephemeral blossom—the sacred tree—to
the Semites the tree was a symbol of the female
principle of nature—tree of life—the Ashera—
horns—the palm represents Astarte, human

sexuality, reward of righteous in temple, the
Jewish state—the olive symbolizes peace—
the vine an emblem of domestic happiness—the
pomegranate symbolizes fertility and life—the
cedar a symbol of height and soundness—the oak
represents strength, protection, fidelity — the
fig an emblem of peace and prosperity—the
lotus symbolizes resurrection—the lily a symbol
of Israel—the almond represents divine forwardness—the myrtle symbolizes joy, peace, tranquillity—the willow a symbol of God's constant
mercies, used to express feelings of joy and
sorrow—wormwood represents moral bitterness.

Representations of natural history in old churches
as object lessons for worshippers—the bestiaries
—primitive man felt a kinship with animals—
animal worship and symbolism—astrological
origin of animal symbolism—forms of animals
determined by sound rather than sight—birds
represent the soul, wings symbolize mind—the
winged figures of Assyrian monuments—bull
symbolism, Maspero and Renan regarded it as
borrowed from Egypt, views of various other
scholars, a symbol of strength in Babylonia and
many other places, and therefore selected by an
agricultural race like the Hebrews to symbolize
their deity—the lion represents sovereignty,
strength, and courage used under figure of
malignant enemy, also Nergal god of burning
sun—the gazelle represents innocent fear,
timidity, and beauty—the snake one of the most
admired and dreaded of animals, poisonous
snakes, representations of a snake with its tail
in its mouth and a disc in many parts of the

CONTENTS

world, an emblem of divine nature in Egypt, Babylonian deities associated with serpent, Tiamat, Rahab, Leviathan, the brazen serpent and power of healing—the horse a symbol of war, winged horses—the ass a symbol of peace-bringing Messiah—the dog represents reproach and humility—the wolf, the unicorn, the leopard, the goat—the dove symbolizes purity and innocence, Holy Spirit, persecuted Israel—the stork a symbol of devoted maternal affection—the raven a bird of ill-omen—the eagle a divine symbol, care for its young, symbol of royalty—the vulture a symbolical bird of prey.

General introduction—some suggest a mathematical foundation for ancient Oriental religions—representative numbering very common amongst Eastern nations—finger method of counting—" five " and " to feel " connected philologically in Hebrew—gematria—everything in life and religion of Babylonia connected with number—gematria amongst Greeks—the Pythagoreans regarded number as a fundamental principle from which the whole objective world proceeds—symbolism of numbers in post-Biblical literature.

Three represents many—frequent occurrence of number amongst Hebrews, Babylonians, Egyptians, Phœnicians, Samaritans, also in Talmud, and Cabbala, Rig-Veda, and rites of Greeks and Romans—the Pythagoreans believed that all and everything is determined through triplicity—number in modern literatures—explanations of Mahler and Wilson—philological considerations.

PROLEGOMENON

I

When Maurice H. Farbridge wrote this volume, he was Langton Fellow and Faulkner Fellow in Oriental Studies in the Victoria University of Manchester. He became interested in this "so important a branch of Biblical and Semitic studies" while he was engaged in the preparation of the article "Symbolism (Semitic)" for Hastings' *Encyclopedia of Religion and Ethics.* He regarded this volume as an introduction to a subject which had hitherto attracted very little attention. This volume itself did not attract the attention it deserved.

In a brief biographical sketch in *The Universal Jewish Encyclopaedia* Farbridge is classified as an educator and author. He was thirty years old when he wrote this study, and in the year following its appearance he delivered a course of lectures in New York at the Jewish Institute of Religion, where he was also acting librarian. In 1927-29 he was Professor of Religion at the University of Iowa, after which he returned to England. His interest in contemporary Judaism is reflected in a number of books: *The Festival Prayer Book,* 1927, prepared for the United Synagogue of America; *Judaism and the Modern Mind,* 1927; *Renewal of Judaism,* 1932. See also *Life—a Symbol,* 1931. Earlier, in 1919, he had written *Industrial Development of Palestine,* based on studies while in the British Foreign Service.

II

Farbridge would no doubt be pleased by the attention given to the subject of biblical symbolism in recent years, not only by historians of religion and psychoanalysts, but also by philosophers and sociologists of religion, by biblical scholars, and by students of the history, religion, culture, and languages of the Near East generally. The bibliographical notations in this Prolegomenon, though more representative than exhaustive, will convince the reader that the study of symbolism no longer attracts little attention. The major bibliographical reference tool for students of symbolism is Manfred Lurker's *Bibliographie zur Symbolkunde,* 1968, with more than 11,000 listings.

The definitions of symbol and symbolism may differ in accordance with the interests of the scholar. Farbridge contents himself with description rather than definition, noting that while its original functions may have been to represent an image, or an idea, or an emotion, the symbol has often ended by replacing the object or idea it was intended to represent. This foreshadows Farbridge's concern with the development of symbolism, to which we shall return in the latter part of this Prolegomenon. For more recent definitions of the nature and function of the religious symbol, see Rollo May, Editor, *Symbolism in Religion and Literature,* 1960;[1] A. N. Whitehead, *Symbolism, Its Meaning and Effect,* 1927 (reissue 1958); and M. Eliade, *Images and Symbols: Studies in Religious Symbolism,* 1961. The symbol is to be compared with—but is not always easily distinguished from—other forms of representative imagery, such as signs and images, or allegory and metaphor, which may have symbolic overtones, sometimes unrecognized. A simple but useful definition is Whitehead's definition of a symbol as something presented to the senses or imagination which stands for something else.[2] It has a figurative quality, carrying non-verbal overtones, often expressing that for which words fail.[3]

The issue of the nature of a symbol is involved in E. R. Goodenough's monumental work, *Jewish Symbols in the Greco-Roman Period,* 1953-69. His concern is symbolism expressed in the art of the period, rather than in its literature. He presents an encyclopaedic collation of Jewish iconic materials, and in the interpretation of them he takes a primary psychological approach.[4] The religious symbol is a thing of power or value, releasing tensions, arousing guilt, or bringing a sense of forgiveness and reconciliation. Its value lies in its power to unify a cluster of ideas, emotions, and drives, and the mythological associations and theological significance given to them are of secondary importance. Pagan symbols could be used in Jewish art because of this fact of emotional impact, which may be different from the interpretation given to the symbol in different periods and cultures. Symbols basically of Dionysiac origin borrowed by the Jews in the art of the Greco-Roman period formed a sort of *lingua franca* among cultures, and had a common denominator of meaning. Such a generalized and seemingly *a priori* meaning of a symbol as this has been questioned. Symbols may have a multiplicity of simultaneous meanings, and when symbols are clearly associated with mythology or are otherwise given verbalized or cultic expression in a culture, they must be interpreted more specifically in these contexts. Symbols may, nevertheless, have a universal validity,[5] and may have a more generalized meaning, and one should beware of interpreting them too narrowly and exclusively in terms of particular myths when they occur apart from the myths. We shall return to this.

The analysis of two main types of symbols, fertility or "life" symbols and aggression or "death" symbols, by Beatrice L. Goff and others, provides a very useful category of interpretation.[6] Scarabs and small images of faience representing Egyptian gods such as Bastet, Bes, Ptah-Sokar, Osiris, or Isis, the House eye, etc., of Egyptian origin, and found in Palestine in both Canaanite and Israelite periods, probably had little or none of their specific Egyptian mythic symbolic significance, and may often have been little more than "life" symbols.[7] Likewise the representation of the palm tree, serpent, and stream in prehistoric Mesopotamian art or on Late Bronze Canaanite painted pottery may have been general "life" symbols.[8] Examples of "death" symbols might be the "dragon" figures on a Chalcolithic fresco at Teleilat Ghassul or the grotesque "monster" figures represented on Chalcolithic ossuaries from Azor. One would not want to be content with such general interpretations when the symbol appears in definite literary contexts, whether in myth, legend, or other forms of literature, for it would be saying little when much more could be said, the much more being perhaps the important thing which could be said.

In this connection Beatrice Goff provides an important classification of stages or levels of symbols; "levels" is the better term, for "stages" suggests chronological development, which is not necessarily involved. The levels are: (1) the symbol is used because it is reassuring, with no explanation of it in words; (2) the symbol is accompanied by a simple explanation; (3) the symbol is accompanied by an elaborate explanation which may take the form of a myth.[9]

III

The myth contains many symbols, or as Rollo May says, the symbols are specific acts or figures, and the myths elaborate these symbols into a story, but both psychologically have the same function.[10] While the story itself is not a symbol, it has symbolic elements.[11] Myth has been described as a carefully chosen cloak for abstract thought, revealing a significant but unverifiable truth.[12] The myth itself has a significance beyond its account of the story involved, which must, like the symbol, be intuitively understood or appreciated. The gods who figure in the myth were not regarded by the ancients as mere symbols, but as realities as well; they did exist. The modern scholar sees them as representational of aspects of reality; the devotees of the gods might make a mythopoeic identification of the deity and the aspects of the natural world which they represented.[13] We may take the action in a myth as itself a mere representation of phenomena in the natural world; e.g., the resurrection of the god representing the revival of nature. But for the ancients who believed that the natural world had a personal aspect and that objects within it possessed power comparable to that of persons (cf. sacred trees, stones, waters, etc., or the seas as the primordial antagonist), the actors and action in the myth *were* the happening in the world of nature, not the cause of it.

Phenomenonologically the essence of a myth is to be seen as the projection of the present order of the world back to the event in the primeval age or to the mythical timeless event. The myth is not just a story, but it, as B. S. Childs states, determinative for the present structure of reality, and this explains the relationship between myth and cult, in which the mythical timeless event is involved at one and the same time in the past and the present.[14] In our sophistication it is difficult for us to understand how the dramatization or recitation of the action of a myth in the ritual could be regarded not merely as a representation but as a re-presentation of the original event depicted in the myth. The ritual recital of the creation epic, the *Enuma Elish*, at the Akitu festival was a re-presentation of the original primordial cosmic conflict. It was not taken as symbolic; it was the happening. The phenomenon of re-presentation appears in the Old Testament, but there it has a historical rather than a mythological context, even though it may use the theme of the myth. In any presentation of biblical symbolism, this aspects of the thought of the biblical world must be taken into consideration.[15] It has been maintained that most of the Ugaritic mythological texts belong to a definite cultic pattern, and can be understood only against the background of the drama that was enacted.[16] All of this points up the fact that the mythical and cultic works were not intended to be mere symbolic representation; it is we, as Kahler says, who derive symbolic meaning from them.[17]

IV

Farbridge mentions Sigmund Freud, C. G. Jung, and Otto H. Rank as adherents of the "Psycho-Analytical School" which was interpreting symbolism along new lines, but he limits his own task to interpreting it from purely Semitic sources. Jung and Freud, whose differences must not be ignored, believed that our minds are rooted in a collective unconscious, and that symbols are involved in a subrational process.[18] Many scholars are dubious about the so-called memory traces of Freud and some of his disciples, and also question Jung's inherited archetypes which are independent of individual experiences and which exist preconsciously.[19] In any case, this is primarily the problem of the psychoanalyst and not of the historian.

The memory traces of Freud's theories are most popularly known through his *Moses and Monotheism*, translated by Katherine Jones (1939, second printing 1955). The work highlights his position that religious phenomena are to be understood on the model of neurotic symptoms of the individual and as a return of long forgotten happenings in the primeval history of the human family. He presumes a common primitive stage of development in which dispossessed older brothers overcame the father and partook of his body in a cannibalistic act. In time a matriarchate developed, and an animal as a substitute for the father was revered as a totem ancestor and killed and eaten at a totem feast. Totemism is thus the worship of a father substitution, and marks the beginning of religion in the history of mankind. Then came human gods whose origin was in the totem which might become a companion of the god. Mother deities reflect another stage in the matriarchate which followed the patriarchate. Monotheism is the religion of the primeval father restored to his historic rites. The Moses story and the origin of Hebrew religion, and therefore much of its symbolism, is traced to this Oedipus Complex born of primordial patricide. Freud presumes that there were two Moses figures, one an Egyptian and the other a Midianite, the former murdered by his people, and the sense of guilt attached to the murder of Moses was the wish fantasy of the Messiah.

One time taken more seriously, this is now recognized as based on anthropological presuppositions palpably false. As we shall see, one can recognize in it a form of schematic hypothetical analysis another form of which Farbridge employs in his explanation of origins, although not with this kind of psychological base. We would not minimize the contribution of depth psychology to the study of symbolism, but Freud's analysis highlights the fact that the problems are not to be solved by depth psychology alone, especially when there are so many data available in the literature of the ancient Near East, and in art forms data are available even for the prehistoric periods.[20] Rollo May, who describes himself as a practicing psychologist, concludes that the individual experiences himself as a self in terms of symbols which arise from three levels at once: (1) from archaic and archetypal depths within himself, (2) from personal events in his psychological and biological experience, and (3) from the general symbols and values which obtain in his culture.[21] It is the last two of these, and particularly the last, which the biblical scholar will find the most fruitful object of his research. The present writer perforce must leave the first to the psychoanalyst.[22]

V

The contemporary emphasis on the phenomenological approach to the study of religion, in this country represented particularly in the writings of M. Eliade, has a significant import for the student of biblical and Near Eastern symbolism; see M. Eliade, *Images and Symbols*, 1961. The "classic" work in this area is perhaps G. Van der Leeuw, *Religion in Essence and Manifestation*, 1938.[23] Eliade takes into consideration biblical data, and it can also be said that frequently students of biblical religion have taken a phenomenological approach without using the term. In the words of E. Jurji, "as regards symbols and rites, phenomenology . . . endeavors to formulate judgements that correspond to the devotee's conception of truth."[24] Phenomenology is concerned with depicting the "essence" of a given religion under study.

Likewise form-critical biblical studies, with their interest in the nature and development of literary forms in their historical life situations, may provide perspective for the study of biblical symbolism, such as number symbolism, or with pronouncements accompanying symbolic action as in cultic situations, or with myths involving significant symbolism.[25] We shall later see how number symbolism may be involved in form criticism. Form criticism has been built upon the pioneering groundwork laid by H. Gunkel (e.g., *Reden und Aufsätze*, 1931).[26] See the presentation by K. Koch, *The Growth of the Biblical Tradition, the Form Critical Method*, translated by S. M. Cupitt, 1969.

Developments in studies of the Israelite cult have illumined understanding of Hebrew religious symbolism, and much of this has been related to form criticism, since the cultic situation often determined the literary form or forms used. Interest in this area was spurred by the publication of S. Mowinckel's *Psalmenstudien II: Das Thronebesteigungsfest Jahwäs und der Ursprung der Eschatologie*, 1922. Of special concern here are the rites and literature associated with the proposed reconstruction of the New Year festival, involving symbolic aspects of the kingship of Yahweh, Israelite kingship, temple arrangements and orientation, and related mythic symbolism found in Hebrew eschatology, in the Psalms, etc.[27] See also the studies of H. Gunkel, Hans Schmidt, J. Morgenstern, and others.[28] Such a festival in Israel, with its parallel in the Babylonian *Akitu* festival, has been regarded by some as a scholar's artificial reconstruction,[29] and some have proposed in its place an annual originally amphictyonic festival of the renewal of the covenant, which involved a considerable amount of the same symbolism.[30] More recently H.-J. Klaus has stressed the primacy of an annual festival on the first day of the feast of booths, celebrating the election of Jerusalem and the Davidic dynasty.[31] There is some validity perhaps in all of these hypotheses, throwing light on the imagery and symbolism of the cult."[32]

Mowinckel's studies gave impetus to the British "Myth and Ritual School," concerned with a pattern of myth and ritual centered in the sacred role of the king and interpreted as part of the common Near Eastern cultural complex. Despite the overstress on similarities and a certain lack of adequate recognition of the distinctive milieu in which the pattern appeared in Israel, many aspects of Old Testament symbolism expressed in Israelite myth and ritual were illumined. This is evident not only in the works of S. H. Hooke and his school, but also in the Scandinavian school under the leadership of I. Engnell, whose interpretations often seemed to read too much into the texts, and who at the same time inspired a great deal of creative scholarship.[33]

VI

The years since the publication of Farbridge's volume have provided extensive new materials for the student of biblical and Near Eastern symbolism. By 1923 the great "golden age" of Near Eastern archaeology between the two world wars had hardly begun. It was not until this period that in Palestinian archaeology a reasonably accurate knowledge of the chronological sequence of pottery and objects was achieved and fairly dependable stratigraphic excavation was employed. Farbridge's conjectures about "the ancient Semitic peoples" often had to be only conjectures. Extensive researches in the development of early cultures have since been made in Egypt, Palestine and Syria, Mesopotamia, Iran, Anatolia, Arabia, and elsewhere. A perusal of E. Anati, *Palestine Before the Hebrews,* 1963, will reveal something of the data significant for a study of symbolism available from prehistoric researches reaching back into the Palaeolithic period. We shall have occasion to refer to Beatrice L. Goff, *Symbols of Prehistoric Mesopotamia,* 1963.

A landmark in the interpretation of Mesopotamian symbolism occurred with the publication of Henri Frankfort's *Cylinder Seals: A Documentary on the Art and Religion of the Ancient Near East,* 1939, republished 1965. The progress made in interpreting Mesopotamian glyptic art is evident when comparing it with W. H. Ward, *Cylinder Seals of Western Asia,* 1910, of which Farbridge makes effective use. The chapter which Farbridge devotes to symbolic representations of the Babylonian-Assyrian pantheon could have served well as an introduction to the subject. A couple of decades later Elizabeth Douglas van Buren in *Symbols of the Gods in Mesopotamian Art,* 1945, collated, classified, and interpreted a mass of data with relevant references to literary sources, producing a classic, basic study of the subject. Earlier, but after Farbridge's work, appeared E. Unger "Göttersymbol," in *Reallexikon der Assyriologie,* IV, 1932-38.[34] Another influential study, Stephen Langdon's *Semitic Mythology* in the series *The Mythology of All Races,* Vol. V, now much outdated both as regards translation and interpretation of relevant texts, did not appear until 1931 (reprinted in 1964).[35] The problems of interpretation of the symbolism of the gods of the Babylonian-Assyrian pantheon are more complex than Farbridge dreamed, and cannot be adequately appreciated apart from Sumerian backgrounds, to which Farbridge paid scant attention. Farbridge makes only passing references to the important deity Tammuz, the Sumerian Dumuzi, the husband of Ishtar, the Sumerian Inanna.[36] Sumerian literature and art are important not only for an appreciation of Mesopotamian symbolism, but for that of a large part of the ancient Near East. See the studies of S. N. Kramer, E. A. Speiser, E. Dhorme, Thorkild Jacobsen, and many others.

One can appreciate something of the plethora of new data available to the student of biblical and Near Eastern symbolism by comparing J. B. Pritchard, Editor, *Ancient Near Eastern Texts Relating to the Old Testament,* 3rd edition, 1969 and *The Ancient Near East in Pictures Relating to the Old Testament,* 2nd edition, 1969,[37] with H. Gressmann, *Orientalische Texte und Bilder zum Alten Testa-*

ment, first published in 1909, or the much expanded second edition which appeared in 1928. Compare also the now seemingly elementary first edition of A. Jeremias, *Das Alte Testament im Licht des Alten Orients,* 1904, with the more extended treatment in the fourth edition of 1930.[38] Much in Pritchard's *Ancient Near East in Pictures* is pertinent for the student of biblical and Near Eastern symbolism, but see especially sections VI, "Gods and Their Emblems," VII, "The Practice of Religion," and VIII, "Myth, Legend, and Ritual on Cylinder Seals." Of import also for the student of symbolism are the Hittite literary and iconographic data, illustrated in the Pritchard volumes, and much of which was unavailable to Farbridge.

The onomastic data from the Egyptian "Execration Texts" of the late twentieth and end of the nineteenth or early eighteenth century, the nineteenth century Cappadocian tablets from Kültepe, the tablets from the eighteenth-century palace archives of the Amorite city of Mari, the Nuzi texts of the fifteenth-fourteenth centuries, the tablets of the same date and the King Idrimi inscription from Alalakh, the Amarna letters, and the Ugaritic materials which illuminate the Canaanite religion and culture of the early fourteenth century provide knowledge of the backgrounds of the patriarchal period pertinent for understanding the religion and therefore the religious symbolism of the patriarchs. Early researches in this area are much indebted to A. Alt's study of the God of the Fathers.[39]

VII

A major advance in the interpretation of the sources and nature of biblical symbolism, particularly as reflected in the cult and literature of Israel and especially in the imagery of its poetry and its eschatology, has been made possible as a result of the recovery of primary literary materials from Canaanite and related cultures. Chief among these are the Ugaritic texts, the first of which were published a little less than a decade after Farbridge wrote. The comparative paucity of data on the basis of which scholars sometimes drew far-reaching and dubious conclusions before the availability of these newer data can now be appreciated. One cannot begin to list here the subsequent studies relevant for the student of biblical symbolism by such scholars as W. F. Albright, G. R. Driver, H. L. Ginsberg, O. Eissfeldt, R. Dussand, T. H. Gaster, Cyrus Gordon, John Gray, Marvin Pope, A. S. Kapelrud, or A. Jirku, to mention rather haphazardly but a few.

Through the Ugaritic texts one can understand something of the nature of Canaanite religious imagery and symbolism phenomenologically, from the inside, as it appeared to the Canaanites themselves, in contrast with the Old Testament presentation of Canaanite religion, which from the viewpoint of its monotheistic insight was pagan and a threat. Common elements in Canaanite and Israelite religious symbolism may be recognized, as well as plausible influences of Canaanite myth and ritual, despite the fact that mythology as such was excluded from normative Israelite religion in the Mosaic tradition as recognized by prophets, priests, and scribes. This did not exclude the use of meaningful Canaanite mythological imagery and symbolism, particularly in cultic and prophetic poetry.[40]

Discussion of the Ugaritic pantheon and its associated symbolism belongs as properly in any treatment of biblical symbolism as a discussion of symbolical representations of the Assyrian and Babylonian pantheon belonged in Farbridge's book. As Albright has pointed out, the pantheon of the epic myths at Ugarit was not localized, in contrast with the divinities of the city in the official pantheon and in sacrificial lists.[41] The gods appear in the epic myth as cosmic rather than local deities, and it is really the imagery and symbolism of the cosmic myths which find their reflection in Old Testament poetry. Such cosmic symbolism and imagery was more easily adopted because of their universalistic character. This can be illustrated in the Old Testament theme of the conflict of Yahweh and the waters, which finds its parallel in the Ugaritic myth of the struggle of Baal and the waters (Sea and River).[42] See also the slaying of Lotan (the Leviathan). In the Israelite literature the theme may be seen not as the re-presentation of an event in the world of nature, but as a primordial event re-presented in past or future events in the drama of salvation history, and the theme may be said to symbolize a cosmic reference in those events, such as the crossing of the Red

Sea, the return from Exile, or the defeat of Israel's enemies in the past or the future, illustrated in Exod. 15, Isa. 51:9-11, Hab. 3, etc. T. H. Gaster comments that words connote as well as denote, and that it is important to get behind the symbol to the thing it seeks.[43] So also the *action* of a myth or a mythological theme may connote as well as denote. When we appreciate phenomenologically the significance of mythological imagery and themes in Canaanite myth, our appreciation of the symbolic reference of similar themes and imagery in the Old Testament may be enhanced.[44]

We cannot here deal with the symbolism of the imagery associated with the deities in the Cannanite pantheon. Even when the imagery may appear to be simply metaphoric it may have a symbolic significance. Thus in the myth of the struggle of the storm-god Baal with the waters, Kothar invokes the *clubs* of Baal and proclaims their names and says:

Thou shalt swoop down in the hands of Baal,
Like an eagle with its talons [or, in his fingers].

Gaster notes that there is more than meets the eye here, for in comparative mythology the eagle is the storm bird and the bearer of the lightning and thunderbolt.[45] The language of myth tends to be replete with symbolic reference.

The Old Testament prophets and poets were not necessarily consciously borrowing from pagan sources such motifs and symbols. These had often become a part of the matrix of Israelite religion, integrated into the religious language of Israel. They took from the depths of Israelite culture themes and symbols which had once had a mythological setting, and which among their neighbors sometimes still had it. The theme of Yahweh's struggle with the seven-headed serpent dragon, the Leviathan/Rahab, and Yahweh's victory over the rebellious waters were integral to the religious imagery of Israel, and may indeed have been so before the days of Moses. The theme of Yahweh's victory over the enemy in the *Endzeit* was mythopoeicly identified with his primordial victory in the *Urzeit* (e.g., Isa. 27:1; 51:9-11), without raising the modern question of literalness. The writers used intuitively the symbolic language of their day. Farbridge raises an unnecessary issue in denying support for the theories of Gunkel, Zimmern, and others that traces of the myth of the Marduk-

Tiamat conflict can be found in names like Leviathan, Behemoth, and Rahab, or that the story had a parallel among the Hebrews (pp. 74–75). For Farbridge, Behemoth in Job 40:15 and Leviathan in 40:25 (Eng. 41:1) are nothing more than the hippopotamus and crocodile. The mythic language used in the description of the Leviathan in Job 40 is today more easily recognized. Farbridge makes no reference to Isa. 51:9–11, and could not know that much of the very terminology used of the Leviathan in Isa. 27:1 would appear in Canaanite literature. He rightly, however, criticizes certain hypotheses which explain origins of verbal images and symbols as borrowings without having passed through the same historical and religious experiences (pp. 18-19).

VIII

The general archaeological data from Palestine and neighboring regions, much larger and more accurately dateable than in 1923, are a rich store of source materials for the student of religious symbolism. The iconographic and other materials from Ugarit, including reliefs, ivories, images, and various other objects, provide art representations of Canaanite symbols. Trees, lions, stags, goats, bulls, doves, stars, serpents, fish, streams, etc., on Late Bronze period painted pottery to which we have already referred frequently may have had a symbolic significance, judging in part from their appearance in religious contexts,[46] even though their symbolic significance may not have been verbalized and though they were at the same time decorative art. Mesolithic sculptured sickle hafts, a basalt pestle with phallic-shaped handle, and an erotic stone figurine recalling scenes on prehistoric Mesopotamian cylinder seals, Neolithic pebble figurines and plastered skulls, Chalcolithic "house" urns and animal-like urns or ossuaries with relief and painted decorations and wall frescoes at Teleilat Ghassul, and prehistoric rock carvings from the Negeb are a part of the early data available from Palestine.[47] Figurines come from many periods.[48] Ivory inlays not only from Ugarit, but from Megiddo, Hazor, Samaria, and elsewhere furnish other data.[49] Faience figurines and scarabs have already been mentioned. Decorative hieroglyphs on scarabs may have added to their efficacy as "life" symbols. Motifs on scarabs and seals include a variety of symbols: e.g., the winged scarab and winged scroll or crested bird or winged sun-disk on the royal jar-handle seals of the late Hebrew monarchy; the ram with winged scarab (?) on a seal of Jotham found at Ezion-geber; the lion on the seal of Shema, official of Jeroboam, from Megiddo; griffin, locust, winged sphinx, winged serpent, and fighting cock on other seals.[50] Some of these may have had specific royal symbolism, to judge from their contexts, e.g., the winged scarab and winged sun-disk which in Egypt have both solar and royal associations (see below, note 86).

Sanctuary arrangements and temple plans and paraphernalia are increasingly illustrated archaeologically and illuminate the religious arts and symbolism of both Canaanites and Hebrews. The varied forms and decoration of cultic (incense?) stands and altars reveal a complex symbolism deserving special study.[51] Temple structures and furnishings have been excavated at Beth-shan, Hazor, Megiddo, Shechem, Jericho, Lachish, Nahariyeh, Arad, and elsewhere.[52] The *bâmâh* or "high-place" of the Old Testament may be identified archaeologically as the large cairn-like stone heaps or altars, some-times associated with temple structures, such as the one from Inter-mediate-Bronze Age Megiddo associated with three broad-room buildings. The *bâmâh* may possibly be associated with veneration of ancestors.[53] Perhaps it also had some cosmic mountain symbolism. Such symbolism is most probable in the case of the great altar of burnt offering before the Jerusalem temple, whose hearth was "the mountain of God" (*har'ēl*) and whose base was "the bosom of the earth."[54] The *maṣṣēbôth,* standing stones or cultic pillars, at ex-cavated sanctuaries at Gebal, Bab edh-Dhra', Gezer, Hazor, Lachish, and elsewhere may often have had a memorial symbolism. There is possibly some link between the *maṣṣēbâh* and the inscribed memorial stela.[55]

The arrangements of the Solomonic temple in 1 Ki. 6-7 (cf. Ezek. 40-42) have numerous analogies in excavated temples, includ-ing the tripartite plan with its elevated inner sanctum, the altar be-fore the inner sanctum, the two pillars before the temple, etc. The temple was the palace of the deity and its inner sanctum his throne room. The symbolism, form, and use of the Jachin and Boaz pillars

(Farbridge pp. 259-60) can now be more plausibly interpreted.[56] The symbolism of the pillars may have been both royal and cosmic. Two pillars were found before the temple of Baal-berith at Shechem, and also at a Late Bronze temple at Hazor and a Kenite (?) Yahweh temple at Arad, as well as elsewhere. The lily-work, cherub, palm-tree, opening flower, pomegranate, and other decorative motifs can be archaeologically illustrated. The "lily-work," perhaps a "life" symbol, decorating the pillars and the Sea of Bronze, is the lotus motif, common in Syro-Phoenician art and having its origin in Egypt. The "opening flowers" ("garlands of flowers"?) may be rosettes or the lotus chain design.[57]

The cherubim had their Egyptian, Canaanite, Hittite, and Mesopotamian analogies. They may be related to and at times the equivalent of the winged sphinx, a human-headed, winged, lion-bodied creature, frequently represented in Canaanite-Phoenician iconographic art, although M. Haran rightly maintains that their form was not fixed in every detail, but within limits was subject to change. Their symbolic significance, evident in their form and in their literary and art contexts, is complex; they are associated with royal, solar, war, and storm attributes of deity and with Yahweh's theophanic glory. Their import is highlighted by their connection with the ark and throne of Yahweh, their appearance as massive statues in the Holy of Holies of the temple, and their association with the Garden of Eden. For the latter see not only Gen. 3:24 but also Ezek. 28:14,16. Some close connection exists between the representation of Canaanite-Phoenician kings on a cherub throne, as on a twelfth-century Megiddo ivory and the tenth-century sarcophagus of Ahiram of Gebal, and the deity enthroned on the cherubim in I Sam. 4:4, etc., and the throne chariot of Yahweh in Ezekiel. Farbridge thinks it hardly credible that the Hebrews, whose religion forbade them to construct an image of anything in the heavens above and the earth beneath, should have borrowed from an alien source a representation of a living creature and have used it in constructing their tabernacle and temple (pp. 264-266). As in the case of mythological motifs, there may often not have been any conscious borrowing of such symbolic art from alien sources. Israel may have considered these representations as a part of the Yahweh cult, although they were probably equally familiar to both Solomon's builders and to the builders of Hiram, king of Tyre, who assisted Solomon, and to the bronze worker Hiram, son of a Tyrian father and Naphtalite mother. The source of the symbolism is of special interest because comparative studies may assist in understanding the import of the symbolism.[58]

The function and symbolism of the ark and tabernacle, only briefly touched upon by Farbridge (pp. 259-261) has been illuminated by the studies of H. Gressmann, R. Hartmann, and others by comparison with Arab nomadic tent shrines, the *qubba, mahmal,* and *'utfa,* and more recently particularly by J. Morgenstern.[59] The specific relationship of the historic tabernacle or ark to these institutions is unclear. Farbridge may be right that the Old Testament makes not the slightest reference to any symbolic meaning of the tabernacle, but it is by implication pregnant with symbolic associations. Farbridge does note that its Hebrew designation, *miškān,* "dwelling," expressed the idea that God dwelt among his people, and that *'ōhel mô'ēd,* "tent of meeting," had reference to the fact that God met his people there. More may be involved in both terms. It has been plausibly deduced (Frank M. Cross) from Ugaritic evidence and the Balaam oracles that the term *miškān* originally meant "tent," later to become a poetic word for "tent," and was used by P to refer to the tent *par excellence,* the tabernacle, and later used in figurative references to the temple. Its root, *škn,* in the early sources meant "to encamp, to tent," and P uses it of the tenting or tabernacling of the earthly presence of Yahweh, to express his immanence, while Yahweh "dwelt" (*yšb*) in the heavens, an expression of his transcendence. This suggests something of the symbolism of the tent in relation to the presence of the deity. It is further suggested that *'ōhel mô'ēd* perhaps means "tent of assembly," and originally referred to the amphictyonic aspects of the tent; compare the meaning and context of *mô'ēd* in Isa. 14:13, in the Ugaritic texts, and in the Egyptian tale of Wenamon.[60] The representation of the tabernacle in the pentateuchal sources is variously presented. In the Yahwist (?) source in Exod. 33:7-11 the *'ōhel mô'ēd* is outside the camp, but the priestly source places the tabernacle in the center of the encampment (Num. 2), as the symbol of the institution of the temple, its description there possibly reflecting the historic sacred tent at Jerusalem at the time of David. It has been conjectured by M. Haran that in the J and E sources there are two tents, one in the center of the camp, an embryo of the house of God and containing the ark, and the other outside the camp, a symbol of the Sinai revelation, the two tents being respectively a hiding place for the godhead and from the godhead.[61]

The relationship of the tabernacle and ark is also a matter of controversy. The priestly representation of the ark as a part of the desert tent sanctuary has been regarded by some scholars as a secondary association, the latter institution being primarily of the desert, and the former an institution of the settled agricultural community.[62] The ark, like the sacred tent, may have served as and had the symbolism of a portable shrine, and the present writer has suggested that there is profitable comparison with the symbolism of the small portable cherub-decorated incense altars in the form of miniature shrines found in excavations, recognizing that there is quite variant material construction and primary function.[63] The ark's association with the institution of warfare and with Yahweh of Armies ([of Israel], "the LORD of Hosts"), its position in the throne-room of Yahweh's temple-palace, its association with the theophanic manifestation of the $K^e v \hat{o} d \ Yahweh$ ("Glory of Yahweh") and analogies with Ezekiel's cherubim throne-chariot in which solar and storm symbolism intermingle suggest something of its rich symbolism. The substance of the primary symbolism of both ark and tabernacle may perhaps be summed up in a category of symbolism which has many manifestations and which is peculiarly evident in the ark, i.e., the notion of the potent presence of the deity, which has been analysed into three aspects by B. A. Levine: (1) the alternatives of presence and absence, (2) the alternatives of presence, absence, and impotence, and (3) the alternatives of exercized and unexercized potency.[64]

IX

There have been significant researches into the symbolism of the Jewish art of the Greco-Roman period. The studies of E. R. Goodenough in this area have already been mentioned. His data are largely the product of archaeological research, for his sources include Jewish tombs, ossuaries, sarcophagi, catacombs, synagogues, amulets, lamps, coins, etc. Farbridge had collated considerable comparative material from the later periods, largely literary data, from Samaritan, Midrashic, Talmudic, Cabbalistic, Greek, Islamic, and Indic sources, but Goodenough's researches dealt with data from a different area of culture, Jewish art, and with much which would not have been available to Farbridge. This is especially true of Greco-Roman and Byzantine synagogue art. The extent of the existence of synagogue art in the Greco-Roman period comes somewhat unexpectedly, although it is being increasingly recognized that art played a not inconsiderable role throughout most of the life of ancient Israel.

At the time Farbridge was working on his volume, H. Kohl and C. Watzinger's *Antike Synagogen in Galilae* (1916) had appeared, but S. Krauss's. *Synagogale Alterümer* (1922) may not have been available to him. In any case, this was not an area in which Farbridge had special interest. The survey of synagogue archaeology, architecture, art, and symbolism of Roman-Byzantine period synagogues by E. L. Sukenik, *Ancient Synagogues in Palestine and Greece,* appeared in 1934. It was preceded, in 1932, by Sukenik's publication of the Byzantine synagogue with its remarkable mosaics at Beth-Alpha at the foot of Mt. Gilboa.[65] Perhaps most remarkable is the mid-third-century A.D. synagogue at Dura-Europos on the Euphrates, with its elaborate frescoes depicting Old Testament themes. The symbolic significance of the particular scenes selected for presentation and of other aspects of the Dura synagogue decoration, including zodiac signs, fruits, flower, and bird designs on the ceiling tiles, is a matter of no inconsiderable controversy.[66] Compare also a certain few biblical scenes represented in Byzantine-period mosaic art, particularly the story of the sacrifice of Isaac.

Although much of synagogue symbolism is rooted in Judaism and especially in the Old Testament, numerous elements of symbolism reflected in the decorative art of the synagogue are drawn from pagan sources, illustrated in the Beth-Alpha mosaics by the symbols of the four seasons, the twelve signs of the zodiac, and the Quadrig and Helios (the four-horse-drawn chariot with the sun-god figure as the driver). A parallel to the Zodiac and Quadrig appears on a Roman mosaic now in the museum at Bonn, Germany. At the Dura synagogue an apparent Orpheus figure, identified by Kraeling and Wischnitzer with David,[67] appears in a Phrygian cap playing to rampant lions (?), recalling the flocks and trees responding to David's lyre, suggesting likewise an Orpheus symbolism, in the version of the 151st psalm as it is found in the Qumran Psalm Scroll. In the later form of the psalm in the LXX, the Orphic elements have been excised.[68]

Goodenough surmounts the problem of borrowing by insisting that the "value" of a symbol lies in its psychological and emotional impact, and that motifs were borrowed because they did not carry a literal meaning. Their values, not their meaning, were appropriated. By contrast Morton Smith, referring to a text copied in Rabbinic circles in which there are prescriptions for making images and prayers to pagan deities, including Helios, suggests that the Helios on synagogue floors may have represented a major deity to whom prayers were addressed for practical purposes.[69]

In any discussion of biblical symbolism today the rich data from the Qumran Scrolls would have to be evaluated. Much here might be more immediately pertinent than the Talmudic references cited by Farbridge. This is a subject obviously beyond the scope of this presentation.

X

Before presenting a critique of selected illustrations of Farbridge's approach to his subject, a word may be said about general procedures in the study of religious symbolism. Farbridge, like ourselves, was a child of his times. His approach was representative of the comparative religion and history of religion studies of his day. His treatment of comparative materials recalls that of J. G. Frazer, the third edition of whose seven-volume work, *The Golden Bough,* came out in 1911-1918. Farbridge ranges widely in his search of parallels, including a few illustrations from the American Indians, although most of them come from Near East related cultures. Like Frazer, Farbridge was interested in primitive religious practice and belief and in evolutionary development from early stages of belief. He makes considerable use of W. Robertson Smith's *Religion of the Semites,* 1889, 2nd ed., 1894 (3rd ed., reissued by KTAV, with a Prolegomenon by J. M. Muilenburg, 1970), to whose anthropological school Frazer belonged. Insofar as comparative religion studies illuminate patterns of thought and variant modes of expression of similar concepts, much may be learned from them, particularly if one keeps in mind the fact that similar symbols or modes of expression may have variant meanings.[70] A wide knowledge of variant contexts and meanings of symbols should be a deterrent against simplistic explanations of their development.

Data for the study of the origin and development of symbols should be taken primarily from the periods and cultural areas more immediately involved. Conjectures derived from presumed primitive psychological behavior and from comparative data from outside the cultural area involved should be recognized for what they are. It is also easy to impose unwittingly on the data one's own philosophy of history which can overly influence the conclusions which are drawn. It is thus easy from today's perspective to see how the early study by K. C. W. Bähr, *Symbolik des mosaischen Cultus,* 1837, reflected the Hegelian idealistic philosophy of history and the theme of development of the time.[71] Similarly, looking back, one can evaluate the stance of Farbridge toward the development of biblical symbolism.

It is now axiomatic that one cannot presume that religion has grown from a primitive animism or polydemonism to henotheism to culminate in monotheism, in nicely graded stages. The magnificent Upper Paleolithic paintings in France's famed Lascaux cave when compared with some aspects of modern art belie theories of gradualism and straight-line development. Albright has long protested against the arrangement of Israelite data in accord with the evolutionary philosophies of Hegel or the English Positivists, most evident in the work of Wellhausen, Robertson Smith, and their followers.[72]

To avoid the pitfalls commonly found in research in art symbols which concentrates on separate symbols and traces their use through cultures of different time and space, Beatrice L. Goff stresses the study of dominant forms of a given period, utilizing the greatest

care in drawing inferences about earlier periods from a knowledge
of later periods.[73] She is, for instance, properly hesitant in using
later Sumero-Akkadian mythological texts in interpreting the symbolism of prehistoric Mesopotamian art forms, particularly in view
of the fact that, in her opinion, the evidence for the development of
the typical Sumerian mythological and epic themes before the
middle or late third millenium is not conclusive, and one has no
clear witness of a long oral development before the written myths
and epics appear. A parallel from Palestinian data would be found
in the strong temptation to interpret the sun, several dragon-like
figures, a human figure, and several masks which appear on a Chalcolithic Ghassulian fresco narrowly in terms of the annual dramatization of the defeat of the dragons of chaos by the god of the sun.
So also it would be unwise to interpret an erotic Mesolithic figurine
from 'Ain Sakri definitely in terms of the *hieros gamos* rite, the
ritual of the sacred marriage.[74] As Frankfort states in his study of
cylinder seals, neither scene nor symbol can be interpreted irrespec-
tive of the age to which it belongs.

There has been large influence of Mesopotamia on the rest of the
ancient Near East. There are also many common elements of culture
in the Near East, because no part of it lived in isolation from the
rest of it.[75] These two factors have relevance in interpreting the
symbolism of any part of the ancient Near East, but both can be
overstressed, as one must confess was done to an extent by the
Myth and Ritual School. Even within the boundaries of the ancient
Near East one can fall into the errors of the older comparative religion approach which tended to stress similarities rather than differences or presume identities on the basis of suggestive analogies.
One can go to the other extreme and be blind to the probable
import of parallels in terminology and motifs.

XI

Significantly, Farbridge's first chapter is devoted to an account
of the development of biblical and Semitic symbolism. Much elsewhere in the volume falls within this same classification. In keeping
with the contemporary scholarship, Farbridge presumed an evolu-

tionary development from the primitive to the more complex, and
the primitive is often that which on psychological grounds, by an-
ology with general human behavior, it seems as though it should
have been. Farbridge presumes that "in the simpler stages of society" man can be taught general truths only by symbols and parables. The necessity for symbolic actions arose as a means of accompanying and supplementing speech, and "scholars are agreed"
that from the very earliest times the audible word has been accompanied by the visible gesture, and in many cases symbolic actions really preceded human speech. This may be true, for animals
perform symbolic actions, but it must be recognized that this is
not something for which direct evidence from "ancient man" can
be cited. The course of development is presumed on psychological
grounds when Farbridge traces the origin of symbolic actions in
covenant ceremonies, affirming that it was "absolutely necessary"
that a verbal agreement should be accompanied by a symbol, for if
the covenant had been mere words it would have been "altogether
worthless," for words easily pass out of memory. "So there arose
amongst all peoples [sic!] various ceremonies which formed a part
of taking an oath or making a covenant." Thus in business transactions there arose the custom of drawing off a shoe in transferring
a possession (Ruth 4:7), showing that there was transferred from
one person to another a sacred obligation; then when the art of
writing became more common in Israel, this practice fell out of
usage, and instead duplicate copies of a document were signed by
witnesses (pp. 7-9).

The chronological sequence of the abandonment of the shoe
symbol with the increased use of writing is dubious, for comparable
symbolic actions are evident at Nuzi, where writing was most common. The shoe transfer was not an aid to memory, but a form of
token payment for which there are analogies in the Nuzi texts, for
which other objects could be used, or might validate a transaction
by circumventing legal obstacles, indicating abandonment of a
right.[76] In Amos 2:6 the symbol is a token payment used to legal-
ize an extortion; compare Sirach 46:19. Although there is no evidence that the custom of using a shoe symbol fell out of practice
at the time when writing became more common, oral contracts

were doubtless proportionately more common in the earlier period. Covenant and business practices of antiquity can be better documented today than when Farbridge wrote, and the import of the oath in treaties and contracts is more clearly understood. Farbridge's concern in this problem is paralleled in today's interest in form critical studies of treaties and covenants in the ancient Near East. See the researches of G. E. Mendenhall, D. R. Hillars, D. J. McCarthy, and others in this area.[77]

In the words of M. R. Lehman, the legally binding oath also "was trapped in symbolic act" to drive home a message of warning and foreboding, emphasizing the significance of the curses to which the parties were subjected. The symbolic act might include the slaughtering of one or more animals, and a common meal in which the parties might be thought to be physically joined together by eating the same food. It has also been suggested that the killing of the animal or animals was taken as invoking a similar fate on the one who broke the covenant. In an Assyrian treaty seven lambs, seven horses, etc., were slain; compare the slaughter of seven ewe lambs at the covenant and oath between Abraham and Abimelech in Gen. 21:25-31; cf. Gen. 15:7-12. At Mari the rite included the slaughter of an ass. See Lehman, *ZAW*, LXXXI (1969), pp. 74 ff. Jer. 34:32 invokes the fate of the animal on the transgressors of the covenant. The making of a covenant or deposit of a contract or covenant at the sanctuary also guaranteed the fulfillment of the oaths and curses which would come upon him who broke the covenant. Farbridge notes important Babylonian parallels.[78]

In a related discussion of prophetic symbolic actions accompanying oracles, Farbridge thinks of them "as a means of attracting attention and impressing their teachings upon the mind of observers," and he is primarily concerned with the question whether they were actually performed or were merely conceived as symbolic visions in the mind of the prophets (pp. 10-12). The dramatic action oracles of the prophets raise many questions, and one of the best recent discussions is G. Fohrer, *Die symbolischen Handlungen der Propheten*, revised edition, 1968.[79] There is more involved than attracting attention and impressing the minds of the observers, even as the words of the prophet were something more than words spoken to be heard. The prophetic word as the word of God had a power of its own (Isa. 55:10, 11; Jer. 5:14). So the symbolic action had a power not to be minimized. Dramatic action oracles must be viewed agaist the whole background of symbolic actions which often had a magical import, particularly in mimetic magic. In the breaking of the bowls on which the names of hostile peoples had been written (the Middle Kingdom Execration Texts, noted above in §VI), there was thought to be a coalescence of the symbol and the thing it stands for; the breaking of the bowls and destruction of the names did real harm to the enemies of Egypt.[80]

The dramatization of the word in symbolic act was an extension of the word. It has been suggested that the dramatized word even more than the spoken word was deemed charged with the power of performance. It may be that the description of a dramatic action ordered by Yahweh, or a mimic of it, could have much the force of an actual detailed dramatization, for a few dramatic action oracles are difficult to imagine being completely carried out (e.g., Ezek. 4:4-8), although we must not underestimate the extent to which the prophet might go. A prophetic symbolic action may be either simply illustrative or predictive; compare Jeremiah wearing the yoke in Jer. 28, or setting the wine before the Rechabites in Jer. 35, with the breaking of the flask in Jer. 19, or Ezekiel going forth with the baggage of an exile through the hole in the wall of his house in Ezek. 12 ("Say, 'I am a sign for you; as I have done, so shall it be done to them.' "). Compare also Ezek. 4:1-4. The prophet was not trying to manipulate God for his own ends, and he was not performing magic, but the sign was no empty sign; the predictive act concerned a predetermined action of God, not one initiated by the prophet. The sign *('ôth)* had something of the aspect of an omen. The import of the predictive dramatic action oracle of the prophet also cannot be adequately understood apart from an appreciation of the contemporary conception of the nature of the prophet, whose word of judgement *was* the word of God, and who had access to the heavenly courts (Jer. 23:18).[81]

XII

Farbridge's explanation of the origin and development of symbolical representations of deities is essentially psychological (pp. 12-16). At a "very early stage" man began to associate animal or human features with various objects of nature. When he made a carved image to represent his deity, it was at first regarded as a sign or representative, and then it came to be regarded as a living being possessed of energy and animation. (How do we know this? Why not the reverse process?). It became not a mere symbol, but was actually the god himself, localized and present in the image. A more adequate explanation than this is that there was a mythopoeic identification of the god and the image, such mythopoeic identifications being a common phenomenon in the ancient Near East, as when the earthly and heavenly temple might thus be regarded as one. Another way to describe it would be that the image acted for and as the god whenever the worshipper addressed himself to the image; it became the god for working purposes, as John Wilson has suggested.[82] No sharp distinction was made between the god and the image, although the godhead was not limitedly localized or limitedly manifest in a particular image. Baal, manifest in or as his image, was still Prince Lord (Baal) of Earth (Ugaritic *zbl b'l arṣ;* cf. Baal-zebul, "Baal-Prince), or Baal-saphon, who dwelt on the mountain of the gods in the recess of the North (=Saphon). The god was not absolutely identified with his image among the neighbors of Israel (p. 15), if we mean by this limitedly identified with his image. Farbridge, by implication, would recognize this elsewhere. We must not minimize the cosmic aspect of the god, i.e., his representation of some important aspect of the world of nature. In this sense also the image was but one way of representing the deity, although prophetic caricature might depict the image as the totality of godhead as viewed by the pagans (e.g., Isa. 44:17; 46:1-7). In Mesopotamia the deity might be manifest in his image in his temple, but the divine presence might also be indicated by sacred symbols *(šurinnu),* representing cosmic phenomena (sun-disk, crescent, etc.) or in the form of weapons, imple-

ments, etc., which could be used on standards or be set on bases
and could represent the deity inside and outside the sanctuary.[83]
Of course the relationship of the deity to the image was not clearly
articulated or a consistent, theologically clarified concept.[84] There
must also have been some relationship between the deity as conceived in the local pantheon (see above, §VII) and as found in the
great epic myths.

Farbridge seems to presume a development from animal deities
to deities in human form. He affirms that animal symbolism may be
traced back to the dawn of history. It can actually be traced back
earlier, as can anthropomorphic symbolism, if certain prehistoric
art forms are symbolic. Farbridge notes that in man's primitive stage
there was no demarkation between man and beast, and man "next"
began to develop a reverence for animals; belief in the mystic
powers of the animal kingdom resulted in zoolotry, and it was in
the East, and especially in Egypt, that animal worship became
popular.[85] Animal figurines found in tombs and private houses in
Palestinian excavations "and all the evidence" seem to show that
originally in early Palestine the gods were regarded as being of
animal form, according to Farbridge. There is in actuality no concrete evidence that early figurines of animals thus discovered were
worshipped as deities, and animal figurines do not seem to appear
earlier than human figurines.

"At a later time," continues Farbridge, as man's conception of
his god developed, there arose a tendency to represent his deity as
possessed of some kind of human form. One must recognize that
when Farbridge wrote, relatively little progress had been made in
archaeological chronology. His "important law in symbolism" (p.
57), is consonant with his developmental theories, but not a satisfactory explanation of many of the composite figures in the Near
East. Also, while it is true that many of the deities had animal symbolism associated with them, the "fly-god" Baal-zebub of Ekron
(2 Ki. 1:2-18) and the "fish-god" Dagon of Ashkelon (p. 56; more
properly Ashdod [1 Sam. 5:2-7] or Gaza [Judg. 16:23]) would
not today be taken as evidence (p. 56), for the god of Ekron was
most likely Baal-zebul (cf. Ugaritic *zbl b'l ars,* "Prince Lord of
Earth") deliberately perhaps corrupted to Baal-zebub,[86] and Dagon

is the well-established grain-god, Dagan, in the Canaanite pantheon. Our more complete data make it impossible to assume in Canaanite, Egyptian, or Mesopotamian culture a primitive stage of animal worship. Farbridge seems to imply that Babylonian animal symbolism is to be traced back to the grinding and groaning produced by the heavy temple doors as they were being shut and opened, these noises suggesting the cries of animals which were kept to guard the gateways, and afterwards the animals were associated not merely with the gateways, but with the temples themselves (pp. 58, 59). This is a broad conclusion to draw from one of the several metaphors found in the Gudea Cylinder A inscription.[87] The suggestion (p. 59) that Ps. 11:1 may reflect the representation of the soul as a bird, as in Egypt, is based on a dubious translation and interpretation; "soul," *nephesh,* is here, as often elsewhere, the self, and best translated "me": "How can you say to me, 'Flee like a bird to the mountains?' " If there is a reflection of the figure of the winged soul or the soul as a bird in the Old Testament, it may be in Ps. 90:10; but if so, it is obscured even there.[88]

In a relatively long discussion of the bull image in Israel (pp. 61-69), Farbridge properly rejects theories that it was borrowed from Egypt. He is also cautious about any influence here from Canaanite sources, although he does not deny the possibility of the appropriation of the symbol. For him the simplest explanation is that after the Exodus and in the days of Jeroboam I there was an attempt to introduce a symbolical representation of Yahweh, and being an agricultural people, the Israelites selected the bull which was regarded as a symbol of strength. Farbridge is generally overly cautious about pagan influence on Israel's religious practices and beliefs. Obvious parallelism with the representation of Yahweh as God of the storm is found in Canaanite imagery: Baal is the "rider on the clouds" (*rkb 'rpt*), as is Yahweh in Ps. 68:4(5) (*rkb b'rbwt*); cf. Deut. 33:26; Ps. 18:11(10). The close associations of the storm-god with the bull in Canaanite, Syro-Phoenician, and Anatolian imagery suggest that something more is involved than is found in Farbridge's explanation, although he is on the right track in insisting on the symbolic aspects of Israel's bull imagery. In an episode in the Ugaritic myth Baal appears as a bull and Anat as a cow, and the latter bears Baal a bull. El is designated as *ṭr il,* Bull-El, and Baal and El appear with a horned headdress.[89] In Syro-Phoenician, Anatolian, and Mesopotamian art the storm god or his symbol may appear standing on the back of a bull,[90] which becomes the pedestal or throne for the deity. It has been suggested that in a somewhat similar way Yahweh was regarded as enthroned above the cherub-decorated ark in the Jerusalem temple, the ark of "Yahweh of Hosts who is enthroned above the cherubim" (1 Sam. 4:4, etc.). Yet there was much difference, for the bull in this position had Canaanitish fertility associations abhorrent to Judah and to Israel's prophet Hosea.[91] It is not surprising that eventually the bulls (oxen) beneath the Sea of Bronze in the Jerusalem temple were removed (2 Ki. 16:17), although being many they could not have been associated so closely with the person of Yahweh. Their arrangement and function, three facing each corner of the earth and supporting the Sea of Bronze which had perhaps some association with the primordial waters, suggest cosmic connotations. Farbridge curiously confuses the animals beneath the Sea of Bronze with the lions, oxen, and cherubim which decorated the panels of the ten stands of bronze and served as supports for lavers (p. 69; 1 Ki. 7:25, 29). As far as the biblical writers are concerned, the symbolism was not articulated. We note that Farbridge also takes the unicorn in the Old Testament as a symbol of strength (pp. 45, 47), but this mythological animal does not appear in the Old Testament or in the ancient Near East; the *re'ēm* in Num. 23:22; Deut. 23:22; Deut. 33:13, 17 is the wild ox.[92]

XIII

Farbridge's concern for tracing origins and development of symbols in accord with the scholarly concern of his day, often resulting in conjectures and generalizations from too few data, may also be illustrated in his discussion of the sacred tree. He illumines certain phenomenological aspects of the symbolism even when his picture of the development may seem to be quite inadequate. He believes that "in all religions" the sacred tree as a visible manifestation of the divine spirit passed through three stages: in the first stage was the

tree of knowledge; in the second the tree, recognized as the home
of the deity, was planted on sacred ground; and in the third it became a symbol such as the Asherah. Were today's evidence for the
goddess Asherah as at Ugarit available to Farbridge, he would hardly continue to maintain that whenever Asherah appears as the name
of a goddess in the Old Testament it is a gloss for Ashtoreth, and
that the Asherah, a post or pole, was a symbol of fertility representing Ishtar (p. 34). In explaining how it happened that a tree came
to be possessed of divine life, Farbridge notes that just as in Greece,
so in Canaan every sacred tree had its fountain, for in the Near
East self-sown wood can only flourish where there is underground
water; possession of divine life was transmitted from the "fountain"
to the tree, and "the next stage" was to regard the tree as symbolizing the divine life which preserves and vivifies all creation. The
critique of this is too obvious to need statement here.[93] In prehistoric Mesopotamian art the tree seems to be little more than a
general "life" symbol. The world or cosmic tree, in connection with
which the symbolism of the cosmic mountain and the navel or
center of the earth as it appears in the Old Testament might well
have been discussed, is mentioned only in passing by Farbridge.[94]

The opposition to an anthropomorphic image of the deity in the
temple cultus, comparable to an image of Baal, Dagon, Marduk,
etc, in which the deity might be manifest in the dramatic ritual of
the cult, was perhaps in part the cause of the development of vivid
representations of the theophanic manifestation of Yahweh in the
cultic poetry of Israel, as well as elsewhere. See Pss. 18, 68, 77; Hab.
3; Judg. 5; Isa. 6. In part we have here word pictures of Yahweh
coming to his people on the festal day. In discussing this, Harrelson
comments that, being unable to make plastic images, the community
developed word images.[95] The verbal symbol takes the place of the
plastic symbol. Form critical studies of the Psalms have helped
point up this aspect of Hebrew cultic poetry, and it may be regarded as a legitimate aspect of the discussion of Hebrew symbolism.

XIV

Farbridge devoted almost one-fifth of his book to the symbolism of numbers.[96] The breadth of his interest and thoroughness of his research are evident in the comparative data invoked from Babylonia, Egypt, the Cabbala, the Talmud, the Samaritans, the Arabs, and the Greeks (especially the Pythagoreans), and from Vedic literature. Here also he is concerned with problems of origins and development as well as the variety of the forms of expression of numerical symbolism.

The antiquity of number symbolism and forms of its early manifestation are demonstrated in Beatrice L. Goff's studies of symbolism in the art of prehistoric Mesopotamia, where she finds the symbolism of two, three, five, seven, and nine as abstract numbers.[97] They emerge as significant forms belonging to that stage of symbolism in which symbols are used because they are reassuring and in which no explanation of their significance in words would have been necessary. Thus the number three as an abstract number appears as three fingers on the hands of demons or men or attached to a swastika design or to the end of tails of quadrupeds. Flowers with three petals, animals with three or five legs, bowls with five spouts, trees with seven or nine branches, incense burners with seven doors, etc., imply some special significance, however vague. The multiplication of symbols is interpreted as a possible reinforcement of the symbol and intensification of its power. Such abstract number symbols appear not only in prehistoric art.[98] They might naturally become attached to specific phenomena and types of phenomena, to receive an articulation and explanation which may not have been originally involved. Most symbolic numbers come to be used so widely that any common denominator of meaning one may find may be too general to be particularly significant.

Farbridge explains the use of round numbers by the fact that representative numbering is common among Eastern nations who have a prejudice [sic!] against counting their possessions accurately, and so it is that round numbers enter largely into many ancient systems of chronology. This explanation may be the result of Farbridge's reaction to his Palestinian experiences. He is well aware, however, of the development of mathematics and science in ancient Mesopotamia. His conjecture that the Hebrews may have had a system of numerical notation can now be demonstrated as a fact.[99]

Questionable and certainly highly conjectural philological or etymological explanations of the origins and significance of the names of numbers, based upon presumed biliteral roots, are presented (e.g., ḥmš, "five"; šlš, "three"; 'šr, "ten", pp. 90-92, 113-114, 143-144). Apart from the conjectural aspect of such etymological speculations,[100] the etymology of a word is not necessarily a guide to its meaning at a later period.[101] Particularly questionable is the philological procedure involved in Farbridge's derivation of qušeṭ, "bow," from the root qdš, "holy, sacred", the form qešet being merely due to assimilation of d and š. Thus qešet and qᵉdēšâh, "sacred prostitute, votary," have arisen from a common stem, and we are justified in regarding the philological connection between the Hebrew words for "votary" and "bow" as showing how the characteristics of Ishtar (a Babylonian goddess) as the goddess of love and passions and as the goddess of war and the bow developed from one another. Neither the etymology nor such etymological and philological explanation of the origins of symbolism is convincing. What about the association of the bow with Anat, the Canaanite goddess of love and war at Ugarit?

Similarly Farbridge's philological association and assumption of common root meaning of šāba', "to be complete," šeba', "seven," and šaba', "to swear" (pp. 136-139). The latter two may be related, but their connection with the first is improbable, and to presume for šāba', "to swear," a stem expressing completeness because in oaths, compacts, and incantations all nature, heaven and earth, were invoked as witnesses is unconvincing. It is an unsupported conjectural sequitur from the questionable assumption that the idea of completeness is involved in the invocation. Compare the recent surmise of M. R. Lehman [102] that šᵉba', "seven," is philologically related to the Hebrew word "to swear" through the fact that the number seven was an essential feature of oath ceremonies, illustrated in the slaughter of seven animals in Gen. 21:25-31, the sacrifice of seven bulls and seven rams in the Balaam incident in Num. 23:1, the seven pairs of clean animals from which Noah made sacrifices at the

time of the post-flood covenant in Gen. 8:20 (cf. 6:2), the seven
rams (and one bull) slaughtered by each novice at the inauguration
of Jeroboam's priests in 2 Chr. 13:9, and in the series of seven
animals associated with an Ashurnirari treaty, etc. (see also 1 Sam.
11:7). The basic meaning of the oath is interpreted to mean that
the fate of the slaughtered animals would befall him who broke the
oath (a viewpoint noted by Farbridge, p. 231), and the verb "to
swear," used in the passive (*hiššābē͑*) literally would mean "to be
subject to the fate of the seven." This is more convincing than Farbridge, but is still a surmise based on one of many aspects of the
rite of swearing.

XV

Farbridge devotes some twenty pages to the symbolism of the
number seven. Interested in origins, he thinks it plausible that
"among the Semites" the symbolic character of seven originated with
the division of the lunar month into quarters. and since Semitic
symbolism is based on the belief that there is an analogy between
all activity in heaven and everything on earth (p. 135), the number
seven regarded as sacred in heaven must be sacred on earth. So in
Babylonia the 7th, 14th, 21st, and 28th "days of the week" [sic!]
arose as specially marked out seventh days, days of evil omen. The
19th day had the same association, but this is interpreted as the
49th day (7 x 7) from the new moon of the previous month.[103]
As Farbridge himself recognizes, this does not really divide the lunar
month evenly. An early Semitic seven-day week cannot be clearly
established. Compare the suggestion of J. and H. Lewy that the
seven-day week was a time unit chosen by the people of the ancient
Near East in accord with the coming and going of the diurnal
winds, derived from the seven wind deities brought forth by Marduk
(*Enuma Elish,* IV, 40-47).[104] See the critique of Mayer Gruber,
who also exposes as conjecture N. H. Tur-Sinai's view of the origin
of the seven-day week in a presumed six-day week in a month of
five six-day periods (*humušta*) mentioned in the Cappadocian texts,
by assuming that the Hebrews transformed the six-day work-week
into a seven-day week by adding a day of rest.[105] H.-J. Kraus sug-

gests that the appearance of seven-day rites in Ugarit may imply the existence of the festival week in Ugarit, and that though conjectural it is not impossible that the Israelites found the institution of the week and the Sabbath already in existence.[106] These are a few of the many variant viewpoints on the origin of the seven-day week and the Sabbath, but at the moment their Hebrew origin seems most probable.[107] Although noting that many scholars do trace the origin of the Hebrew Sabbath to Babylonia, Farbridge properly cautiously does not indicate his agreement. Even if one presumes that it might have arisen outside of Israel, it cannot be proven.[108]

The significance of the number seven in the Ugaritic texts involves the issue of the seasonal aspect of Baal, his role as an annual dying and resurrecting deity.[109] A. S. Kapelrud in a study of seven in Ugaritic literature concludes that seven is often used by itself, or along with eight, to indicate completeness, and thus may be a round number; e.g., seven . . . eight sons of Keret, seven chambers . . . eight chambers whence El lifted up his voice, seven-year periods of drought. Seventy is similarly used, and sixty-six and seventy-seven or seventy-seven and eighty-eight may be used in poetic parallelism. Seven is used at Ugarit in four ways: (1) as a number loaded with strength and danger, (2) as an indefinite number, (3) to indicate intensity and quality rather than quantity, (4) to indicate fulfillment, completion, finishing. Kapelrud concludes that the representation of Baal's resurrection after seven years in the Ugaritic texts does not vitiate the existence of the yearly cycle in the Ugaritic cult.[110]

In the graded numerals in the oracles of Amos, chs. 1 and 2 ("For three transgressions . . . for four") Farbridge interprets three to mean many or enough and four more than enough (p. 100). Three and four occur in graded numerical expressions at Ugarit, e.g., in Krt 125:84, 95, "Three months that he is sick, Four that Krt is ill." We may contrast with the Amos 3:1 ff. type of graded numerical idiom the reflective graded numerical saying such as Job 5:19; Prov. 6:16-18; 30:15-16, 18-19, 21-23, etc., in which the items listed show the second number is that which is intended, and there seems here to be no symbolic or mystic meanings to the numbers. In Amos 1:3 ff. there is only one crime involved, and the ascending enumeration is used for climactic effect to emphasize the enormity of the crime, as Knierim has suggested.[111] We cannot, however, be certain that Amos in chs. 1 and 2 did not select numbers three and four in part because they total seven. It has been suggested by D. N. Freedman that an important clue to the structure of Amos' oracles may lie in the use of numbers for fixing the lengths, order, and relationship of important parts of the oracles. In chs. 1 and 2 there are seven peoples who are to receive Yahweh's judgment, and in the last of the series Israel is charged with three pairs of sins and an extra sin to produce a total of seven. "For three transgressions . . . for four" is repeated seven times, and the oracle concludes in vss. 14-16 with different groups of fighting men listed in groups of three and three plus one. Ch. 3:3-8 lists seven sets of things which naturally go together, and in ch. 6 is a series of seven deadly sins to match the deadly sins of ch. 2.[112]

To Farbridge's comments on gematria in the Old Testament we may add the frequently suggested illustration of the 600,000 fighting men in the Exodus party, taken to be the numerical value of the letters *bny yśr'l*, Sons of Israel, multiplied by 1000 (Exod. 12:39; cf. 38:26). Gematria has been taken by P. W. Skehan as a key to the structure of the book of Proverbs, in which the editor has brought the number of proverbs in the Solomonic collection (10:1-22:16) up to 375, the numerical equivalent of *šlmh*, Solomon, and has made the sayings in the Words of the Wise in 22:17-30:33 add up to 118, the numerical equivalent of *ḥkmym*, wise men,, while the number of the lines in chs. 25-29, the Hezekiah collection, is 140, the numerical equivalent of *yḥzqyh*, Hezekiah. The total number of lines in the work is 930, the numerical equivalent of Solomon, David, and Israel.[113] The 318 retainers of Abraham (Gen. 14:14) have been variously interpreted, including as a gematria, the numerical value of Eliezer. It has also been recently interpreted by S. Gevirtz as a simple application of prime numbers.[114]

Two studies of quite different character imply deliberate numerical systems over larger portions of Scripture. The first, by K. Stenring, advances the thesis that twelve books of the Old Testament (the Pentateuch, Joshua, Judges, Samuel, Kings, Chronicles, Ezra 1-3, 7, Jeremiah, and Ezekiel; cf. the 12 tribes, 12 months, etc.)

contain a deliberately concealed chronological system incorporated into the final editing around 240-230 B.C., to increase the sacredness and secret character of the writings and to create a chronological cipher which conceals magical and sacred matters from the ordinary reader. The Cabbala and the Qumranian concern for chronological data are invoked as a parallel. It involves the use of three calendars, each calculated from the first day of creation. A systematic collocation of all the data in Kings and Chronicles produces a pattern of forty rulers distributed over 70 intervals of time.[115] The conclusions of E. R. Thiele regarding the chronology of the Book of Kings would tend to cast doubt on such a theory of editing.[116] The other study is that of E. Laubscher, who finds special symbolic significance in the numbers three, four, six, seven, and eight (e.g., six has a profane, human reference; seven a sacred celestial reference; eight symbolizes something new; etc.). He finds the numerical symbolism not only in the use of the numbers, but particularly in the number of times certain words belonging to various categories of symbolic meanings occur in the New Testament, in the book of Revelation, or in the Old Testament, although his primary concern and area of study relates to the New Testament.[117]

XVI

Farbridge's discussion of burial and mourning customs can be supplemented by a great deal of Palestinian archaeological data, including those for the prehistoric period. See, for example, Joseph Calloway, "Burials in Ancient Palestine, from the Stone Age to Abraham," BA, XXVI (1963), pp. 74-90, and other studies.[118] Many types of burials and variant mortuary practices are evident. Symbolic actions accompanying mourning for the dead may be illustrated in the Baal and Anat texts at Ugarit. At the death of Baal, El descended from his throne to sit on the earth, poured ashes and dust on his head, wore sackcloth, lacerated cheek, chin, forearms, chest, and back, roamed the mountains in mourning, and raised his voice in lamentation, and the goddess Anat at a ritual feast at Baal's burial also lacerated herself, wept, wore sackcloth, ranged the hills, and offered sacrifices (see, e.g., 67:VI:10-30; 62:1-29;

etc.). The description of the mourning rites reflects Canaanite practices, which were much the same as in ancient Israel.[119] The Keret and Aqhat texts also have light to shed on mourning practices.

Farbridge is interested in explaining the origins of some of these mourning rites. We may doubt that in Hebrew usage the practice of self-mutilation or cutting oneself had any association with making a covenant with a living or dead person, although Farbridge seems to suggest that this is a possible explanation of the expression "to cut a covenant" (pp. 230-232). He notes the suggestion that self-mutilation may have been to provide nourishment for the dead, and thinks it possible that there arose after a time a custom of substituting the mourner's own blood by that of a slaughtered animal. Perhaps all that can be said of the rite of self-laceration in mourning is that it was to benefit the spirit of the departed in some way.[120] Farbridge's apparent support of the view that "among the Semites" the idea of sacrifice was really based upon the idea of forming a covenant by means of blood is too generalized, for by contrast, in Mesopotamia, it is doubtful whether the blood of victims was ever used in the ritual of sacrifice, and the communion or "peace offering" and burnt offering did not exist in Mesopotamia.[121]

The use of ashes as well as dust in mourning is explained in what Farbridge (pp. 250-252) thinks a much more interesting and plausible way than Robertson Smith's view that the ashes were probably the ashes of the victim sacrificed at the grave, namely through the assumption that the Hebrew for ashes ('pr) is almost identical with the word for dust ('pr), and that the words are really synonymous. While similarity in etymology may have little to do with the use of ashes as well as dust, Farbridge, Jastrow, and others are right in recognizing that the two words may be at times synonymous, for 'pr can clearly mean dust. Cf. 'mr and 'pr in parallelism in Ugaritic, in a mourning context (67: VI; 14).

Taking his lead from Jastrow, Farbridge has a curious explanation of the origin and development of the use of dust in mourning. Plausibly interpreting the two men with baskets on their heads on the Vulture Stele as carrying dirt for a burial tumulus (see J. B. Pritchard, *The Ancient Near East in Pictures*, #299), he suggests that the practice of sprinkling dust on the head arose when a change took place in the manner of burial, and no longer did one carry a basket of dirt to the burial mound, but earth was placed on the head as a symbol of mourning, and then sprinkled up into the air (pp. 252-253). This is unsupported conjecture, especially in the light of the very complicated history of funerary rites. Increased knowledge may make possible more accurate interpretation of scenes on ancient monuments. This may be illustrated by a bronze tablet on which Farbridge finds "a clear idea of the Babylonian conception of the underworld," including the representation of a funeral ceremony and the goddess of the lower world, Allatu, on a horse in a barque (pp. 215-216); it turns out to be a representation of the exorcism of a demon or evil spirits from a sick man seen on his bed, and the Allatu figure in the nether world is the female demon Lamashtu on an ass which will carry Lamashtu to the boat floating on the waters which surround the earth.[122]

The Ugaritic texts provide a primary source for the Canaanite view of the lower world and figures associated with it.[123] Farbridge is hospitable toward the viewpoint that many symbolical mourning customs have their origin in hero worship which "formed part of the religion of the ancient Semites," and relates this to the Rephaim of the Old Testament. The word *rp'um* at Ugarit would seem to be equivalent of *rp'ym*, Rephaim, of the Old Testament, but whether we have at Ugarit in the *rp'um* the Old Testament Rephaim as the shades of the dead, or the gods of the earth (the underworld), or a sacred guild associated with the king and his office is unclear.[124] If, as is possible, there are at Ugarit two separate categories of the Rephaim, one constitutng an ethnic term and the other the shades of the dead, the relationship between the two is as uncertain as the relationship between the comparable meanings of Rephaim in the Old Testament. Farbridge believes the word Rephaim, which later came to be applied to all the dead, originally referred to distinguished dead heroes. As an analogy he notes that just as many of the early kings of Babylonia were deified and worshipped as gods when they were alive, so they continued to be worshipped in the same manner after death. It is probable to him that the term Sheol got its name meaning "place of inquiry" from the fact that these dead hero-divinities were often consulted for oracles,[125] and the mourning customs of

wearing sackcloth, offering sacrifices at the graves, etc., were originally intended as symbols of respect to a dead hero, in whose honor
they had also been performed in his lifetime (pp. 218-220).[126] One
could wish for more connecting links in the evidence. Considerable
obscurity surrounds the problem of deification of Mesopotamian
kings. That the determinative for deity before the name of the Babylonian king implies deification has been described as a gross ra-
tionalization, and there is some question whether he was ever worshipped, although offerings were made to the king's statue, and one
can speak of a cult of the deceased kings.[127] That, however, many
symbolic mourning customs had their origin in hero worship or
worship of hero-divinities lacks any kind of concrete demonstration.

Particularly as a comparative religion study, Farbridge's treatment of burial and mourning customs has merit, and it illustrates
something of the breadth of his interests. He has gathered together
much relevant material.[128]

XVII

Obviously this Prolegomenon cannot be a complete response to
what Farbridge regarded as an introduction to a neglected subject
on which to write an exhaustive work would be, in his words, a
life task itself. One might visualize as an alternative to such a
life task a multi-volume Dictionary of Biblical Symbolism, written
not by one, but by many scholars. The larger Near Eastern, Iranian,
Anatolian, and Greco-Roman world would have to be involved in
it. It should be adequately illustrated, as Farbridge's book would
be were it published today. This is not to recommend such a pro-
ject, but to indicate something of the scope of the subject. Farbridge could not have done otherwise than elect to discuss selected
aspects of biblical symbolism. Also, from among several possible
approaches to his subject he elected to approach his subject as a
historian of religion and student of comparative religion.

Farbridge raised many issues for which available data could not
provide a satisfactory solution. Many are still unanswerable. Although
it is the symbolical representations of the Assyrian-Babylonian pantheon that he picks out for distinctive attention, he is not an ad-
herent of the pan-Babylonian school. He has too much respect for

the insights and originality of the Israelites to fall into this error. Despite his concern for the development of biblical symbolism, he lays little emphasis on chronology. This is one of several aspects of relevant biblical researches which today receives more adequate attention. In Palestinian archaeology, for example, it is the difference between the confused stratigraphy and chronological analysis of R. A. S. Macalister at Gezer (*The Excavation of Gezer, 1902-1905 and 1907-1909,* Vols. I-III, 1912) and the refined excavation techniques and chronological criteria of the current Hebrew Union College Biblical and Archaeological School excavations at the same site initiated in 1964-65. Near Eastern prehistoric archaeology also has come into its own since the days of Farbridge, providing data for the student of symbolism. Studies in anthropology, art, literature, history, and linguistics have had their contributions to make, as well as psychology and psychoanalysis.

In the first part of this Prolegomenon we have presented something of the developments in biblical symbolism since Farbridge prepared his study, discussing particularly aspects of biblical symbolism in which the reader might have special interest, and associating the discussion with Farbridge's interpretations. In the latter part of the Prolegomenon we have concerned ourselves largely with items which would indicate something of the nature of the approach of Farbridge and place it in the perspective of recent studies. The complexity of the available data have at times made Farbridge's solutions seem to be a simplification of the situation, although the mass of data collated by Farbridge is an indication of the breadth of his interests and comprehension. It is hoped that the reprinting of Farbridge's study will inspire further creative concern in this area of biblical studies, and will perhaps compensate for the fact that his study has not received the attention that it deserves. The present writer must express gratitude for his own increased interest in the area of biblical symbolism which has resulted from work on this volume.

Herbert G. May
Oberlin College
Oberlin, Ohio
The Divinity School
Vanderbilt University
Nashville, Tennessee

March 15, 1970

NOTES

1. In that volume see particularly Rollo May, "The Significance of Symbols," pp. 11-49; Erich Kahler, "The Nature of the Symbol," pp. 50-74; Paul Tillich, "The Religious Symbol," pp. 79-98; and A. N. Whitehead, "Uses of Symbolism," pp. 233-50.

2. *Symbolism, Its Meaning and Effect*, p. 9.

3. P. Tillich, *loc. cit.*

4. See especially Vols. IV, IX, and XXII for statements of methodology, also "Symbolism in Hellenistic Jewish Art: The Problem of Method," *JBL* (1937), pp. 103-14; M. Smith, "Goodenough's Jewish Symbols in Retrospect," *JBL*, LXXXVI (1967), pp. 53-68; Paul Friedman, "On the Universality of Symbols," in Jacob Neusner, ed., *Religions in Antiquity, Studies in the History of Religions*, XIV, 1968, pp. 609-18; E. J. Bickerman, "Symbolism in the Dura Synagogue," *HTR*, 58 (1965), pp. 127-51.

5. See Friedman, in J. Neusner, *op. cit.*, p. 610.

6. *Symbols of Prehistoric Mesopotamia,* 1963, p. xxxiv See also P. Friedman, *op. cit.*, p. 610; E. J. Bickerman *op. cit.*, p. 151, and his comment that the perennity of symbols is conditioned by the perennity of the condition of man, who is "tormented by the two grimmest tyrants, Hope and Fear."

7. The solar aspects of Egyptian scarab symbolism or the Egyptian myth of the loss and restoration of the eye of Horus may not have been popularly known in Canaan. The seal or signet did have important royal connotations in Palestine (Jer. 22:24; cf. I Ki. 21:8; see below, p. 18 and note 83), but the obvious popularity of Egyptian figurines as amulets suggests that Egypt, as the land of mystery and the occult (cf. the Joseph story) gave special potency to amulets and motifs of Egyptian origin.

8. See H. G. May, "The Sacred Tree on Palestinian Painted Pottery," *JAOS*, LIX (1939), pp. 251-59.

9. Beatrice L. Goff, *op. cit.*, p. xxxvii.

10. Rollo May, *op. cit.*, p. 34.

11. P. Tillich, *op. cit.* pp. 83-89.

12. H. and H. H. Frankfort, *et al.*, *The Intellectual Adventure of Ancient Man*, 1946, p. 7. See the important discussion of myth and story in T. H. Gaster, *Myth, Legend, and Custom in the Old Testament*, 1969, pp. xxv-xxxix, especially p. xxxv. Also, John L. McKenzie, *Myths and Realities*, 1963, p. 182.

13. H. and H. H. Frankfort, *op. cit.*, pp. 8-12.

14. B. S. Childs, *Myth and Reality in the Old Testament*, 1960, pp. 17-21.

15. B. W. Anderson, *Creation versus Chaos*, 1967, pp. 17-18; M. Noth, "The Re-Presentation in the Old Testament in Proclamation," in Claus Westermann, ed., *Essays in Old Testament Hermeneutics*, trans. by J. L. Mays, 1963, pp. 76-88 ("Die Vergegenwärtigung des Alten Testaments," in *Probleme alttestamentlicher Hermeneutik*, 1960); H. Zirker, *Die kultische Vergegenwärtigung der Vergangenheit in den Psalmen*, 1964. For an appreciation of the phenomenon in religions in general, see M. Eliade, *Cosmos and History; The Myth of the Eternal Return*, 1954. See also W. Pannenberg, "Redemptive Event in History," in C. Westermann, *op. cit.*, pp. 314-35

16. T. H. Gaster, *Thespis. Myth, Ritual, and Drama in the Ancient Near East*, new and rev. ed., 1961; A. S. Kapelrud, *The Ras Shamra Discoveries and the Old Testament*, 1965, pp. 47-49, who holds the entire annual cycle represented in the texts was presented in the cultic drama; *Baal in the Ras Shamra Texts*, 1952, pp. 13-27. T. H. Gaster speaks of the texts as the *libretti* of sacred dramas and as myths projected from ritual: "Divine Kingship in the Ancient Near East," *Review of Religion*, 1945, pp. 272-73.

17. E. Kahler in R. May, ed., *op. cit.*, pp. 65-67.
18. See C. G. Jung, "Concerning Two Ways of Thinking," in his *Psychology of the Unconcious* (1937), trans. by B. M. Hinckle from *Wandlungen und Symbole der Libido.*
19. Paul Friedman, *op. cit.*, p. 611. E. J. Jurji, *The Phenomenology of Religion,* 1963, pp. 103-5. Friedman calls attention to the view of E. Jones ("The Theory of Symbolism," in *Papers on Psychoanalysis,* 1948) that the stereotype in symbolism is due to the uniformity of the fundamental and perennial interests of mankind.
20. See S. W. Baron, Bruce Mazlich, H. L. Philip, "The Freudian Hypothesis," in R. J. Christen, H. E. Hazelton, editors, *Moses and Monotheism, The Genesis of Judaism,* 1969, pp. 39-58. Rollo May, *op. cit.*, pp. 33-34. Cf. H. M. Orlinsky, "Moses," in *Great Jewish Personalities in Ancient and Medieval Times,* ed. S. Noveck, 1959, p. 17: "(Sigmund Freud's study of Moses . . . is now regarded by many as a naive venture, constituting in reality a more important source of information for the analysis of Freud himself than of Moses)".
21. R. May, *op. cit.*, p. 22
22. For a general psychological approach, see Werner Wolff, *Changing Concepts of the Bible; A Psychological Analysis of Its Words, Symbols, and Beliefs,* 1951. The author describes his as a cultural as over against an individual analysis, concerned with a layer of expression patterned by categories different from our own, a semantic approach to be contrasted with an anthropological, historical, and theological approach.
23. See also M. Eliade, *Patterns in Comparative Religion,* transl. by Rosemary Sheed, 1958, where the extensive bibliographies provide some impression of the number and scope of significant studies pertinent to the subject of Farbridge's work. See also P. Ricoeur, "The Problem of the Double Sense as Hermeneutic Problem and as Semantic Problem," in *Myth and Symbols, Studies in Honor of M. Eliade,* edited by J. M. Kitagawa and C. H. Long, 1969, pp. 63-79. B. S. Child, *Myth and Reality, Studies in Biblical Theology #27,* 1960. W. G. Oxtoby, "Religionswissenschaft Revisited," in J. Neusner, ed., *op. cit.*, 590-608.
24. *Op. cit.*, p. 1.
25. *Op. cit.*, pp. 30-32, 42-43.
26. W. Klatt, *Hermann Gunkel: zu seiner Theologie der Religionsgeschichte und zur Entstehung der formgeschichtlichen Methode,* 1969. See the subsequent studies of A. Alt, M. Noth, G. von Rad, C. Westermann, K. Baltzer, H. G. Reventlow, K. Koch, J. Muilenburg, R. Murphy, R. Knierim, etc. A proposed *Interpreter's Handbook of Old Testament Form Criticism* has been announced.
27. See also S. Mowinckel, *The Psalms in Israel's Worship,* 1962; *He That Cometh,* 1956. See the critique in A. S. Kapelrud, "Sigmund Mowinckel and Old Testament Study," *Annual of the Swedish Theological Institute,* V (1967), pp. 4-29.
28. Hans Schmidt, *Die Thronfahrt Jahwes am Fest der Jahreswende im alten Israel,* 1927; *Die Psalmen,* 1934; *Der heilige Fels in Jerusalem,* 1933; H. Gunkel and J. Begrich, *Einleitung in die Psalmen,* 1933; J. Morgenstern, "The Gates of Righteousness," *HUCA,* VI (1929), pp. 1-37; J. Hollis, "The Sun Cult and the Temple at Jerusalem, in S. H. Hooke, *Myth and Ritual,* pp. 87-110; H. G. May, "The Departure of the Glory of Yahweh," *JBL,* LVI (1937), pp. 309-21.
29. See discussion by N. H. Snaith, *The Jewish New Year Festival,* 1947; H. H. Rowley, *Worship in Ancient Israel,* 1967, pp. 184-212.
30. G. von Rad, *Das formgeschichtliche Problem des Hexateuchs, BWANT, IV,* 1938; A. Weiser, *The Psalms, The Old Testament Library,* 1962 (transl. by H. Hartwell from *Die Psalmen,* 1959); *Glaube und Geschichte im Alten Testament und andere ausgewählte Schriften,* 1961, pp. 303-21. For descriptive bibliography,

see H. F. Hahn with H. D. Hummel, *The Old Testament in Modern Research,* 1966, pp. 119-56, 285, 286.

31. H.-J. Kraus, *Worship in Ancient Israel,* 1966 (transl. by G. Buswell from *Gottesdienst in Israel; Studien zur Geschichte des Laubhüttenfestes,* 1954).

32. H. Ringgren, "Enthronement Festival or Covenant Renewal," *Biblical Research,* 7 (1962), pp. 45-48. A. S. Kapelrud, "The Role of the Cult in Old Israel," in J. P. Hyatt, ed., *The Bible in Modern Scholarship* (1965), pp. 44-46; H. G. May, *ibid.,* pp. 71-73.

33. S. H. Hooke, ed., *Myth and Ritual,* 1933; *The Labyrinth,* 1935; *Myth, Ritual, and Kingship,* 1958; I. Engnell, *Studies in Divine Kingship in the Ancient Near East,* 2nd ed., 1967; J. Willis, ed., transl., *A Rigid Scrutiny, Critical Essays on the Old Testament by I. Engnell,* 1969. G. Widengren, *Sakrales Königtum im Alten Testament und im Judentum,* 1955; A. R. Johnson, *Sacral Kingship in Ancient Israel,* 2nd ed., 1967. T. H. Gaster, "Divine Kingship in the Ancient Near East," *Review of Religion,* 1945, pp. 267-81; G. W. Ahlström, *Ps. 89,* 1957. Compare H. G. May, "Pattern and Myth in the Old Testament," *JR,* XXI (1941), pp. 285-99. See critique in H. Frankfort, *Kingship and the Gods,* 1948, 1955; K. H. Bernhardt, *Das Problem der altorientalischen Königsideologie im Alten Testament (VT Suppl.,* VIII), 1961. The interpretation of royal symbolism, both related to God and the king, involves many facets of Israelite literature and cult.

34. See also the much earlier work of Carl Frank, *Bilder und Symbole babylonisch-assyrischer Götter,* 1906.

35. Compare, e. g., Stephen Langdon's published text and translation of the Sumerian myth he entitles "Sumerian Epic of Paradise, the Flood, and the Fall of Man" (*PBS,* X [1915]) with S. N. Kramer, "Enki and Ninhursag, A Sumarian Paradise Myth," *BASOR Suppl. Studies I,* 1945. See also S. N. Kramer, *The Sacred Marriage Rite, Aspects of Faith, Myth, and Ritual in Ancient Sumer,* 1969. See pertinent classified bibliographical references in H. W. Saggs, *The Greatness That Was Babylon; A Sketch of the Ancient Civilization of the Tigris-Euphrates Valley,* 1962.

36. Compare, e.g., Thorkild Jacobsen, "Toward the Image of Tammuz," *History of Religions,* I (1961), pp. 189-213; the figure of Tammuz is analyzed in terms of the loci, the phenomena in the external world, in which the life of the god was encountered; the identification of the associated phenomena is but the beginning of the understanding of the symbolism. See discussion of the origins of Sumerian Mythology, B. L. Goff, *Symbols of Prehistoric Mesopotamia,* pp. 212-64.

37. Also J. B. Pritchard, ed., *The Ancient Near East; Supplementary Texts and Pictures Relating to the Old Testament,* 1969, supplementing the second ed. of *Ancient Near Eastern Texts* and the first ed. of *Ancient Near East in Pictures.*

38. Farbridge did not succumb to the pan-Babylonian theories of Jeremias (and of H. Winckler) or his emphasis on astral symbolism.

39. A. Alt, *Der Gott der Väter,* 1929. So also J. Lewy, "Les Textes paléo-assyriens et l'Ancien Testament," *RHR,* CX (1934), pp. 50 ff. See H. G. May, "The Patriarchal Idea of God," *JBL,* LX (1941), pp. 113-28; M. Haran, "The Religion of the Patriarchs; An Attempt at Synthesis," *Annual of the Swedish Theological Institute,* IV, 1965, pp. 30-55; W. F. Albright, *Yahweh and the Gods of Canaan,* pp. 152-207; F. M. Cross, "Yahweh and the God of the Patriarchs," *HTR,* LV (1962), pp. 225-59; "The Divine Warrior in Israel's Early Cult," in A. Altmann, ed., *Biblical Motifs; Origin and Transformation,* 1966; A. Malamat, "Mari and the Bible," in J. M. Grintz and J. Liver, eds., *Studies in the Bible,* 1964; A. S. Kapelrud, "The Role of the Cult in Old Israel," in J. P. Hyatt, ed. *The Bible in Modern Scholarship,* 1964; G. E. Wright, "History and the Patriarchs," *Expository Times,* July 1960, pp. 3-7, etc. etc.

40. M. Dahood (*Psalms I, The Anchor Bible,* 1966, p. xxxv) recalls that the

adaptation of mythological motifs by prophets and psalmists does not diminish the significance or the originality of prophecy and psalmody, but sets off the omnipotence and majesty of Yahweh. See D. N. Freedman, "The New World of the Old Testament," circulated address delivered May 7, 1968; J. H. Patton, *Canaanite Parallels in the Book of Psalms*, 1944; W. F. Albright, *Yahweh and the Gods of Canaan*, 1968, pp. 1-62, 110-207. Whether or not the term "Canaanite" is proper for the Ugaritians (A. F. Rainey, "The Kingdom of Ugarit," *BA*, XXVIII, 1965, pp. 102-25) is somewhat irrelevant for our purposes.

41. *Yahweh and the Gods of Canaan*, pp. 115-52. See J. Nougayrol in *Ugaritica V*, (1968), pp. 42-64; H. Cazelles, in *VT*, XIX (1969), pp.499-500.

42. J. A. Montgomery, "Ras Shamra Notes IV: The Conflict of Baal and the Waters," *JAOS*, LV (1935), pp. 268-77; W. F. Albright, "The Psalm of Habakkuk," in H. H. Rowley, ed., *Studies in Old Testament Prophecy*, 1950, pp. 1-18; T. H. Gaster, "The Battle of the Rain and the Sea," *Iraq*, IV (1937), pp. 21-32; *Myth, Legend, and Custom in the Old Testament*, pp. 240-41, 668-78, 747-50; F. M. Cross and D. N. Freedman, "The Song of Miriam," *JNES*, XIV (1966), pp. 237-50; F. M. Cross," The Song of the Sea and Canaanite Myth," *Zeitschrift für Theologie und Kirche*, V (1968), pp. 1-25; B. W. Anderson, *Creation Versus Chaos*, pp. 23-26, 132-43; H. G. May, "Some Cosmic Connotations of *MAYIM RABBIM*, 'Many Waters,' " *JBL*, LXXIV (1955), pp. 9-21. S. E. Loewenstamm, "The Ugaritic Myth of the Sea and Its Biblical Counterparts," in *W. F. Albright Volume, Eretz-Israel*, IX (1969), pp. 96-101 (Hebrew). Whether the Ugaritic theme of Baal and the Waters represents a conflict about creation or about kingship is not clear; perhaps both symbolisms are involved: see L. Fisher, "From Chaos to Cosmos," *Encounter*, 26 (1965), pp. 185-87; cf. M. K. Wakeman, "The Biblical Earth Monster in the Cosmogonic Combat Myth," *JBL*, LXXXVIII (1969), pp. 313-20.

43. T. H. Gaster, *Thespis; Ritual, Myth, and Drama in the Ancient Near East*, p. ix.

44. The bibliography is encyclopaedic, but see more recently M. H. Pope, *El in the Ugaritic Texts (VT Suppl. II)*, 1955; A. Jirku, *Der Mythus der Kanaanäer*, 1966; J. Gray, *The Legacy of Canaan: The Ras Shamra Texts and Their Relevance to the Old Testament*, sec. rev. ed., 1965; W. F. Albright, *Yahweh and the Gods of Canaan*, 1968; A. S. Kapelrud, *The Violent Goddess; Anat in the Ras Shamra Texts*, 1969. For the texts, see Cyrus Gordon, *Ugaritic Textbook*, 1965.

45. *Thespis*, p. 158.

46. The reference here is not limited to the distinctive bichrome pottery paintings of the Late Bronze I period described by C. Epstein, *Palestinian Bichrome Ware*, in *Documenta et Monumenta Orientalis Antiqui*, XII, 1966. For the appearance of these motifs in a religious context, note the goats eating from the sacred tree, the lions, palm trees, etc., on a Taanach pottery cultic stand, palm trees, lions, streams, etc., on a Megiddo incense altar, or the stags and sacred trees on a jug from the Lachish fosse temple. See below, note 51.

47. See E. Anati, *op. cit.*, pp. 159-67, 181-214, 255, 265-66, 288-91, 303-10, etc.

48. J. B. Pritchard, *Palestinian Figurines in Relation to Certain Goddesses Known Through Literature*, 1943; cf. E. Douglas van Buren, *Clay Figurines of Babylonia and Assyria*, 1930; K. Galling, *Biblisches Reallexikon*, cols. 200-230.

49. G. Loud, *Megiddo Ivories*, 1939; J. W. and G. M. Crowfoot, *Early Ivories from Samaria*, 1938; J. B. Pritchard, *Ancient Near East in Pictures*, Figs. 231-41; idem, art. "Ivory" in *IDB;* M. E. L. Mallowan, *Nimrud and Its Remains*, I, II, 1966.

50. Olga Tufnell, art. "Seals and Scarabs," *IDB*, IV, pp. 254-59; A. Reifenberg, *Ancient Hebrew Seals*, 1950; N. Avigad, "A Group of Hebrew Seals," in *W. F. Albright Volume, Eretz-Israel*, IX (1969), pp. 1-9, Pls. 1,2. The Jotham seal from

Ezion-geber with ram cannot with certainty be ascribed to King Jotham; see K. Galling in *ZDPV*, 83 (1967), pp. 131-34.

51. See, e.g., the newly discovered Taanach cultic or incense stand, belonging to the late tenth century, on which appear the bull with winged sun-disk flanked by voluted columns, a naked "Astarte"-type goddess flanked by lions, goats feeding on each side of a sacred tree, winged sphinxes (cherubim), griffins, etc., with its registers reminiscent of reliefs on orthostats associated with Syrian temples, as at Carchemish. See Paul Lapp, "The 1968 Excavations at Tell Ta'annek," *BASOR*, No. 195 (1969), pp. 42-44 (cf. *Qadmoniyot, II,* 1969, pp. 16-17 [Hebrew]), and reference there to Y. Yadin, "Symbols of Deities at Zinjirli, Carthage, and Hazor," *Yediot,* 31 (1967), pp. 29-63 (Hebrew). Cf. H. G. May, *Material Remains of the Megiddo Cult,* 1935, pp. 13-23.

52. See G. A. Barrois, art. "Temples" in *IDB,* IV; G. E. Wright, "The Significance of the Temple in the Ancient Near East, Part III, The Temple in Palestine-Syria," *BA,* VII (1944), pp. 66-68 (See Part I, "The Egyptian Temple," by H. H. Nelson, and Part II, "The Mesopotamian Temple," by A. L. Oppenheim, on pp. 42-63). See reports on sites noted above in *BA, IEJ,* etc., and the detailed excavation reports.

53. W. F. Albright, "The High Place in Ancient Palestine," *VT Suppl. IV* (1957), pp. 242-58.

54. Ezek. 43:13-17. W. F. Albright, *Archaeology and the Religion of Israel,* 1942, p. 150; *Yahweh and the Gods of Canaan,* pp. 203-206. See also the altar-hearth as *'r'yl ('ry'l)* in Ezek. 43:14, 15, suggesting association with Akkadian *Arallu,* the lower world.

55. See K. Galling, *Biblische Reallexikon,* Cols. 500-503. In the Ugaritic text 2 Aqhat 1:27, 45 there is a reference to setting up a stele (?) of *'il'ib,* which has been taken to refer to an ancestral god or a departed ancestor. See below, note 126.

56. W. F. Albright, "Two Cressets from Marissa and the Pillars Jachin and Boaz," *BASOR,* 85 (1942), pp. 18-25; H. G. May, "The Two Pillars before Solomon's Temple," *BASOR,* 88 (1942), pp. 19-27; G. E. Wright, "Solomon's Temple Resurrected, *BA,* IV (1941), pp. 17-31; *Biblical Archaeology,* rev. ed., 1962, pp. 132-45; "The Stevens' Reconstruction of the Solomonic Temple," *BA,* XVIII (1955), pp. 41-44; P. L. Garber, *The Howland-Garber Model Reconstruction of Solomon's Temple, Revised and Reprinted by AIA,* 1960. For the symbolism of the names of the pillars, see R. B. Y. Scott, "The Pillars Jachin and Boaz," *JBL,* LVIII (1939), pp. 143-50. For symbolic aspects of the Jerusalem temple, see also E. L. Ehrlich, *Die Kultsymbolik im Alten Testament und im nachbiblischen Judentum, Symbolik der Religion,* III, 1959, pp. 18-33. See also the interpretation of the microcosmic character of the temple of Baal in Ugaritic texts and the temple of Yahweh, both constructed on Mt. Saphon (cf. Ps. 48), and both built in terms of seven (that of Baal seven days, that of Yahweh seven years), L. Fisher, "The Temple Quarter," *Journal of Semitic Studies,* VIII (1963), pp. 34-41.

57. Illustrated on the Samaria ivories; see above, note 49.

58. W. F. Albright, "What Were the Cherubim," *BA,* I (1938), pp. 1-3; M. Haran, "The Ark and the Cherubim, Their Symbolic Significance in the Biblical Ritual," *IEJ* (1959), pp. 30-38, 89-94 (note the interpretation of the ark as both the throne and the footstool of Yahweh); "The Ark of the Covenant and the Cherubs," *Eretz-Israel,* 5 (1958), pp. 83 ff. (Hebrew).

59. H. Gressmann, *Die Lade Jahwes,* 1920; R. Hartmann, "Zelt und Lade," *ZAW,* 37 (1917-18), pp. 209-39; H. Lammens, "Le culte des Bétyles et les processions religieuses chez les Arabes préislamites," *Bulletin de l'Institut Français d'Archéologie Orientale,* XVII (1920), pp. 39 ff.; J. Morgenstern, *The Ark, the Ephod, and the Tent of Meeting,* 1945; cf. M. Haran, " 'OTFE, MAHMAL and

KUBBE, Notes on the Study of Origins of Biblical Cult Forms: The Problem of Arabic Parallels," in *D. Neiger Memorial Volume*, 1959, pp. 1-7 (Hebrew).
  60. F. M. Cross, "The Tabernacle," *BA*, X (1947), pp. 45-68, reprinted in G. E. Wright and D. N. Freedman, eds., *Biblical Archaelogist Reader*, I (1961), pp. 201-28. See also H.-J. Kraus, *Worship in Israel*, pp. 131-33.
  61. M. Haran, "The Nature of the *'Ohel Mo'edh* in Pentateuchal Sources," *JTS*, V (1960), pp. 50-65. For a study of the symbolical significance of the inner ritual complex of the tabernacle, see M. Haran, "The Complex of the Ritual Acts Performed Inside the Tabernacle," in *Scripta Hierosolymitana*, vol. VIII, *Studies in the Bible*, (1961), ed. C. Rabin, pp. 289-97.
  62. R. Hartmann, *loc. cit.*
  63. H. G. May, "The Ark—A Miniature Temple," *AJSL*, LII (1936), pp. 215-34.
  64. B. A. Levine, "On the Presence of God in Biblical Religion," in J. Neusner, ed., *Religions in Antiquity*, pp. 76-78. Compare the discussion of the ark's symbolism as token of Yahweh's presence with his people in M. H. Woudstra, *The Ark of the Covenant from Conquest to Kingship*, 1965.
  65. *The Ancient Synagogue of Beth-Alpha*, 1932.
  66. C. H. Kraeling, *The Synagogue, The Excavations at Dura-Europos, VIII*, Part I, 1956; E. R. Goodenough, "The Synagogues of Palestine," in *Jewish Symbols of the Greco-Roman Period*, I, pp. 178-267 (see also II, pp. 70 ff.; IV, pp. 65 ff.; VIII, pp. 167 ff.); R. Wischnitzer, *The Messianic Theme in the Paintings of the Dura Synagogue*, 1948; H. G. May, "Synagogues in Palestine," *BA*, VII (1944), pp. 1-20; E. L. Ehrlich, *op. cit.*, pp. 86-96. See also the important monumental Roman period synagogue at Sardis, G. M. A. Hanfmann, "The Ancient Synagogue of Sardis," *Papers, Fourth World Congress of Jewish Studies*, I, 1967, pp. 37-42 and reports in *BASOR*.
  67. C. H. Kraeling, *op. cit.*, p. 370; R. Wischnitzer, *op. cit.*, p. 95.
  68. J. A. Sanders, *The Psalm Scroll of Qumran Cave 11*, 1965, pp. 54-63.
  69. M. Smith, "Goodenough's Jewish Symbols in Retrospect," *JBL*, LXXXVI (1967), pp. 53-68. Cf. T. H. Gaster, "Pagan Ideas and the Jewish Mind," *Commentary*, 17 (1954), pp. 185-90.
  70. T. H. Gaster, *Myth, Legend, and Custom in the Old Testament*, pp. xxi-xxiii.
  71. See the analysis of Bähr as predecessor of the Wellhausen approach in H.-J. Kraus, *Worship in Israel*, 1965, pp. 1-2.
  72. W. F. Albright, *History, Archaeology, and Christian Humanism*, 1964, pp. 135-43; *From Stone Age to Christianity*, sec. ed., 1957, pp. 84-96.
  73. *Symbols of Prehistoric Mesopotamia*, pp. xxxvi-xxxvii, 212-64.
  74. A. R. Mallon, *et al.*, *Tuleilat Ghassul*, I, frontispiece; E. Anati, *op. cit.*, p. 161.
  75. W. S. Smith, *Interconnections in the Ancient Near East; A Study of the Relationships between the Arts of Egypt, the Aegean, and Western Asia*, 1965. C. H. Gordon, *The Common Background of Greek and Hebrew Civilizations*, 1963, 1965; *The Ancient Near East*, 3rd ed., 1965.
  76. E. A. Speiser, "Of Shoes and Shekels," *BASOR*, 77 (1940), pp. 15-19. Note in the Amos oracle also the reference to the garment taken in pledge (Amos 2:8), and the legislation in Deut. 24:12, 13; an ostracon found south of Jaffa is a letter of a man objecting because his garment taken the day before the Sabbath while reaping was not returned: J. Naveh, "A Hebrew Letter from the Seventh Century B.C. [Mesad Hashavyahu]," *IEJ*, X (1960), pp. 129-139; XIV (1964), pp. 158-159; J. D. Amusin and M. L. Heltzer, "The Inscription from Mesad Hashavyahu," *IEJ*, XIV (1964), pp. 148-57; F. M. Cross, Jr., *BASOR*, No. 165 (1962), pp. 33-46; S. Yeivin, *Bibliotheca Orientalis*, XXIX (1962), pp. 3-10.
  77. G. E. Mendenhall, "Covenant Forms in Israelite Tradition," *BA*, XVI (1954), pp. 50-76; *Law and Covenant in Israel and the Ancient Near East*, 1955.

D. J. Wiseman, *The Vassal-Treaties of Esarhaddon*, 1958. D. R. Hillers, *Covenant: The History of a Biblical Idea*, 1969. D. J. McCarthy, S.J., *Treaty and Covenant (Analecta Biblica XXI)*, 1963. Jonas Greenfield, "Some Aspects of Treaty Terminology in the Bible," *Fourth World Congress of Jewish Studies*, Vol. I, 1967, pp. 117-119. M. R. Lehmann, "Biblical Oaths," *ZAW*, LXXXI, 1969, pp. 74-91.

78. For relevant texts see "Hittite Treaties," in Pritchard, *Ancient Near Eastern Texts*, pp. 201-206; "Akkadian Treaties from Syria and Assyria," *Supplementary Texts and Pictures*, pp. 95-105 (531-41).

79. See also H. W. Robinson, "Prophetic Symbolism," in *Old Testament Essays*, 1927, pp. 1-17; "Hebrew Sacrifice and Prophetic Symbolism," *JTS* (1942), pp. 129-139. B. D. Napier, "Prophet, Prophetism," *IDB*, III, pp. 912-913.

80. H. and H. H. Frankfort, *et al., The Intellectual Adventure of Ancient Man*, p. 12.

81. See J. Muilenburg, "The 'Office' of the Prophet in Ancient Israel," in J. P. Hyatt, ed., *op. cit.*, pp. 74-97.

82. H. and H. H. Frankfort, *et al., op. cit.*, pp. 63-64.

83. See E. Douglas van Buren, *Symbols of the Gods in Mesopotamian Art*, pp. 1-7; A. L. Oppenheim, "Assyria and Babylonia," *IDB*, I, pp. 298-99. Farbridge pays considerable attention to these symbols as they appear on the Kudurru or Boundary Stones; see J. Pritchard, *Ancient Near East in Pictures*, Figs. 454, 518-21.

Farbridge refers to the possible Egyptian origin of the winged sundisk symbol, offering Joel 2:2 (?) as a possible Old Testament illustration (pp. 177-78). More likely is Mal. 4:2 ("the sun of righteousness shall rise with healing in its wings"), although the association with healing complicates the interpretation. See T. H. Gaster, *Myth, Legend and Custom in the Old Testament*, pp. 698-90, 736-37. In its Egyptian form the wings had a primary association with the falcon (=Horus) and so with Pharaoh. From its origins in Egypt it can be traced, with variations in form, in Canaan, Phoenicia, and Syria, in Anatolia among the Hittites, in Assyria associated with Ashur, and in Persia where Ahura-Mazda is seated in the center of the disk, as various cultural elements effected its representation and significance. It occurs on an Ugaritic relief, on a Megiddo ivory, on a 10th century cultic stand from Taanach, and probably on royal jar-handle stamps from the late Judean monarchy. See H. Frankfort, *Cylinder Seals*, pp. 207-15; D. Diringer, "The Royal Jar-Handle Stamps," *BA*, XII (1949), pp. 70-85; J. B. Pritchard, *Hebrew Inscriptions and Stamps from Gibeon*, 1959, pp. 18-23; E. Douglas van Buren, *Symbols of the Gods in Mesopotamia*, pp. 87-104.

84. H.-J. Kraus, *op. cit.*, p. 150.

85. Contrast J. A. Wilson, *The Burden of Egypt*, 1951, p. 305. (the worship of animals was no feature of the earlier Egyptian religion), and discussion by H. Frankfort, *Ancient Egyptian Religion*, pp. 8-14, where it is noted that hybrid animal-human forms in the Egyptian cult are not transitional forms between a cult of animals and anthropomorphic forms, for the earliest preserved statues of Min were anthropomorphic, and to the very end of Egypt's dependence gods were believed to be manifest in animals.

86. T. H. Gaster, art. "Baal-zebub," *IDB*, I, p. 322; A. S. Kapelrud, *Baal in the Ras Shamra Texts*, pp. 60 ff.; cf. F. C. Fensham, "A Possible Explanation of the Name of Baal-Zebub of Ekron," *ZAW*, LXXIX (1967), pp. 361-64 (=Baal, the Flame, comparing Ugaritic d̲bb).

87. See I. M. Price, *The Great Cylinder Inscriptions A and B of Gudea*, 1927, pp. 31-32.

88. T. H. Gaster, *Myth, Legend, and Custom in the Old Testament*, pp. 769, 850-51.

89. See e.g., J. B. Pritchard, *Ancient Near East in Pictures*, Figs. 490, 493.

90. Cf., e.g., J. B. Pritchard, *ibid.*, Figs. 500-502, 519-21.

91. W. F. Albright, *Yahweh and the Gods of Canaan*, pp. 197-98. See O.
Eissfeldt, "Lade und Stierbilder," *ZAW*, LVII (1940), pp. 190-215); W. Harrelson,
art. "Calf, Golden," *IDB*, I, pp. 489-90; M. Weippert, "Gott und Stier," *ZDPV*,
LXXVII (1961), pp. 93-117.
92. F. S. Bodenheimer, art. "Fauna," *IDB*, I, p. 251; Odel Shepherd, *The Lore
of the Unicorn*, 1930.
93. See the extensive bibliography on the sacred tree in M. Eliade, *Patterns in
Comparative Religion*, pp. 324-27. E. Douglas van Buren, *Symbols of the Gods in
Mesopotamian Art*, pp. 22-29. E. O. James, *The Tree of Life*, 1966. W. L. Reed,
The Asherah in the Old Testament, 1949.
94. M. Eliade, *Images and Symbols*, ch. 1. A. J. Wensinck, *The Ideas of the
Western Semites concerning the Navel of the Earth*, 1916; *The Tree and Bird as
Cosmological Symbols in Western Asia*, 1921, pp. 25-35. G. Widengren, *The King
and the Tree of Life in Ancient Near Eastern Religion*, 1951. For the navel of
the world concept, see more recently Samuel S. Terrien, "The Omphalos Myth
and Hebrew Religion," *VT*, XX (1970) (in press); G. R. H. Wright, "The
Mythology of Pre-Israelite Shechem," *VT*, XX (1970), pp. 75-82; T. H. Gaster,
Thespis, 170-71; M. Eliade, *Patterns in Comparative Religion*, 374 ff.; B. S. Childs,
Myth and Reality in the Old Testament, pp. 83-93.
95. W. Harrelson, *From Fertility Cult to Worship*, 1969, p. 71; see also G. von
Rad, *Old Testament Theology I* (1962), pp. 364 ff.
96. See A. Heller, *Biblische Zahlensymbolik*, 1936. M. Pope, art. "Number," in
IDB, III, pp. 560-67. See bibliography M. Lurker, *op. cit.*, Nos. 8169, 8170, 8194,
8197, 8188, 8182, 8231, 8244. And now see K. Minninger, *Number Words and
Number Symbols:A Cultural History of Numbers*, 1970.
97. *Symbols of Prehistoric Mesopotamia*, pp. 8, 61, 82, 106, 146, etc.
98. For illustrations of abstract number symbols in 21st Dynasty Egypt, see
B. L. Goff, "The Significance of Symbols; A Hypothesis Tested with Relation to
Egyptian Symbols," in J. Neusner, ed., *Religions in Antiquity*, pp. 476-505.
99. Y. Yadin, "Ancient Judean Weights and the Date of the Samaria Ostraca,"
Scripta Hierosolymitana, III (1960), pp. 1-17; G. E. Wright, *Biblical Archaeology*,
rev. ed., 1962, p. 163.
100. For example, that *'éser*, "ten," is philologically connected with Hebrew śr,
"prince," and that this is part of the data helping us to understand why the
number ten and its multiples symbolize greatness, exaltation, and magnitude is
less probable than other conjectures, e.g., that Arabic cognates suggest a root idea
of a group, band, or a whole.
101. J. Barr, *The Semantics of Biblical Language* (1961), pp. 100-60; see also
Barr's discussion of numerals, pp. 96-100.
102. *ZAW*, LXXXI (1969), pp. 78-82.
103. See also, more recently, Julius and Hildegard Lewy, "The Origin of the
Week and the Oldest West Asiatic Calendar," *HUCA*, XVII (1942-43), pp. 3, 103.
104. *Op. cit.*, pp. 19-20. See also pp. 75-109, the reconstruction of the pentecontad
calendar, and J. Morgenstern, "The Calendar of the Book of Jubilees, Its Origin
and Its Character," *VT*, V (1955), pp. 35-76.
105. N. H. Tur-Sinai, "Sabbat und Woche," *Bibliotheca Orientalis*, VIII (1951),
pp. 14-24.
106. *Worship in Israel*, pp. 85-87. It is not clear why the statement that the
Sabbath was to be observed "to Yahweh" (Exod. 20:10; Lev. 23:3) suggests that
a traditional institution was taken over by the Yahweh faith.
107. There is no evidence of the connection of the Babylonian *Šabattu* with the
days of evil omen or that the 15th of every month bore that designation. See
T. H. Gaster, *Festivals of the Jewish Year*, 1952, p. 264. It has been maintained
that the Sabbath had its origin in an early West Semitic pentecontad calendar

current before 1000 B.C., based on a basic unit of a week of seven days in a year
of 365 days, divided into seven pentacontads or fifty-day periods (7 x 7 plus 1),
plus two festival periods of seven days each (the feasts of ingathering and of unleavened bread), plus one additional day. See H. and J. Lewy, *op. cit.*, pp. 1-152;
J. Morgenstern, art. "Sabbath" in *IDB*, IV, pp. 135-41.

108. R. de Vaux, *Ancient Israel, Its Life and Institutions*, pp. 475-83.

109. See C. Gordon, *Ugaritic Literature*, 1949, pp. 4-5. The annual resurrection
of Tammuz in the myth, sometimes regarded as doubtful, now seems definitely established: S. N. Kramer, "Dumuzi's Annual Resurrection; An Important Correction
to 'Inanna's Descent,' " *BASOR*, 183 (1966), p. 31.

110. A. S. Kapelrud, "The Number Seven in the Ugaritic Texts," *VT*, XVIII
(1968), pp. 494-99. See also A. Bea, "Der Zahlspruch in Hebräischen und
Ugaritischen," *Biblica*, XXI (1940), pp. 196-98. See M. H. Pope, art. "Number,"
IDB, III, 561-67.

111. In an unpublished study of "I will not turn it back" in Amos chs. 1, 2 by
R. Knierim. For detailed discussion of graded numerical sayings and bibliographies,
see W. M. W. Roth, *Numerical Sayings in the Old Testament; A Form Critical
Study*, *VT Suppl.*, XIII (1965).

112. See D. N. Freedman, "The New World of the Old Testament," address
given on inauguration as Professor of Hebrew and Old Testament Literature, May
7, 1968. He finds that five and combinations of three and two are also important
in the organization of the oracles. If such an arrangement is deliberate, there is
no evidence of the involvement of numerical symbolism.

113. P. W. Skehan, "Wisdom's House," *CBQ*, XXIX (1967), pp. 484-86
(178-80); cf. R. E. Murphy, "Form Criticism and Wisdom Literature, *CBQ*, XXXI
(1969), pp. 482-83.

114. See S. Gevirtz, "Abraham's 318," *IEJ*, XIX (1969), pp. 110-113.

115. K. Stenring, *The Enclosed Garden, With Introduction by G. J. Larsson*,
1965. For a critique rejecting the hypothesis, see J. Meysing, "L'énigme de la
chronologie biblique et qumranienne dans une nouvelle lumière," *RQ*, VI (1967),
pp. 229-51; rebuttal by G. Larsson, "Is Biblical Chronology Systematic or Not?"
RQ, VI (1969), pp. 499-516.

116. E. R. Thiele, *The Mysterious Numbers of the Hebrew Kings*, rev. ed., 1965.

117. E. Laubscher, *Phänomene der Zahl in der Bibel*, 1955. See also L. Stal-
naker, *Mystic Symbolism in the Bible Numerals*, 1952, a layman's collation and
classification. As a curiosity, reference may be made to R. McCormack, *The
Heptadic Structure of Scripture*, published in the year that Farbridge's work appeared, and described by a reviewer as illustrating the desire at all costs to
be heptadic.

118. E. Anati, *Palestine Before the Hebrews*, pp. 90-109 (Middle Paleolithic),
pp. 170-78 (Mesolithic), pp. 254-56, 278-83 (Neolithic), pp. 288-92 (Chalcolithic), etc. K. Kenyon, *Archaeology in the Holy Land*, 1960; see p. 321 for index
of her discussion of burial customs from the Mesolithic to the Iron Age. Eric
M. Meyers, "Secondary Burials in Palestine," *BA*, XXXII (1970), pp. 2-29.

119. See J. Gray, *The Legacy of Canaan*, pp. 53-54, 183.

120. See T. H. Gaster, *Myth, Legend, and Custom in the Old Testament*, pp.
590-602. For discussion of this and other rites associated with the dead, see J.
Morgenstern, *Rites of Birth, Marriage, Death, and Kindred Occasions among the
Semites*, 1966, pp. 105-179.

121. See R. de Vaux, *Ancient Israel, Its Life and Institutions*, pp. 432-35; *Studies in Old Testament Sacrifice*, transl. by J. Bourke and R. Potter, 1964. See
also, R. Ringgren, *Sacrifice in the Bible*, 1962; H. W. Robinson, "Hebrew Sacrifice and Prophetic Symbolism," *JTS*, XLIII (1942), pp. 129-39. There were many

common elements in Israelite and Canaanite sacrificial rites and terminology.

122. See also another "Pazuzu plaque" reproduced in J. B. Pritchard, *Supplementary Texts and Pictures*, Fig. 857 (from *Nimrud*, M. E. L. Mallowan, *op. cit.*, I, p. 119, Fig. 60).

123. See, e.g., N. J. Tromp, *Primitive Conceptions of Death and the Netherworld in the Old Testament*, 1969, pp. 209, and bibliography noted there.

124. J. Gray, *The Legacy of Canaan*, pp. 92-93: "The Rephaim," *PEQ*, LXXXI (1949) pp. 127-39; see also *Ugaritica*, VI, pp. 299-300. For identification of *rp'um* with "gods of the earth-underworld," see Tromp., *op. cit.*, pp. 176-80.

125. Compare the suggestion that Sheol etymologically denoted "examination, ordeal," and that originally ša'al was the name of an underworld god or goddess. See the discussion in N. J. Tromp., *op. cit.*, p. 22.

126. The difficult issue of ancestor worship is involved. Compare Albright's view that the *bâmôt* or high places were strikingly parallel to Greek hero shrines and the interpretation of the god *'Il'ib* at Ugarit as the patron of ancestor worship (*Yahweh and the Gods of Canaan*, pp. 141-42, 204-6). In a passage in the Aqhat epic, this has been taken as a reference to ancestral spirits, ancestral gods, or an ancestral god. See text and discussion in J. Gray, "Social Aspects of Canaanite Religion, *"VT Suppl.,"* XV (1965), p. 173. For a presentation of the data see Gaster, *Thespis*, pp. 274-75. Note the designation of the spirit of the dead as Elohim, god, in 1 Sam. 29:13.

127. A. L. Oppenheim, art. "Assyria and Babylonia," *IDB*, I, p. 295. See also H. Frankfort, *Kingship and the Gods*, pp. 224-26, 297-312.

128. In connection with this and other subjects treated in this Prolegomenon, there are many studies of specific aspects of the subjects which might have been included in our bibliographical data. To give but one example at this point, see the discussion of the role of the desert as a notion parallel to the Nether World among the Sumerians and the Eastern and Western Semites by A. Haldar, *The Notion of the Desert in Sumero-Accadian and West Semitic Religions*, 1950.

PREFACE

IT was whilst engaged in the preparation of the article Symbolism (Semitic) for Hastings' *Encyclopedia of Religion and Ethics*, that I realized the necessity for a work entirely devoted to so important a branch of Biblical and Semitic Studies. To write an exhaustive work on so wide a subject would be a life-task in itself, but I was induced to prepare this volume in the hope that it may serve as an introduction to a subject which has hitherto attracted very little attention, and concerning which very few contributions of scientific value have been published.

It was recognized long ago that the language of the Bible—especially in the prophetical writings of the Old Testament—was not always intended to be taken literally, but when interpreted symbolically conveys important truths presented in the form of parable. As a means of presenting abstract ideas this form of language was most suited to the infancy of the world's religious era. The discovery of symbolism in the Bible was then carried to great extremes, and every syllable and letter of its contents was believed to contain some hidden symbolical meaning which became the basis for the doctrines of various religious creeds and sects. Whilst, however, several of these went to the most absurd lengths and thereby tended only to bring discredit on the opinions which they held, yet their efforts can be described as the abuse of a principle which is in itself right and, within its proper limits, is calculated to lead to a clearer conception of ancient Hebraic thought.

I am well aware that two schools among ethnologists are seeking to interpret symbolism on new lines—the Historical School associated with the names of Dr. H. R. Rivers (see his " Symbolism of Rebirth " in *Folk Lore*, March, 1922), Dr. G. Elliot Smith (see his *Evolution of the Dragon*, 1919), and Mr. W. J. Perry (see his *Children of the Sun*, 1923) ;

and the Psycho-Analytical School, associated with the names of Dr. Sigmund Freud (see his *Totem and Taboo*, 1919), Dr. C. G. Jung (see his *Psychology of the Unconscious*, 1919), and Dr. Otto Rank (see his *Myth of the Birth of the Hero*, New York, 1914, and his *Psychoanalytische Beiträge zur Mythenforschung*, 2nd ed., Leipzig, 1922). But, on the whole, I have felt that my first task should be to collect the material available and attempt to interpret it from purely Semitic sources.

If we compare many of the religious symbols of the ancient Hebrews with those of other Semitic nations, we find that there is a close and intimate connexion between them. In fact, the starting-points of many religious forms which expressed themselves in symbols were the same throughout, although on being transferred from the polytheistic religions of their neighbours to the monotheistic teachings of the Hebrews they passed through the fire of Divine purification. So that whilst there is a close similarity between Hebrew and other Semitic Symbols, those of Israel survived, and their influence lived long after other Semitic States had vanished and their power was well-nigh forgotten. And this was entirely due to the fact that this small Semitic people which had once been a nation of slaves in Egypt brought new religious ideals to the world of men who sought after God.

I wish to express my profound indebtedness to my senior colleague, Professor Maurice A. Canney, M.A., who has always been my " guide, philosopher, and friend ". He has read a considerable part of the work in MS., and it affords me pleasure to express my gratitude for many helpful suggestions.

I also feel deeply grateful to the Rev. B. Rodriguez Pereira, B.A., who has favoured me with his kind and liberal assistance in correcting the proofs and in the preparation of the index.

M. H. F.

UNIVERSITY OF MANCHESTER.
June, 1923.

ABBREVIATIONS

BDB. = The Oxford Hebrew Lexicon (Briggs, Driver, Brown).

CT. = Cuneiform Texts from Babylonian Tablets in the British Museum, 1896.

JE. = Jewish Encyclopædia.

K. = Kouyunjik Collection of Cuneiform Tablets in the British Museum.

KAT. = Die Keilinschriften und das Alte Testament, Eberhard Schrader, 3rd ed., Berlin, 1903.

KB. = Keilinschriftliche Bibliothek, Eberhard Schrader, Berlin, 1889, etc.

MDP. = Délégation en Perse. Mémories publiès sur la direction de J. de Morgan, Paris, 1900–13.

PSBA. = Proceedings of the Society of Biblical Archæology.

RBA. = Jastrow's Religion of Babylonia and Assyria (English edition).

ThLZ. = Theologische Literaturzeitung.

ZA. = Zeitschrift für Assyriologie.

ZATW. = Zeitschrift für die Alttestamentliche Wissenschaft.

ZDMG. = Zeitschrift der Deutschen Morgenländischen Gesellschaft.

ZNTW. = Zeitschrift für die Neutestamentliche Wissenschaft.

CHAPTER I

THE DEVELOPMENT OF BIBLICAL AND SEMITIC SYMBOLISM

CHAPTER I

THE DEVELOPMENT OF BIBLICAL AND SEMITIC
SYMBOLISM

Symbolism originated in the efforts of intuitively intelligent human beings to convey ideas and information by the use of certain signs. In the simpler stages of society mankind can be taught general truths only by symbols and parables. Whereas the idiomatic phraseology which characterizes a restricted form of expression is wholly inadequate or else misleading and obscure when utilized in the domain of spiritual analyses, the symbol often illumines the understanding beyond the bounds of human intellection. In religion, as in art and literature, symbolism corresponds with a necessity of the human mind which has never been able to content itself with pure abstractions.

The tendency to give a substantial visible form to an abstract idea is so deeply rooted in humanity that it must be looked upon as responding to a human necessity. It is only very rarely that purely intellectual conceptions can satisfy us—they must be given some external palpable and visible form to exert their greater influence. Creeds are inadequate to express the emotional side of religions, and, in consequence, creeds never do fulfil the desire for full expression of the sentiment of wonder worship in man. In the words of Dean Inge: "The truth is that the need of symbols to express or represent our highest emotions is inwoven with human nature, and indifference to them is not, as many have supposed, a sign of enlightenment or spirituality. It is in fact an unhealthy symptom. We do not credit a man with a warm heart who does not care to show his love in word or act, nor should we commend the common sense of a soldier who saw in his regimental colours only a rag at the end of a pole." [1] As Victor Hugo says in *L'Homme qui rit:* " Il est presque impossible d'exprimer dans leur limites exactes les évolutions abstruses qui se font dans le cerveau. L'inconvénient des mots, c'est d'avoir plus de contour que les idées. Toutes les idées se mêlent par les bords ; les mots, non. Un certain côté diffus de l'âme leur échappe toujours. L'expression a des frontières la pensée n'en a pas." This explains why we find almost all early religions becoming mythic, and explaining their mysteries by allegories or national incidents. Lord Bacon has more than once declared that as hieroglyphics preceded letters, so parables are older than arguments.

According to Porphyry " The ancients were willing to conceal God and divine virtue by sensible figures, and by those things which are visible yet signifying invisible things ".[2] For instance, the world, sun, hope, eternity, were symbolized by round things ; whilst the heavens were represented by a circle, a segment of which indicated the moon. This fact was recognized by humanity in the incipiency of its spiritual teachings, and we can thus understand why even at present our thoughts about the highest and deepest subjects deteriorate in our attempts to express them with precision, and why great ideas as well as deep feelings are very often more convincingly conveyed to many people in music than in words.

Similarly a pictorial representation of an idea or thought often produces a much better effect than a description of it in words. And as art has always preceded language, pictorial art has always produced

---

[1] *Christian Mysticism*, p. 259.

[2] It is of interest to note that many ancient Oriental writers were compelled to make use of symbolism as a mask as the only possible means of imparting mystical truth when plain speaking would have been dangerous. See *Studies in Islamic Mysticism*, by Nicholson, pp. 232, 257.

a much more lasting impression on the memory than written or spoken words, and it was by its symbolical ornamentation and architecture that spiritual and religious truths were taught and explained. Early Christian art was full of symbols whose uses and meanings were discussed in various treatises. Didron, in his work on Christian Iconography, writes : " For those men of the Middle Ages, for those Christians of lively susceptibility, but who yet knew not how to read, the clergy provided rondes-bosses, bas-reliefs, and pictures where science on the one hand and doctrine on the other were personified. A sculptured arch in the porch of a church, or an historical glass painting in the nave presented the ignorant with a lesson, the believer with a sermon—a lesson and a sermon which reached the heart through the eyes instead of entering at the ears. The impression, besides, was infinitely deeper, for it is acknowledged that a picture sways the soul far more powerfully than any discourse or description in words."

We thus find that not only in the ancient East but even in mediaeval England symbolism permeated the whole life of the people, and entered into the observances of chivalry, the very armour of the valiant knight being full of symbolical meanings which it was his duty to know. The abbot had his rebus worked into the capitals or bosses of his abbey, and even the merchant placed his sign or the emblem of his trade outside his warehouse.

Various definitions have been given of the word " symbol ". It has been defined by some scholars as " a representation which does not aim at being a reproduction ", by others as " a form of representing a thought or fact which is difficult to express by words alone ", by others again as " an image couched in the language of human experience which is not to be understood literally by the trained intelligence, but only as the best available expression of transcendent spiritual realities ". But whatever definition may be given of the term, it is of the utmost importance to notice that while its original functions may have been used merely to represent an image, an idea, or an emotion, its importance has often grown and developed so considerably that the symbol has ended by replacing the very object or idea it was intended to represent, thus acquiring much greater importance than that which was originally assigned to it.[1]

In later times the great classical example of " symbolic statements " is to be found in Plato's stories which, although appearing as simple narratives, can easily be understood to be valuable only because they are the vehicles of certain thoughts and ideas. The Alexandrian Jews like Philo made use of this form of symbolism as one of their methods in their interpretation of the Old Testament; whilst in later times Jewish philosophers like Spinoza looked upon this method as a bridge between what they thought to be intellectually true and spiritually edifying for humanity.

But as man found that words are altogether inefficient to give expression to the infinite contents of the human soul, and as in primitive society the art of writing as giving lasting and permanent expression to one's ideas and thoughts had not yet developed, there arose the necessity for symbolical actions as a means of accompanying and supplementing human speech. One can gather the necessity for symbolical actions from our present-day forms of intercourse amongst men. Even nowadays speech is often accompanied by gesture; and various parts of the body, the hands or the head in particular, are used to illustrate or emphasize one's thoughts or meaning. How much more must these gestures have been necessary in early times when human speech had not yet reached the stage of development it has attained to-day! Scholars are agreed that from the very earliest times " the audible word has been accompanied by the visible gesture ". In fact, in many cases symbolical actions really preceded human speech, for the thoughts

[1] G. Ferrero, *Les lois psychologiques du symbolisme*, Paris, 1895.

which stir man's mind to adopt such actions are already
there and express themselves forcibly before he possesses
sufficient verbal power to make them clear to his neighbour ;
so that the symbol shows clearly all that he does and is
before he is able to express his thoughts in words. Again
the symbolical action served another purpose. At a period
when the art of writing had not yet developed the symbol
took its place and was used as a means of creating an
indelible impression on the mind of man.

We can thus see how there arose in the intercourse of
mankind the necessity for symbolical actions of every kind.
If two men had made a covenant binding each other by
mere words to preserve it, the covenant would have been
altogether valueless. Words rustle past like the wind and
soon pass out of memory. It was absolutely necessary,
therefore, that the verbal agreement should be accompanied
by a symbol which would produce a profound and lasting
impression on the mind, and would indicate clearly to both
parties the punishment they would receive in case they
violated it. Thus there arose amongst all peoples various
ceremonies which formed part of the taking of an oath or
the making of a covenant.

For example, amongst the Hebrews the one who took an
oath lifted up his right hand towards heaven and thus
pointed to the throne of the deity who was invoked as
a witness to the truth and as the avenger of falsehood.

This explains why the phrase " to lift up the hand " was
used to denote the taking of an oath. But there were other
more elaborate and impressive symbolical ceremonies.
Sometimes an animal was killed and divided into two pieces
and the parties walked between them to show that they
invoked a similar doom of destruction upon themselves if
they proved unfaithful to their oath. (Gen. xv,
Jer. xxxiv, 18 f.)

Another custom was for the person who took the oath
to place his hand under the " thigh " of the adjurer.
(Gen. xxiv, 2 ; xlvii, 29.) This practice arose from the

fact that the genital member which is meant by the euphemistic expression " thigh " was regarded as especially sacred being the symbol of perpetuity and union in matrimonial life. As a matter of fact it was actually an object of worship amongst many nations of antiquity. No more impressive ceremony could therefore have been performed in early days than for a man to touch the symbol of creation and the source of that issue who may, at any future date, be called upon to maintain an oath which has been taken, or revenge one which has been broken. Thus we read of Joseph taking an oath by placing his hand upon the organs of generation and so does Eliezer with Abraham. Even at the present day this form of oath is to be found amongst certain Arabian tribes [1] who actually swear by the " phallus of Allah ".

There are numerous references in Babylonian literature to the ceremony connected with the taking of an oath or the making of an agreement. The judge administered the oath at the shrine of Shamash (the sun-god who was also the great judge of the universe), in Sippar, or before the dragon which was sculptured on the doors of the temple of Marduk at Babylon. In the case of a contract not to alter the stipulated agreement, the oath was followed by the words " whoever shall alter or dispute the words of this tablet ". The punishment for so doing is not stated, but this was because it was considered too terrible to mention. A kind of " magical conjuration " was employed sometimes, but the meaning of this is not yet understood. These very words and ceremonies thus represented clearly to all concerned the potency and efficiency of the oath which had been taken.

Again, on the annulment of a former agreement, the cancelling of a deed, the dissolution of a partnership or the payment of a debt, a ceremony took place, part of which consisted in the breaking of a tablet. The symbolism connected with such a ceremony is obvious.

[1] Nork, *Mythologie*, i, 154.

Let us consider a few further examples. Amongst the ancient Hebrews business transactions took place publicly in the market-place so that the presence of the whole community, or at least ten of the elders, served to confirm them. (Gen. xxiii.) Now, if a mere verbal agreement had been made between the two parties it would have been soon forgotten. As an aid to the memory, therefore, there arose the custom of drawing off the shoes in transferring a possession or domain. (Ruth iv, 7.) The idea was that the person who gave up a possession should show by removing his shoe that he was thus divesting himself of something before the witnesses. This could then be regarded as a public declaration that he was withdrawing from the property and handing it over to another person. In the book of Ruth the delivering of a shoe signified that the next-of-kin transferred to another a sacred obligation.[1] When the art of writing became much more common in ancient Israel this practice fell out of usage, and, instead, as a means of perpetuating the transaction, two copies of a document, signed by the witnesses, were prepared. One copy was for public use, whilst the other was sealed and only opened officially if any doubt arose as to the genuineness of the former.

Another reason for the importance of these symbolical actions was the firm belief that they were being executed in the presence of the deity who could therefore constantly be invoked as a witness to their permanency. Such a belief existed in Babylonia also, and, therefore, when legal documents—particularly those dealing with the ownership of land—were drawn up there were carried at the head of the stelae the symbols of the chief gods of the pantheon. At times, also, symbols of various gods were sculptured upon a stone monument to show that it was under the protection of the gods whose symbols were represented.

---

[1] In order to symbolize the marriage contract in Babylonia the officiating minister bound sandals on the feet of the newly wedded pair. See Chap. VII.

But it was mainly in the domain of religion that these signs and symbols were employed, for in man's relationship with the great Eternal all human words and expressions, however beautiful and perfect, are altogether inadequate to express his inmost feelings. Religion depends for its inexhaustible power upon symbols of its life and as soon as these symbols are performed they help to emphasize its existence to both its adherents and opponents.

This leads us on to the numerous symbolical actions which were employed by the Hebrew prophets as means of attracting attention and impressing their teachings upon the minds of observers. When Saul accidentally tore Samuel's robe, the prophet interpreted it as indicating that Saul's kingdom would be torn away from him. Ahijah tore his garment into twelve pieces and gave ten to Jeroboam to symbolize the partition of Solomon's kingdom. Zedekiah, a false prophet, put on horns in order to show that Ahab would push the Syrians with horns of iron. In Zechariah xi we read that the prophet took a staff as an emblem of the two Israelitish kingdoms, and broke it to symbolize the breaking of brotherhood between Israel and Judah. Isaiah walked about naked and barefoot for three years as a sign that the king of Assyria would lead away, captive, the Egyptians and Ethiopians naked and barefoot.

Such symbolical actions are particularly common in Jeremiah and Ezekiel. In order to show to the people that Jerusalem would be destroyed, Jeremiah shattered an earthen vessel before the people. On another occasion he placed bands and bars upon his neck and then sent them to the kings of Edom and Moab and their allies (who were trying to persuade Zedekiah to rebel against the king of Babylon) with the announcement that the yoke of Babylon would be laid upon all those countries. Ezekiel removed all his goods from his house as a sign of the approaching exile. He also shaved his head and destroyed the hairs, with the exception of a few, to illustrate the fate in store for the nation.

Now, in considering the special symbolical actions of the prophetic books we are confronted with very great difficulty, for scholars are divided in their views as to whether these actions were actually performed in their literal sense or were merely conceived as symbolic visions in the minds of the prophets. It seems almost certain that there are a number of such actions which could not have been performed literally, and a brief discussion of some of these from the Books of Jeremiah and Ezekiel may give some indication as to the difficulties in arriving at a definite decision. In Jer. xiii, 1-11, God tells the prophet to go to the Euphrates and hide his linen girdle in a rock. After a while he is told to remove the girdle and then finds it to be marred. The lesson is that just as a girdle from its nature clings to a person, so Israel is closely united to God.

On the one hand, it may seem unlikely that Jeremiah should have undertaken a journey from Jerusalem to Babylon, a distance of about 200 miles, in order to bring out this point to the people. But it is possible that the journey *was* actually performed. (1) We know that the prophet was absent from Jerusalem during part of Jehoiakim's reign, and, as we have no account of his whereabouts during this period, it is possible that he had made the journey to Babylon during this time. (2) In Jer. xxxix, 11, we are told that Nebuchadrezzar behaved most friendly towards him on the capture of Jerusalem. This could be explained by the suggestion that king and prophet had met previously and that it was on this occasion of the prophet's visit to Babylon.

In Ezek. iv, 5, we are told that the prophet lay upon his side for 390 days. How can this be taken literally ? Did any person actually count the number of days ? In iv, 12, we are told that he used human excrement for fuel in baking some barley cakes. Surely it cannot reasonably be suggested that the prophet would have inconvenienced himself by going to such extremes merely in order to bring home to the people some divine message which he could very well have preached in a much more suitable manner. There are some scholars, however, chief of whom is Klostermann, who argue that these symbolical actions *were* performed.[1] The dumbness of Ezekiel (iii, 24–7), they suggest, was due to a temporary loss of speech, and they explain similar performances by somewhat similar suggestions. Against this it may be argued that the very fact that the divine command to the prophet to carry out a symbolical action is introduced by the words " Give to the rebellious house a parable and say to them, Thus saith the Lord God, set on the cauldron and pour water into it, etc." (Ezek. xxiv, 3), suggests that Ezekiel does not carefully distinguish between symbolical actions actually performed and merely spoken parables.   Again, in some cases instead of being informed that the symbolical action was actually performed we are given an account rather of its symbolical meaning (Ezek. iv, 16 ; v, 5 ; xii, 19).   These arguments, as well as the belief that many of the symbolical actions referred to in the book of Ezekiel could not actually have been performed, have led many scholars to regard the symbolisms of the Book of Ezekiel which are not definitely stated to have been performed as merely a kind of *meshalim* or parables centring round the prophet as the representative of Israel.[2]

But in our attempts to trace the development of religious symbolism, we must consider, also, the origin of symbolical representations of the deity amongst the ancient Semites.   The human mind constantly craves to express its religious conceptions by some physical forms, and as it is in the nature of man to desire to have within his reach an object which represents to him something which he loves or

---

[1] See his article, " Ezechiel : ein Beitrag zur besseren Würdigung seiner Person und seiner Schrift " : in *Studien und Kritiken*, 1877, pp. 391 ff. ; also L. Gautier, *La Mission du prophète Ezechiel*, 1891, pp. 85 ff., and Kraetzschmar, *Ezechiel*, 1900.

[2] See König, " Zur Deutung der symbolischer Handlungen des Propheten Hesekiel " : *neue kirchliche Zeitschrift*, 1892 ; also Toy, " Ezekiel " : in *SBOT*, and Hühn, *Die Messianischen Weissagungen*, 1899, p. 160.

adores, it was only natural that at a very early stage of civilization man should have begun to set up images and symbols of the gods he worshipped and should have kept them in his own home.

As a result of excavations in Palestine numerous statuettes, images of goddesses, and bas-reliefs have been discovered in private houses. Some primitive peoples in their anxiety to have their patron gods as near to them as possible went even further and engraved a portrait or image of their gods on their bodies. It was this which gave rise to tattooing.

Now, at a very early stage in this development man began to feel the need of representing the root sources of all phenomena of nature which appeared to him so superhuman and mysterious by means of natural or artificial objects. He thus began to associate human or animal features with various objects in nature.[1] But after a time the previous significance of the image was entirely forgotten and a new myth was invented to explain its meaning. This accounts for the origin and development of many symbols. In Babylonia, for example, the numerous symbols or emblems by which the different gods of the pantheon were recognized arose through the characters which these gods had assumed in mythology.

Whether the sacred image which man made to represent his deity was worshipped in one form or another, in the first stage it was looked upon as a sign or representative of some divine personage.[2] Then it came to be regarded as a living being possessed of energy and animation. The image was treated as possessing personal consciousness and power, and its worshippers talked to it and prayed and sacrificed to it just as though it were a real conscious being. The image was thus " a receptacle for the spirit of the god ", and was

---

[1] For example, the spirits which inspired terror in the hearts of the Babylonians were symbolized by a human body crowned with the head of an angry lion with dog's ears.
[2] Tylor, *Primitive Culture*, ii.

the object in which the god had made his abode and thus displayed his presence to his adorers.

A careful study of image worship amongst the Semites will convince us that to the Semitic peoples the image was not a mere symbol or representation of the form of the god for whom it stood. It was actually the god himself. The god was localized and present within the image so that he became identical with the image and was the very image itself. A few examples from Babylonian history will help us to understand this point.

When the Elamites were conquered at the time of Hammurabi, the Babylonians carried off the images of certain Elamite goddesses in order to obtain their favour, and at a later time when trouble occurred in Babylonia it was described as having been caused by the anger of these goddesses on account of their having been taken into exile. Again, in one of the Tell el Amarna letters the goddess Ishtar and her statue are actually identified. Tushratta, the king of Mitanni, at the request of the king of Egypt, sent him the statue of Ishtar of Nineveh, together with a letter in which Tushratta exhorts Amenophis to treat Ishtar with honour and allow her to return with joy just as though the statue was the goddess herself. The letter reads as follows : " Thus saith Ishtar of Nineveh, the lady of all lands," " Unto Egypt, into the land which I love, will I go." Tushratta exhorts Amenophis to pay her due honour and to send her back, saying : " Verily now I have sent her and she is gone. Indeed, in the time of my father, the lady Ishtar went into that land : and just as she dwelt there formerly and they honoured her, so now may my brother honour her ten times more than before. May my brother honour her, may he allow her to return with joy."

This belief continued right to the very latest period of Babylonian history, and was one of the causes which brought about the conquest of Babylon. Nabonidus, busy with his historical and archæological researches, and regardless of the feelings of his people, wished to centralize the cultus of Babylon. He therefore collected all the old images of the country into Babylon and thus removed the gods from their own local homes. This action outraged the feelings of the priesthood, and thus when the great hour of danger came he found himself lacking in the support which was so essential for the preservation of his kingdom.

Now that we have seen the extent to which the god was absolutely identified with his image amongst neighbours of the Hebrews we can understand why the making of any visible representation of the deity was so violently opposed by the religious leaders and teachers of the Hebrews. If these images had been mere symbols and had been employed as such, in all probability they would not have been treated with so much scorn and contempt by the Hebrew prophets, and the making of images would not have been so violently opposed by them. But apart from the fact that the religious leaders of Israel believed that God's unique greatness made any visible representation of him impossible, they were afraid that if the Hebrews borrowed any visible representations of their god from the neighbouring peoples and regarded this at first as a mere symbol and nothing more it would not remain so permanently but would eventually be worshipped as a localized image of the God of Israel and actually identified with him.

The Hebrew prophets, therefore, express their utmost scorn both for idols and their worshippers. They describe idols as nothing. If a man cries to them out of his trouble they can neither answer him nor save him (Isa. xli, 24 ; xlvi, 7). They heap up their utter derision upon those who are so foolish as to make a god for worship from the same piece of timber which they use in obtaining fuel to prepare their food. And they emphasize the folly and uselessness of man worshipping sticks and stones made by his own hand.

It is true, of course, that although the image may be realistic it can be interpreted in such a way that it becomes a pure symbol. But the teachers of Israel realized that " man cannot with impunity bring down the invisible God to the sphere of the visible. He thereby empties the idea of God of its ethical content and it loses for him its sanctifying, elevating, disciplinary, and purifying power." They realized that the danger in ancient Israel was that any material symbol of the deity would not be regarded by the masses of the people as an aid to devotion but as a kind of fetish which would bring about an utter degeneration in their religious and national life, and it was for this reason that they opposed, so violently, the making of any material symbol of the deity.

But although the prophets prohibited visible symbolical representations of the deity they did not hesitate to use verbal imagery and symbolism, for the metaphor is in the sphere of words what the symbol is in the sphere of things, and words may just as well be described as symbols as images and statues.   It is to be regretted, however, that an utter misunderstanding of many of the metaphors of the Bible and too literal an explanation of their origin and development have given rise to the fantastic theories of many critical scholars ; whilst the erroneous interpretations of many poetical expressions, which are found not only in Hebrew but in many Semitic and non-Semitic languages, have been employed as proof that to the Hebrews their God was identical in character with other Semitic deities.

Whether we agree with Renan [1] in entirely excluding the Semites from the domain of mythology or with Bunsen that there are myths belonging to the Hebrews (which they borrowed from other races) but no Hebrew myths, we are bound to state that Goldziher's view that " not only Genesis but also the narrative portions of the other Books of Moses, of Joshua, and Judges, are mythical " [2] is certainly altogether beyond the bounds of plausibility.

It is true that in poetical language we find modes of expression which have been preserved from a much earlier period, and that the language of Hebrew poetry and

[1] *Histoire générale et système comparé des langues Sémitiques*, p. 7.
[2] *Mythology among the Hebrews*, p. 420.

metaphor can therefore be used as a means of tracing back their mythological ideas to an early age

But in our zeal to discover the mythological ideas of the Hebrews we must be on our guard against creating and discovering myths from language which is purely metaphorical and poetical.

Let us consider a few examples. Kuenen argues that because the God of Israel is spoken of as a god of fire and light, and is said to have appeared to Moses in the burning bush ; since fire is said to proceed from his mouth and smoke from his nostrils (Ps. xviii, 9), and there are so many references to fire in connexion with theophanies, he must have been regarded as a fire deity and worshipped as such. He therefore arrives at the conclusion that there must have been some relationship between the God of Israel and Molech which gave rise to these expressions. A theory founded on such a basis seems to show a lack of sympathy with the psychology and *Weltanschaung* not only of the Hebrews, but of primitive man generally. In the first place fire is used as a divine symbol by nearly all nations of antiquity.

Man saw there was a fire burning in the sky. There was the fire of the sun's disc and the fire of lightning. Life itself was a fire burning in the body, the extinction of which resulted in death. He therefore came to regard fire like other great natural phenomena, as an emblem of divine power. In the words of Tylor " no material phenomenon seemed to primitive man to be so plainly divine as fire." Surely it was only natural that to the child-like feeling of the Hebrews of remote antiquity, the wondrous nature of fire growing and moving like a divine being, its destructive energy and the torment which it inflicts, should render it a fit symbol of the divinity and thus be symbolically identified with God Himself.[1] This explains why the fiery appearance is part of the endowment of the *summus deus* in so many Old Testament narratives.

[1] Fire or flame was also used in a metaphorical sense to express excited feeling and divine inspiration.

One is reminded of the Rabbinical passage, which says : " The Torah given by God was made of an integument of white fire, the engraved letters were in black fire, and it was itself of fire and mixed with fire, hewn out of fire, and given from the midst of fire." (*Yer. Sotah*, viii, 22.)

Surely the fact that the Hebrews and Canaanites both represented their deities as appearing in fire does not necessarily prove that there must have been any borrowing of religious ideas. "A man is not the less intelligent inventor of a new word or a new metaphor because twenty other intelligent inventors elsewhere may have fallen on a similar expedient."

Man's first attempt to express his conception of unseen things results in metaphor, so that all religious language is metaphorical, and if the Hebrews employed religious phraseology which is very similar to that used by their neighbours, this is no proof that their religion passed through the same stages of development.

But to return to Goldziher and the methods he employs. In his *Mythology of the Hebrews* he traces back nearly all the Old Testament names to their original meanings, and then uses them and the narratives in which they occur as mere symbols of old mythological ideas, which have been worked over by a later monotheistic writer from a previous age of polytheism. Now, whilst one may be prepared to agree that many Hebrew names and metaphors may have arisen from mythology, surely this is no indication that at a much later period they were still employed in the same original sense. The mythological ideas on which the metaphor was based must have been forgotten entirely, and the expression must have been used by the Hebrews as a verbal image or symbol without any thought as to its original meaning. The fact that the Christian still calls the first day of the week "Sunday" is no indication that in speaking of "the Lord's day" he is including an Anglo-Saxon deity, from whom the word was originally derived, as part of his theology.

On coming in contact with the Canaanites, the Hebrews learned their theological terms, which embraced their theological conceptions, and made use of them in connexion with their own religion, without their having passed through the same historical and religious experiences. Furthermore, it was only natural that the similarity of the languages of both peoples should have also influenced the Hebrews in making use of the religious terminology of their neighbours and applying them to their own religion. It is in this way, also, that one can explain the imagery and symbolism borrowed from mythology which appear in so many names and metaphors connected with the pure worship of Israel.

Even if a hero bears a name which appears of mythological origin it does not necessarily follow that he himself and the narratives recorded about him merely belong to the domains of mythology. So that whilst Barak means " lightning ", Deborah " a bee ", and Jael " a wild goat ", this cannot be taken as proof that they were not typical Hebrew names during the early period of Hebrew history and that the narrative in the Book of Judges is purely mythical.

Whilst it is unnecessary for us to exaggerate the importance which symbolism played in the religions and civilizations of the ancient Semites, we must admit that the key to a profound understanding and faithful explanation of the ancient Oriental world is hidden in a mysterious system of symbolism which is still exceedingly difficult to interpret. To the Semites all nature was invested with profound sacredness, for it was through this material form that the divine manifested himself to man. In fact, it was regarded that God had constructed both worlds on similar principles, so that the visible world was merely the dial-plate of the invisible. Everything on earth was regarded as a faint shadow cast by the vast heavenly reality. The kingdoms of this world were but the miniature exhibitions, the fleeting shadows of the eternal kingdom above. And it is of interest to note that even the Cabbalists later affirmed

that everything that is in the kingdom of earth is found also
in the kingdom of heaven. We can thus understand why
nature should have played so significant a part in creating
and moulding Semitic symbolism, why so many mental
and spiritual ideas which we have from the Near East are
capable of being understood by us only through the medium
of figures borrowed from external nature, and why it should
have lent to the ancient Orientals imagery for the poetical
and symbolical expressions of their highest thoughts and
deepest feelings. All the letters of the Hebrew alphabet
were originally borrowed from objects in nature. The
signs of the Zodiac by which animals were made to express
the various changes of the revolving year owe their origin
to a like tendency, and the science of heraldry is founded
on the same principle—the originally figurative nature of
all language.

Now, it is clear that so long as symbols remain the image
of some object or perceptible phenomenon the mental
operation which produced them can always be recon-
stituted. But in the domain of abstract ideas the field of
analogy is as vast as that of individual fancy. How could
we ascertain the origin of so abstract a symbol as the
representation of the world under the form of a serpent
biting its tail, if the texts did not inform us that in the
cosmogony of Egypt, of Babylonia, of Greece, and of
India the earth was believed to be circumscribed by an
ocean or celestial river, whose circular course is compared
to a serpent? Many symbols common to the different
races of mankind can hardly be said to have originated
independently amongst them. They have no doubt been
carried from one race to another by its migrations and
conquests. Many of them came from the ancient East,
through the connexion between Babylonia and Egypt.
Then came the internationalization of Hinduism, the
intercourse between the countries of the Indian Ocean and
the Mediterranean, and finally the influence exerted by the
nations of classical antiquity upon modern thought and

life. A few examples may here be given to illustrate how symbols have been modified in the course of their migrations by the people by whom they have been adopted in order to represent their own religious ideas.

The Mesopotamian type of the sacred tree was adopted by the Persians to represent their tree of immortality, by the Buddhists to symbolize their tree of wisdom, and by the Christians to symbolize their tree of temptation. When the Persians conquered Babylonia they converted many Babylonian symbols to represent their own religious ideas. Ahura Mazda appropriated the symbol of Ashur, the Babylonian Demons represented the *devas* which personified all that is impure and false; whilst the trees of Mesopotamian art now represented the Iranian Holy Tree.

We find that Semitic colonists on the border of Egypt used Egyptian symbols in representing their own deities. In the Cairo Museum there is a stele of the Persian period which was found at Tell Defenneh, the probable site of the Biblical Tahpanhes and the Daphnæ of the Greeks, where the Jewish fugitives, fleeing with Jeremiah after the fall of Jerusalem, founded a colony. Near them was a flourishing Aramæan and Phœnician settlement. One of the local gods of Daphnæ is represented on the stele standing on the back of a lion and clothed in Asiatic costume, with a Syrian tiara crowning his hair. There is also a brazen fire-altar before the god and a sacred pillar being anointed by the officiating priest. All of these characteristics show clearly its Syrian workmanship. But the god holds in his left hand a purely Egyptian sceptre, whilst in his right hand is a Babylonian symbol—the weapon of Marduk and Gilgamesh.[1] Again, it has been thought by many scholars that some of the decorated motives on potsherds recently discovered at Susa are the ancestors of some of the sacred emblems which, after being

[1] H. Max Müller, *Egyptological Researches*, pp. 30 f., pl. xl.

developed on Elamite soil, reached Babylonia during the Kassite period.

Let us now trace in the briefest outline how many of our present-day symbols in general, and our modern ideas of the symbolism of numbers in particular, have developed throughout the ages and owe their origin and foundation to the ancient East.

Beginning with Mesopotamia, we find that the cuneiform archive found at Tell el Amarna, in Egypt, which contains a diplomatic correspondence between the monarchs of that country and of Mesopotamia, written about 1500 B.C., proves conclusively the early and active intercourse between the inhabitants of both countries at this early period in the history of civilization.

Furthermore, the latest finds at Lachish, in Palestine, show that the language of Babylonia and the cuneiform script were a current means of intercourse amongst these regions of Western Asia. When we come to India we find that that country borrowed many of its principal symbols from Mesopotamia, from Persia, and even from Greece. India has always been regarded as the home of religious syncretism, and it has generally been admitted that the Indian alphabets are of Semitic origin; whilst in the centuries following the expedition of Alexander it was Greek art which influenced the development of Indian architecture. We have now learned that at the Tell el Amarna period and the period of the Hittite Kings at Boghaz Koi there was a general spread of Babylonian culture in the Nearer East. The elements of Babylonian astronomy found their way into India, and in the course of time exerted very considerable influence upon Indian thought and culture, because, already, centuries previously, commercial relationship between East and West had caused India to become prepared for the reception of Eastern culture. The Babylonian Deluge Narrative, in all probability, influenced the Indian Flood Story, and attempts have also been made to show how the Marduk

Myth exerted considerable influence on the cult of India ; whilst the Babylonian and Vedic stories of the creation have also been identified. An extension of Babylonian mathematics to India and the East of Asia has been considered within the bounds of possibility, and proofs have already been adduced to show that the numeral system of Indian literature based on the Sexagesimal principle owes its origin to Babylonian influences. Sir George Birdwood asserts that nearly all Indian symbols are of Mesopotamian origin (*Journal of Royal Asiatic Society*, London, 1886, vol. xviii, p. 407).

Whilst in earlier times many scholars would have considered it derogatory to Greece to assume that its culture had been considerably influenced by the ancient Orient, it is generally acknowledged to-day that the beginnings of the material civilization of Greece owe almost all their entire origin to the ancient East. Furthermore, even in the domain of religion, as ancient native traditions failed more and more to satisfy their increasing curiosity and thirst for knowledge, they were compelled at a time of acute intellectual progress to draw more and more upon foreign sources. The Semitic Ashtoreth and Adonis, her lover, later the Thracian Bendis and the Phrygian Cybele, as well as other similar foreign deities, were adapted by means of their genius to native traditions. And when we come to the symbolism of numbers we find that just as in Babylonia the individual gods had their own sacred numbers, so Apollo was symbolized by the number one, Artemis by two, Aphrodite by six, Athene by seven, Poseidon by eight, etc. But it is through the Pythagoreans mainly that our present-day ideas concerning the symbolism of numbers have been formed, for, as we shall see later, Pythagoras must have borrowed many of his ideas from the Oriental peoples amongst whom he travelled ; and it was through his disciples and followers that these ideas have influenced us so profoundly in modern times.

CHAPTER II
TREES, PLANTS, AND FLOWERS

CHAPTER II
TREES, PLANTS, AND FLOWERS

It is perhaps correct to say that in the whole range of symbolism no emblem is more widespread or has exerted greater influence upon the institutions of mankind than the branch or tree. Primitive man was impressed by the huge proportions of trees, their age, and the usefulness of their fruits. Furthermore, the tree was to early man his village meeting-place, and his protection from the fierce heat of the sun or the cold or the rain. We can thus understand how after a time he came to regard it as an object of veneration and worship.

Tree-worship and tree-symbolism were particularly common amongst the ancient Semitic peoples, perhaps because to them more than any other section of the human race every element of nature was full of potent spiritual forces. It seems quite clear that as groves were the haunts of wild beasts trees came to be regarded as demoniac beings amongst all the Semitic peoples, and they were thus adored as divine in every part of the Semitic area. " The pines and cedars of Lebanon, the evergreen oaks of the Palestinian hills, the tamarisks of the Syrian jungles, the acacias of the Arabian wadies, besides such cultivated trees as the palm, the olive, and the vine were all venerated by the ancient Semites."

As man was driven to learn the properties of plants and flowers in the earliest period of his existence he soon found that according to their usefulness, their taste, or any peculiarities in their growth, they became a real language to him, and the names which he gave them became symbols of these phenomena. Thus the antiquity of floral symbolism probably dates back to the very earliest times when man sought to express through the instrumentality of flowers his love of purity and beauty, or to typify through their aid the ardour of his passionate desires.

The presence of flowers as symbols and language on the
monuments of Assyria, Babylon, Egypt, and other Oriental
countries, and the graceful floral adornments which were
sculptured on the temples of the Græco-Roman period,
demonstrate how great was the part which the symbolism
of flowers and plants played in the early history of civilization. The flower represented to the Oriental all the
mysterious phenomena connected with birth, reproduction, and fecundity ; whilst warmth and life which are
obtained from the sun were symbolized by various
symbolical flowers. The numerous trees, herbs, and flowers
mentioned in the Bible, and the care with which they were
so assiduously cultivated in ancient times, have justifiably
caused Palestine to be described by many as " the flowery
land ". One is immediately reminded of the Song of
Solomon, where many plants are introduced as metaphors.
We read of " the flower of the field ", " the lily of the
valleys ", " the lily among thorns ", " the orchard of
pomegranates ", " myrrh and camphor ", " spikenard and
cinnamon ". Many scholars regard " the lily of the
valleys ", which is compared to the lips of " the beloved ",
as the scarlet anemone which responds so readily to the
sun, throwing back its petals and baring its heart.

In Assyrian monuments we frequently meet with flowers
and the fruit or cone of the pine as sacred symbols carried
by the priests, and Layard has shown that there is
a close connexion between the cone of the cypress and
the worship of Venus in the religious systems of the East.
The ancient Hebrew writers drew considerable inspiration
from the transient flower and ephemeral blossom. In the
carvings and embroidery of the Temple and Tabernacle
flowers had an important place, as also in the ornamentation
of the metal-work (Exod. xxv, 31 ; xxxvii, 17 ; 1 Kings vii,
26, 49). Finally one may note that the use of many trees
and flowers as symbols on the coinage of Palestine in post-
Biblical times caused them to be indelibly stamped upon
the minds of the people.

In all religions the belief in the sacred tree as a visible manifestation of the divine spirit really passed through three stages. In the first stage we have the tree of knowledge, in the second stage the tree recognized as the home of the deity was planted in sacred ground, whilst in the third stage the tree became a symbol such as the *Ashera*, which was the adjunct of the Canaanitish shrine. According to Phœnician traditions the first beings consecrated the plants which grew on earth, made gods of them, and offered libations and sacrifices to the things on which they lived.[1] Furthermore, they regarded the whole universe as a revolving cosmic tree.

In Egyptian mythology Nut, the goddess of the heavenly ocean who pours out the waters of life, was regarded as having her abode in the tree of the sky. Around Memphis there was a district known as " the land of the Sycamore ", where various trees were regarded as symbols of Hathor and Nut, whilst the famous sycamore trees of Egypt, the sycamores of the South, were looked upon as symbols of the body of Hathor.

Coming now to the Hebrews we find that in the early period of the history of Israel sacred oaks or terebinths played a very important part, and there are many occasions when God or His angel revealed Himself to one of the old patriarchs at an oak or terebinth. God appeared to Abraham at the oak of Shechem, and the latter built an altar there (Gen. xii). Later, when three angels appeared to Abraham he was sitting beside the oaks of Mamre by the door of his tent (Gen. xviii). Similarly an angel came and sat under the oak of Ophrah, and Gideon, who was busy threshing the wheat, brought him the flesh and broth of a kid and unleavened cakes to eat. But the angel of God brought forth a flame with his staff and after that vanished ; whilst Gideon built an altar on the spot (Judges vi, 11, 21). Many modern scholars argue that Abraham carried on his propaganda for his monotheistic religion by joining his

[1] Eusebius, *Praeparatio Evangelica*, i, 9.

form of worship to existing sanctuaries and cults, having a special preference for the sacred tree. We read in Gen. xxi, 33, that he planted a tamarisk-tree in Beersheba and called there on the name of God.

Furthermore, the sacred tree constantly represents the word and will of the deity. God called Moses from the midst of the burning bush at Horeb (Exod. iii, 1). Before David attacked the Philistines he consulted the oracle of the mulberry-trees ; whilst a palm-tree near Bethel was the place where Deborah gave her responses. In Judges ix, 37, a holy tree near Shechem is called the tree of soothsayers, and the " tree of the revealer " in Gen. xii must have been the tree of a Canaanitish oracle.

The modern Arabs call sacred trees *manahil* and look upon them as places where angels play about and sing. All men are advised to treat them with the utmost reverence and to hang beads upon them. A sick man who sleeps under such a tree will probably be restored to health.[1]

In a Babylonian bilingual hymn the god Tammuz is identified with the sacred tree. The following is an extract from the hymn :—

Line 1.   In Eridu a stalk [of the vine] grew over-shadowing ; in a holy place did it become green ;

Line 2.   Its root was of white crystal, which stretched towards the deep ;

Line 3.   Before Ea was its course in Eridu, teeming with fertility ;

Line 4.   Its seat was the central place of the Earth.

Line 5.   Its foliage was the couch of Zikum the primeval mother.

Line 6.   Into the heart of its holy house which spread its shade like a forest no man entered.

Line 7.   There is the home of the mighty mother who passes across the sky.

Line 8.   In the midst of it was Tammuz.

---

[1] Doughty, *Travels in Arabia Deserta*, i, 448 seq.

In Babylonian magic the cedar, which was supposed to be under the special protection of Ea, played an important part. Sayce compares it with the rowan ash of Northern Europe. The Persians believed that the sacred tree called " tree of life " is planted by Ahura Mazda and is protected by the waters of a celestial sea. On Assyrian monuments we often find representations of trees before which kings or priests are standing or kneeling in an attitude of adoration. Those trees probably became sacred through various reasons. Sacrifices may have been offered there, some saint may have lived underneath them, or they may have been of special value to the community, and so, after a time, owing to their usefulness a halo grew around them, and they came to be looked upon as things to be revered.

How was a man to show his reverence for such sacred trees ? Obviously by removing some of his clothing and valuables and placing them upon the tree, thereby symbolizing his readiness to sacrifice his all to the deity which it represented. It thus became customary in Palestine in ancient times, as it is still nowadays, to hang various objects upon trees as marks of reverence. Pliny writing about the time of Jesus said that trees were the temples of the gods and that country people hung coloured rags and other offerings on holy trees. There is a tree in Arabia which may perhaps be identified with the acacia. It is referred to in tradition as *dhat anwat*, tree to hang things on, and at annual pilgrimages the people of Mecca used to hang on it ostrich feathers, garments, etc. Sacred trees thus came to be worshipped in every part of the Semitic area, and were hung with unguents and votive offerings ; whilst their leaves, which were their divine power, were used for medicinal purposes.

Primitive man looked upon the functions of a plant as symbolizing the life of a human being, liable to temporary successions of inactivity in winter and of reanimation in spring. We can thus understand how to the Semites the tree, on account of its fecundity and universal renovation, became a symbol of the female principles of nature And the sexual relations of all plants were regarded as symbolizing human sexuality and the renewal and communication of life. Similarly, it was believed that the acacia is really a woman, and her menstruous blood is symbolized by its gum.[1]

Furthermore, the palm-tree was associated with Astarte, and we have many cylinders which have representations of a tree, accompanied in some cases by the image of a nude woman with her hands turned towards her breasts. This is doubtless another symbolical representation of Ishtar, the goddess of the passions. The tree thus came to be widely worshipped as a symbol of the great mother-goddess. On a coin of Myra, in Lycia, we find the foliage of a tree representing the bust of a goddess, and on the coins of Heliopolis we have a cypress representing the figure of Astarte.

Just as in Greece, so in Canaan every sacred tree had its fountain, for in the East self-sown wood can only flourish where there is underground water. It was only natural, therefore, that the tree which drew strength and life from the fountain at its roots, and by which it was watered, should itself become possessed of divine life. The next stage, therefore, was to regard a tree which nourishes its remotest leaves and twigs as symbolizing the divine life which preserves and vivifies the whole creation. In the Apocalypse (xxii, 2), to quote but one instance, we read of the tree of life which bare twelve manners of fruits and yielded her fruit every month, and whose leaves were for the healing of the nation. This is interesting when considered in connexion with the tree-symbolism of the Celts. The mistletoe, which was one of the chief features of their worship, was called by them *uile* " all-heal ". Its berries were used by the

---

[1] Tylor, *PSBA.* xii, 383–93.

priests as a remedy for various diseases, and as antidotes
to the effects of poison ; whilst the juice was said to heal
wounds, and was drunk by women to ensure having children.
The Egyptians believed that deities such as Selkit, Nut,
and Hathor inhabited the sacred sycamores, and in *The
Book of the Dead* we have references to the manner in which
the soul, in the course of its journey to the next world,
receives a supply of bread and water from the goddess
of the tree.

We have numerous texts from the Semitic Babylonians
testifying to the prophylactic reputation possessed by
many cone-bearing plants. In Assyria there was a " plant
of life ", which was the gift of the gods. Assyrian kings
often compared their rule with the qualities of this plant
of life, and Esarhaddon, for example, expresses the hope
that his rule may be as tolerant as this plant. Gilgamesh,
also, desires to bring a magic plant to Erech to renew his
youth. The cedar, employed in magic rites and incantations, which were for the purpose of restoring life and health,
came to be regarded essentially as a " tree of life ". Isaiah
refers to the day when the branch of God will be beautiful
and glorious. A rod will come forth out of the stem of
Jesse, and a branch shall grow out of its roots, and this
will inaugurate a period of peace and happiness (Isa. xi).
Zechariah (vi, 12–13) describes a future period of happiness
under a similar figure.

But to return to our discussion of the tree as symbolizing
the female principle in nature. The question now arises
as to whether we can connect this with the Ashera, so
often referred to in the Bible. First, as to the appearance
of the Ashera. By comparing some of the passages
in the Bible where the word occurs we can obtain some idea
as to this. It seems in most cases to signify a wooden
post, which was planted near the altars of various gods.
The passage in Deut. xvi, 21, which is usually translated
" an ashera, any tree ", should perhaps be translated
" an ashera of any kind of wood ", whilst from Judges vi, 25,

where we are informed that it could furnish fuel for the
sacrifice of a bullock, it seems that the post was of considerable size.   One explanation of the Ashera is that in earliest
times the altars stood under actual trees, the place of which
was taken later by a dead post or pole, but the influence
of tree worship in Palestine was already so great that
the sacred tree or its substitute, the pole, came to be looked
upon as a symbol of the deity.

Robertson Smith says, " when we find that no Canaanite
high place was complete without its sacred tree standing
beside the altar, and when we take along with this the
undoubted fact that the direct cult of trees was familiar
to all the Semites, it is hardly possible to avoid the
conclusion that some elements of tree-worship entered
into the ritual even of such deities as in their origin were
not tree-gods." Now, Baal was worshipped in Canaan
as the god of fruitfulness, and the peasants' harvests
were really his gift. The fact, therefore, that in some
passages of the Bible where the idolatry of the Hebrews
in Canaan is referred to, Ashera is mentioned with Baal
would further support the view that the ashera was
a symbol of fertility representing Ishtar, the goddess of
the female principle, and that this symbolism arose
through the place of the living tree being taken by a dead
post or pole planted in the ground like an English maypole.
This view is supported by the present writer, and it should
be added that modern scholars regard the text in the
Biblical passages where ashera occurs as the name of
a goddess (e.g. Judges iii, 7 ; 1 Kings xviii, 19) as being
glossed for Ashtoreth. There was a Semitic goddess
Asheri referred to in the Tell el Amarna letters of the
fifteenth century B.C., and in a Sumerian hymn published by Reisner, but she was apparently a different deity.

Although we read of various trees being held sacred
amongst the Semites, there is, on the whole, little evidence
of a *particular* tree being identified with a special deity.
In Phœnicia, the cypress was sacred to Melcarth and

Astarte. The Venus of Lebanon bore the local name of the cypress,[1] and there is a story told of Apuleius who, wishing to paint the son of Venus in his mother's lap, represented him in the foliage of a cypress.[2] However, tree symbolism of a definite nature seems to have been particularly strongly rooted in those areas where the Semitic races came into contact with the Aryans. Attis, whose worship was exceedingly popular in Phrygia, was symbolized by a pine-tree with his image attached. Adonis, who was really Tammuz under another name, was born from a myrrh-tree ; whilst Dionysus was worshipped in Greece as " Dionysus of the Tree ". There is a symbol of the mother-goddess Cybele very similar to the sacred tree of Babylonia. According to Frazer,[3] Osiris, Tammuz, Adonis, Attis, and Dionysus were all tree-gods, and the ceremonies connected with their worship symbolized the annual death and revival of vegetation.

We have an early Sumerian hymn in which a mystical tree is described as the abode of the gods. On Babylonian cylinders there are often representations of palms, pomegranates, vines, and cypress-trees. The simple symbol of the early Babylonian monuments becomes rather complex on the Assyrian monuments, and on either side of the tree there are usually representations of a priest or a king in an attitude of worship, or else there are symbolical representations of animals, winged bulls, etc. The winged circle, which is often above the tree, represented, according to Lenormant,[4] the primeval cosmogonic pair, the creative sun and fertile earth, and thus symbolized the divine mystery of generation. The Babylonian symbol of the mystical tree was well known to the

---

[1] Mövers, *Die Phönizier*, vol. i, chap. 15.
[2] Layard, *Mémoires de l'Academie des Inscriptions et Belles Lettres*, 1854, vol. xx.
[3] *The Golden Bough*, vol. i, p. 60.
[4] *Les origines de l'histoire*, vol. i, p. 88.   See also Menant, *Les Pierres gravées de la Haute Asie*, pt. ii, who shows how the sacred tree became one of the most sacred symbols in the Assyrian religion.

Phœnicians, and is found wherever their art penetrated, in Cyprus and on the pottery of Athens and Corinth. The symbolism in connexion with the temple of Solomon (1 Kings vi, 29, 35) and the references in the Book of Ezekiel, xli, 18, to a palm-tree between a cherub, are thought to have been based upon the Babylonian sacred tree.

The Babylonians also believed in a world-tree, whose roots stretched down into the abysmal deep where Ea, the god of the subterranean deep, was all-supreme, nourishing the earth with the streams that forced their way upwards. At first it seems that this sacred tree was the cedar, but later it was displaced by the palm. In Genesis, the tree figures both as a tree of life and tree of knowledge, to eat the fruit of which makes men as gods, knowing good and evil. Ezekiel (xlvii, 12) refers to the tree " whose leaf shall not fade, neither shall its fruit be consumed : it shall bring forth new fruit according to his months, because the waters thereof issue out of the sanctuary, and the fruit thereof shall be for meat and the leaf for healing ". One may compare with this the tree yggdrasil, which grew on the Scandinavian Mountain Asgard, and whose roots were watered by the well of life. Its limbs spread over the whole world, and three of its roots stretch across the heaven and hold it up. Sayce thinks that the Babylon tree of life was an amalgamation of two actual trees, the cedar and the palm.

Various theories have been put forward in order to explain the horns which seem to be supporting the Assyrian sacred trees. It is possible that they were not introduced by the Assyrian artists simply as symbols of divinity, but as Bonavia suggests, because they saw them tied on real date-trees for the purpose of producing hybrids and variations through the raising of plants from the crossed seeds. In any case, the different varieties of date-trees gave rise to many myths and superstitions concerning the different kinds of dates. Furthermore, the horns were tied to the dates in order to draw the evil eye away from them, a practice still adopted in Southern Italy.

Bonavia thinks that the Assyrian sacred date-tree, with its supporting horns, was probably taken up by the Greeks and modified into ornaments for friezes. He says : " There are numerous architectural and decorative designs, which, I think, are traceable to the Assyrian date-tree and its horns. The Prince of Wales's feathers are perhaps also a descendant of the same motive. There are in it the three elements held together by means of a crown, which may be a modification of the ligature." [1]

In any case, partly from the powers ascribed to horns in general and partly from the custom of scaring noxious beings by noise, the blowing of horns became a common method of driving off demons or of producing magical results. This explains its symbolical use amongst the Hebrews on various occasions, and it will be remembered how, through the blowing of rams' horns, the walls of Jericho were even gathered in.

In connexion with tree-worship and tree-symbolism, it is important to note how in various Semitic religions Paradise was always connected with a miraculous tree or trees. In fact it has been suggested that the mystical tree was the main idea connected with Paradise, and that the conception of a garden in which this tree was placed grew up around it. Then each nation emphasized a specific feature of the garden according to its own stage of culture. The Bible, like the sacred books of the Parsis, gives an account of Paradise as the home of the first parents, and the two mystical trees of the Biblical paradise find their common counterpart in the sacred cedar of the Babylonians, which was a tree of life employed to restore strength and vitality to the body and was also regarded as the revealer of the oracle of the gods. The name of Ea, the god of wisdom, was written upon it. According to the

---

[1] *The Flora of the Assyrian Monuments*, p. 154.

Koran, as well as the Talmud, Paradise is the dwelling-place of the righteous. In Mohammedan tradition, it is situated in the seventh heaven, and in the centre is a wonderful tree of enormous size, with boughs full of delicious fruits. In the Talmud, there is an upper paradise and a lower one, and the souls of the righteous ascend every sabbath and festival from one to the other. In the second book of Esdras we read of " twelve trees laden with different fruits and fountains flowing with milk and honey ".

The Hebrew tradition of a tree of life is often referred to in the Bible. We read in Proverbs (xi, 30) : " The fruit of the righteous is a tree of life ", and again (xiii, 12) : " Hope deferred maketh the heart sick ; but when the desire cometh it is a tree of life." The poet also compares wisdom to a tree of life, for he says : " She is a tree of life to them that lay hold upon her " (iii, 16–18).

We will now proceed to consider in greater detail the symbolical meanings attached to some of the more important trees, plants, and flowers referred to in the Bible and in Oriental literatures.

On Assyrian monuments we often see a prominent cone-shaped object held by winged genii pointing at a sacred tree whilst the genius almost always holds some kind of basket in the other hand. Various explanations have been put forward as to the meaning of this object. Bonavia thinks it resembles a citron and the figures holding it may have been intended to represent some ceremony in which the citron played a part. Tylor thinks that the date-tree to which the cone-object is pointed represented a palm-grove, that the cone-like object in the hand of the genius represented the male inflorescence of the date-palm, and that the basket in the other hand was there merely for a further supply of male flowers. D'alviella regards the whole scene as a phallic emblem symbolizing fecundity. On the other hand, it is possible that the scene symbolized a sprinkling of holy water by means of the fir-cone used as an "aspergillum"—a very old method of scaring away evil spirits which were plentiful in Assyria. In any case, it is important to note that the Assyrians regarded the palm as a symbol of the mother goddess Astarte, and of generative nature, which represented human sexuality and the renewal and communication of life. And it has been suggested that palm culture became so important in Mesopotamia that it may have caused the palm-tree to be regarded as a sacred tree, and may then have also become conventionalized as a symbol of worship.[1] Herodotus,[2] in a description of Chaldæa, says : " Palm-trees grow in great numbers in the whole of the flat country ; most of them bear a fruit which supplies the inhabitants with bread, wine, and honey. They are cultivated like the fig-tree, particularly in the following respect. The natives tie the fruit of the male palm, as the Greeks call it, to the branches of the date-bearing palm, in order to let the gall-fly enter the date and ripen them and prevent the fruit from falling off."

From various passages in the Bible it is clear that palm-trees were far more plentiful in Palestine in ancient times than at present. Jericho was called the city of palm-trees, and masses of them were found round the sea of Galilee and in the ravine of the Jordan. The palm was taken by the Hebrews as a symbol of the righteous man. In Ps. xcii, 12, we read : " The righteous buds forth like a palm-tree, he grows like a cedar of Lebanon. Planted in the house of the Lord they flourish in the forecourts of our God. Even in old age they bud forth afresh, they are full of sap and grow green." There are many reasons to account for this symbolism and why the habits of the tree were taken to illustrate the character of the righteous.

The palm flourishes in a barren soil, and its verdure seems to spring from the scorching dust. It has thus

---

[1] Jastrow, *RBA.*, 663.
[2] i, 193.

been described as "a friendly lighthouse, guiding the traveller to the spot where water is to be found". It is remarkable for its beauty, and its very foliage is the symbol of joy and exultation. It is a lofty tree, a straight tree, always growing so long as it lives, and always bearing fruit as far as possible from earth and as near as possible to heaven. It is a most useful tree. The weary traveller is refreshed by its fruit, and it announces water when his soul fails for thirst. The tree grows slowly but steadily from century to century, uninfluenced as other trees either by the copious rains of winter or the burning sun of summer. Finally, its best fruit is borne in old age; the finest dates being often gathered when the tree has reached a hundred years.

We can now understand why it is so often mentioned in connexion with the architectural ornaments of Solomon's Temple as well as in the symbolical vision of Ezekiel's temple. We read in 1 Kings vi, 29, how all the walls of the holy of holies were covered round about with these trees. "They were there not only as ornaments, but as highly suggestive symbols of the reward of the righteous who, as a result of patience in well-doing, would have a flourishing old age."

It was customary in ancient times to plant such trees in the courts of temples and palaces. On Assyrian monuments we often see representations of a king seated in a chariot amidst a grove of palm-trees. It was probably because it was regarded as illustrating fertility and blessings that its leaves are referred to in the Apocrypha as symbols of triumph (2 Esdras ii, 44 ; 1 Macc. xiii, 51). The tall, graceful stalk of the tree suggested to the Arab poets a figure of their lady love, and the same imagery is also found amongst the Hebrews (Cant. vii, 8–9).

Palm-trees were often represented in the bas-reliefs to indicate some part of Babylonia. In later times, the tree was considered as characteristic of Judaea, as a symbol of the Jewish state, probably because it was the first country where the Greeks and Romans met with it in proceeding southward.[1] This explains why the coins of the Roman conquerors of Judaea had inscribed on them a weeping Jewess sitting under a palm-tree, with the inscription *Judaea Capta*. The palm as a symbol was very often exhibited on Jewish coins in post-Biblical days. One need only refer to the half-shekel of Simon Maccabeus, which had on the reverse side a palm-tree between two baskets filled with various fruits.

Tertullian described the olive as a symbol of peace even older than Christianity itself. In this he was, of course, quite correct, for its healing qualities and its well-known property of calming roughened water caused an olive twig to appear as an attribute in allegorical figures of peace. One need only refer to the Old Testament account of the dove sent forth by Noah, which returned across the waters, and lo! in her mouth was an olive leaf plucked off as a sign that the wrath of God was appeased.

Again, the evergreen freshness of the tree, the enormous quantity of oil it produces, the fact that it was so necessary for lighting and medicinal purposes, as well as for food, caused it to be regarded as one of the main necessities of life. Its timber is also of a rich amber colour. This explains why the prophets spoke of the olive-tree as a symbol of beauty and strength. In Jer. xi, 16, we read : " The Lord called thy name a green olive-tree, fair, and of goodly fruit." Similarly in Hos. xiv, 7 : " His branches shall spread and His beauty shall be as the olive-tree." Perhaps this also explains some further symbolisms in connexion with Solomon's temple, for we are told in 1 Kings vi, 23, that the door and post of the temple as well as the cherubim, were all made of olive wood.

The vine, which was the emblem of the nation, is referred to in the parable of the vineyard in Isa. v. Together with the olive and fig-trees, it is mentioned as an image

---

[1] Tacitus not only bears testimony to the fertility of Judaea, but particularly notes the growth of its palms (*Hist.* v, 6).

of beauty, wealth, and prosperity. Dwelling under the vine and fig-tree is taken as an emblem of peace and tranquillity (Mic. iv, 4 ; Zech. iii, 10), whilst a fruitful vine is associated with domestic happiness (Ps. cxxviii, 3). On the other hand, Israel, when unfaithful, was compared to the wild vine—not of genuine stock. In Jer. ii, 21, the prophet, speaking in God's name, says : " I had planted thee a noble vine, wholly a right seed ; how then art thou turned into the degenerate plant of a strange vine." In Deut. xxxii the enemies of Israel are likened to the " vine of Sodom ", in other words, one whose roots and juice are tainted by the corruption typified by Sodom.

The pomegranate is frequently referred to in Semitic literatures, is often represented on Assyrian and Egyptian monuments, and was a religious symbol in many ancient cults. The references in the Bible show that it was one of the common fruit-trees in Palestine (Deut. viii, 8 ; Joel i, 12, etc.). Solomon compares the temple of his bride to a piece of the fruit (Cant. iv, 3), and her whole person to an orchard of them (iv, 13). The barrenness of the tree was, therefore, taken as a symbol of desolation. It has even been suggested that the Hebrew for pomegranate, *rimmon*, is connected with the divinity bearing the same name, and this has been taken as further proof of its sacred symbolism (Kohut, *Memorial Studies*, 120–5). The fact that the pomegranate contains hundreds of seeds accounts for its being regarded amongst many ancient peoples as a symbol of fertility and life, and the pomegranates which were represented on the pillars of Solomon's temple probably had a similar idea underlying them. " The network with pomegranates " of the temple of Solomon (1 Kings vii, 41–2) and the pomegranate on the garments of Aaron (Exod. xxviii, 33–4) were no doubt symbolical. On Assyrian monuments we often find an ornament resembling a pomegranate.

The cedar-tree, distinguished for its exalted and vigorous growth, is referred to in the Bible as a symbol of height.

Ezekiel, when describing the cedar, speaks of its high stature, its numerous boughs, its long branches, and its shadowing shroud (Ezek. xxxi, 3–9). It is sound to the very core, the roots of the tree are expansive, and being firmly fixed in the soil, it is enabled to withstand the violence of storms. Like a palm-tree, it loves the water, and is an evergreen. It is always covered with leaves, and its bark and leaves are highly aromatic, and the " smell of Lebanon " has become a proverb for fragrance. This explains why the righteous are represented as growing like the cedar-trees of Lebanon (Ps. xcii, 12) ; and Israel is compared to the cedar-trees beside the waters (Num. xxiv, 6). Tristram says : " The cedar is to the vegetable what the lion is to the animal world. Of all the monstrous presumption, the most outrageous was the proposal of the thistle to ally itself with the cedar (2 Kings xiv, 9). It was the crowning insolence of the boast of Sennacherib, ' I am come up to the height of the mountains, to the sides of Lebanon ; and I will cut down the tall cedars thereof ' (Isa. xxxvii, 24). Everyone who has seen these noble trees recognizes the force of the glorious and majestic imagery of the prophets. With their gnarled and contorted stems, and their scaly bark, with their massive branches spreading their foliage rather in layers than in flakes, with their dark green leaves shot with silver in the sunlight, as they stand, a lonely group, in the stupendous mountain amphitheatre they assert their title to be monarchs of the forest."

One may mention that in Babylonian and Assyrian literature we frequently hear of palaces and temples being made of cedar wood. Enannatum I constructed the roof of his temple with cedar wood ; whilst Shalmaneser II, of Assyria, informs us that in reconstructing the temple of Anu he roofed it over with beams of cedar. Tiglath Pileser III also built a palace of cedar wood.

Oaks probably occupied a conspicuous place in the landscape in some parts of Palestine. The strength of

the oak is referred to by Amos in speaking of the Amorite
(Amos ii, 9). The oaks of Bashan, in particular, were
famous for strength and beauty, and when God threatens
judgment upon the nations He refers in a special manner
to the oaks. " Howl, O ye oaks of Bashan " (Zech. xi, 2).
" The day of the Lord shall be upon all the oaks of Bashan "
(Isa. ii, 12–13). We have already noted some instances
in which oaks are referred to in the Old Testament. " The
Bible story of the oak is unvarying in its meaning—
strength, protection, fidelity, protest against false teachings.
Its roughened trunk and stalwart appearance suggest
a kind of homely dependability, honour, and courage."
In Gen. xxxv, 4–8, we read how Jacob hid the idols under
the oak near Shechem, where they would no longer harm
the people. It was appropriate, also, that the durability
of a solemn agreement should be symbolized by having
it made under an oak. When Joshua charged the people,
and announced to them the law he put up a stone of
witness under an oak (Joshua xxiv, 26). Deborah, the
nurse of Rebecca, is buried under the shelter of an oak-
tree ; whilst Saul is buried with his sons by the valiant
men under the oak in Jabesh. The man of God who came
to warn Jeroboam of his sin is found sitting under an
oak on his return home, whilst Absalom, punished for his
treachery, is caught in its branches. Whilst one cannot
enter here into the numerous stories in the mythologies
of many peoples connected with the oak, one should note
that it has always been venerated and regarded as sacred.

The fig, which was common in Palestine, and con-
stituted an important article of food in Eastern countries,
was employed to indicate the peace and prosperity of
a nation (1 Kings v, 5 ; Mic. iv, 4) ; whilst the failure,
destruction, and falling of figs are mentioned as indications
of God's judgments (Ps. cv, 33 ; Isa. xxxiv, 4 ; Jer. v, 17).
This imagery is probably due to the fact that this tree acts
as an excellent means of protection from the rays of an
Eastern sun.

In Egypt, the lotus, which is a very fertile plant and is virtually self-productive, became the symbol of the reproductive power of all nature. " The plant grows in the water, and amongst its broad leaves puts forth a flower in the centre of which is formed the seed-vessel, shaped like a bell or inverted cone, and punctuated at the top with little cavities or cells in which the seeds grow. The orifices of these cells being too small to let the seeds drop out when ripe, these shoot forth into new plants in the places where they were formed, the bulb of the vessel serving as a matrix to nourish them until they acquire such a degree of magnitude as to burst it open and release themselves, after which they take root wherever the current deposits them." [1] We can thus see how it came to be regarded as a symbol of resurrection and re-creation. From Egypt this symbolism spread to India and the Far East, and it was looked upon everywhere as the flower of Eastern poetry and religion. The three great deities, Brahma the creator, Vishnu the preserver, and Siva the destroyer were represented as seated upon a great lotus.

In Babylonia, the lotus is frequently found on bronze dishes and ivories from Nimroud. It is also sometimes engraved on a seal. We often see representations of unicorns, griffins, or other types of monsters approaching the sacred tree as if they intended plucking a fruit or flower. In the story of Gilgamesh we read how on reaching the gates of the ocean the hero encounters a forest of trees bearing fruits of crystal and emerald. Gilgamesh attempts to pluck a fruit, and then withdraws from the garden, when he discovers that the door is closed. On a Phœnician bowl, discovered at Amathus, in Cyprus, there is a representation of the sacred tree between two persons, who seem to be plucking a lotus flower. The most plausible explanation of all this symbolism seems to

---

[1] Maurice, *Indian Antiquities.*

be that the lotus flower which grows upon the sacred tree and opens itself to the sun's rays every morning, was regarded as a symbol of resurrection, and it therefore represented the " flower of life ".

The lily of the Old Testament may be discussed in connexion with the lotus for it is quite possible that they are the same flower. The Hebrew for lily, *Shushan* or *Shoshannah*, probably originates from a similar Egyptian word denoting a lotus. Furthermore, the word *Shoshan* is used in a figurative sense of the capitals of the pillars and of the molten sea in the temple (1 Kings vii, 19–26), and it has been suggested that the Hebrew writer probably had in mind the lotus flower which was frequently used in Egyptian decorative art. We may also note that the place which the lotus held in Oriental symbolism has been taken by the lily in European symbolism. It is possible, however, that the lily of the Bible is a term used to express the common wild flowers with which the eyes of the people were familiar, for the Arab peasants now apply the name *Susan* to any brilliantly coloured flower resembling a lily.

In any case, the lily was always regarded as a highly symbolical plant, and for this reason many legends have clustered around it. In the Song of Solomon there are many vague references to it. Hosea (xiv, 5) says " Israel shall grow as a lily ". " As the water-lilies grow vigorously in the waters under the shining of the southern sun, so Israel, fed by the refreshing streams of living water, shall flourish under the shining of the sun of righteousness."

A considerable amount of symbolism is connected with the lily in later Jewish literature, where it is nearly always compared to Israel. It symbolizes the trust in God which Israel should have in all afflictions, for its heart is directed upwards even when it grows amongst thorns. It was also employed in Cabbalistic literature as a symbol of resurrection.

The Hebrew for almond (*shaked*) signifies " the waker ",

as it is the first tree to wake to life in winter. It therefore
occurs as a symbol of the divine forwardness in bringing
God's promises to pass.   In Jer. i, 11, God shows the
prophet an almond-tree to prove that He is hastening to
perform His word.   The expression in Eccles. xii, 5, " the
almond-tree shall flourish," is symbolical, meaning that
the old man's hair shall turn white like the almond-tree.
The seven-branched candlestick was taken from the shape
of the almond, and its fruit served as a model for certain
kinds of ornamental carved work.   In speaking of the
candlestick of the tabernacle, Moses says its bowls were
like almonds (Exod. xxv).   In Num. xvii we read that
the chiefs of the tribes had almond rods.   The rod is
always used as a symbol of authority.   And these rods
were perhaps emblematical of the vigilance which became
them as leaders of the people.

The myrtle is one of the best known of Bible plants.
It is referred to in four passages in the Old Testament
(Isa. xli, 19 ; lv, 13 ; Zech. i, 8–10 ; and Neh. viii, 15), and
was regarded as a symbol of joy.   The passage in
Lev. xxiii, 40, translated in the English Versions
" boughs of thick trees ", has always been regarded by
Jews as meaning " branches of myrtle ".   Many travellers
refer to the rich colouring of its dark green and shining
leaves, affording in hot countries a pleasant shade under
its branches and diffusing an agreeable odour.   Furthermore, it forms a stimulant tonic, and is useful in various
complaints connected with debility.   This explains why
it has always been appreciated from the very earliest
times.   Isaiah (lv, 13), therefore, refers to a new period,
when " instead of the thorn shall come up a fir-tree, and
instead of the briar shall come up the myrtle-tree, and it
shall be to the Lord for a name, of an everlasting sign
that shall not be cut off ".   Instead of the wild, neglected,
thorny briar, which was a mark of desolation, there shall
come up the myrtle, which can only flourish in cultivated
soil, and is a symbol of peace and happiness.   Similarly,

in the vision of Zech. i, we read of some guardian
angels at night sent down to visit the earth amongst
the grove of myrtle-trees. When questioned as to the
welfare of the inhabitants of the world, they reply : " We
have walked to and fro to the earth, and behold all the
world sitteth still and is at rest."

The myrtle was probably used as an emblem of peace
and tranquillity because it often grows in a shaded valley
where all is calm and tranquil. We learn from classical
literature that garlands of myrtle were worn at feasts,
as the myrtle was sacred to Aphrodite, and was the symbol
of conjugal love. Kittel has, therefore, suggested that
the name Hadassah, the Hebrew for myrtle, which Esther
bore (Esther ii, 7) was a symbolical name.

The willow, which is represented in Palestine by several
species, seems to have been in different ages symbolical
of two directly opposite feelings, and was associated with
the joyous and sorrowful days of the ancient Hebrews.
On the first day of the Feast of Tabernacles, the Hebrews
were commanded to take boughs of goodly trees, branches
of palm-trees, and the boughs of thick trees and willows
of the brook, " and to rejoice before the Lord seven days."
Again, in Isa. xliv we are told that Israel's offspring
shall spring up as willows by the water course. In other
words, the constant supply of water which the willows
of the brook receive is a symbol of God's constant mercies.
This accounts for its uses as a symbol in days of joy.
On the other hand, in Ps. cxxxvii, 2, where the sorrows
of Israel are so beautifully depicted, it is no doubt the
weeping willow that is referred to. The willow bends
over the stream and appears to weep, as the Jews wept
when they remembered their home and distant land.
The tree is referred to in all poetry as the emblematical
tree of tears and sorrowful associations, and its very leaves
are described as being of a mournful hue.

Wormwood is used in Hebrew metaphorically to denote
the moral bitterness of distress and trouble (Deut. xxix, 17 ;

Jer. ix, 14 ; xxiii, 15 ;   Prov. v, 4 ; Lam. iii, 15, 19 ; Amos v, 7). Its Hebrew designation *la'anah* is preserved amongst the Arabs to this day in the form *la'ana*. It thrives in sterile and sandy places, and the seeds as well as the leaves are extremely bitter. So striking is the simile furnished by this outcast of the field in some passages of the Old Testament, that the Hebrew expression " gall and wormwood " has become a stock phrase in many European languages.

CHAPTER III
THE ANIMAL KINGDOM

CHAPTER III

THE ANIMAL KINGDOM

Every student of ancient churches has noticed how frequently animals and other representations of natural history are to be found carved therein, and has, no doubt, been tempted to ask whether these sculptures or paintings are mere grotesque creations of the artist's fancy or whether they have a deeper symbolical meaning. Fortunately the reply to this question is supplied from natural history books of the Middle Ages known as bestiaries. These works, which had a greater circulation than any other book except the Bible, deal with the supposed habits and appearance of various animals and birds. They also contain illuminated miniatures of each animal dealt with, and explain the moral lessons which the animal's behaviour teaches. The builders of a church were thus able to use these sculptures as symbols for instructing all future worshippers. An early compilation of such allegorical interpretations of the nature of plants and animals, made up partly from antique materials, is still extant in the *Physiologus*, which was the natural history of the Middle Ages and the basis of all later bestiaries.

Animal symbolism can, however, be traced back almost to the dawn of history, and we have considerable material which proves that it was extant at a very early period in the history of the Semites. We find bulls, lions, serpents, dragons, and other kinds of mythological monsters entering largely into the religious decorations of the Assyrians, and being used as means of symbolizing ferocious protective spirits at the beginning of their history. In Babylonia we meet with the enamelled lions as well as the dragons and bulls on the gates of Ishtar ; whilst the winged bulls and colossal lions at the doorways of the Assyrian palaces were placed there also as divine guardians.

In his primitive stage man felt a distinct kinship with
animals, and there was no line of demarcation between man
and beast. There is a saying among the North American
Micmacs that in the beginning of things men were as animals
and animals were as men.[1] Animals were thus represented
in fables and folk-tales as carrying on conversations, and
as being moved by the same motives as the human beings
who narrated the stories.[2] Man next began to develop a
distinct reverence for animals. He now regarded the beasts
which prowled through the interminable forests not only
as brutes whose rapacious strength was to be feared, but
also as mysterious forces capable of benefiting or injuring
humanity by means of some secret occult influence.
Auguries were drawn from the movements of birds, and the
approach of certain animals was always a symbol of good
or evil. It was this belief in the mystic powers of the animal
kingdom that resulted in zoölatry or animal-worship, and
it was in the East and especially in Egypt, more than in
any other part of the world, that animal-worship became
popular. We hear of various beasts, birds, or fish being
worshipped in different districts, and although many
animals were regarded on the whole as anthropomorphic,
they were often represented in art as a man or woman with
the head or body of a bird or beast. Furthermore, the
craving of human nature for the mysterious and the
marvellous was well provided for in ancient religions,
and the usual appearances and productions of nature
offered to the fancy, in various parts of the world, similar
means of diversifying fictitious narratives by the introduction of prodigies.

But this animal-worship was often explained as being
symbolical, for it was not the beast but the qualities which
he personified that were adored. Porphyry distinctly
says that " under the semblance of animals the Egyptians
worship the universal power which the gods have revealed

[1] Leland, *Algonquin Legends*, p. 31.
[2] McCulloch, *Childhood of Fiction*, pp. 38–41, 247–78.

in the various forms of living nature ".[1] Similarly, we must note the view of Apollonius of Tyana, that these beasts were not deities but symbols of deities.[2] According to Maspero these animals were actually worshipped as deities till the second Theban Empire, when the priests began to attribute to them a symbolical sense.[3] In any case, we must note that amongst the Egyptians, the Babylonians, and Assyrians symbolical zoology as the natural outgrowth of the doctrine of metempsychosis attained its greatest development.

This notion of animal symbolism, as we have already noted, was in no way restricted to the ancient East, but found expression also in Europe right through the Middle Ages in heraldry, where all kinds of animals were represented on coats of arms as emblems of qualities supposed to be peculiar to individuals or hereditary in families. The chieftain thus attempted to strengthen the courage of his friends and to strike terror into the heart of his enemies by adorning his escutcheon with the beast whose ferocity he feared or the bird whose rapidity of flight he coveted.

Similarly, in patristic theology the animal kingdom was a collection of symbols of religious dogmas, which were to be held up to the religious man as models for imitation. This was proved from the passage in Job xii, 7 : " Ask the beast and it will teach thee, and the birds of heaven and they will tell thee." No doubt this belief was further strengthened by symbolisms such as those in the Book of Daniel, where the successive Empires which dominated the Eastern world from the sixth to the second century are represented by the forms of animals.

The animal symbolism of the Semites, and particularly the composite animal types, can also be explained in an entirely different manner. As a result of excavations in

---

[1] *De Abst.* iv, chap. ix.
[2] Le Page Renouf, *Hibbert Lectures*, pp. 6, 7.
[3] *Revue de l'histoire des Religions*, vol. i.

Palestine, numerous figurines have been discovered of bulls, cows, and doves, etc., in tombs and private houses, and all evidence seems to show clearly that originally amongst the early inhabitants of Palestine the gods were regarded as being of animal form. In Ezek. viii the prophet enumerates the three main forms of idolatry rampant in Judah, and amongst these he refers to the animal-worship embracing reptiles and beasts. W. R. Smith[1] has also drawn attention to the fact that there existed both amongst the Hebrews and Arabs the vestiges of a primitive form of animal worship, and he points out that the Hebrews gave names to families and tribes after animals and birds. " All the great deities of the Northern Semites had their sacred animals, and were themselves worshipped in animal form or in association with animal symbols down to a late date," and he thinks, therefore, " that this association implied a veritable unity of kind between animals and gods." One need only refer to the fly-god (Baal-zebub) of Ekron, the fish-god (Dagon) of Ascalon, and the cow-headed Ashtoreth of Zidon.

As we have noted already, a real spirit of kinship was supposed to exist in early times between man and animal. At Thebes there was an annual sacrifice to the ram-god Amen, at which the worshippers expressed their sympathy with the animal victim thus symbolizing their kinship with it, whilst an image of Amen was draped over with the skin of the sacrificed animal to symbolize further the close relationship between animal and god.

Again, the kinship between man and animal was symbolized by the way in which the worshipper attempted to identify himself with the animal victim which he brought as a sacrifice. At Hierapolis every person who wished to offer sacrifices had to bring a sheep first. After partaking of some of its flesh, he placed its skin on the ground, knelt on it, and placed the head of the sheep over his own head.

---

[1] *Religion of the Semites*, 1894, p. 288.

He thus represented himself as a sheep both in his outward appearance and also by having taken some of the flesh of the animal into his body. When, however, the sacrifice was not offered on behalf of an individual but for the whole community, it was the priest who identified himself with the victim and clothed himself in its skin. This now helps us to understand why the priest who performed the symbolical purification ceremony previous to the burial of the body of the dead clothed himself in fish costume, for he was supposed to represent Ea the water-god and the great source of symbolical purification whose symbol was a fish.

Now at a later time, as man's conception of his god developed, there arose a tendency for him to represent his deity as possessed of some kind of human form also. There is an important law in symbolism, to which we may now refer. " When two signs or two plastic types in any given neighbourhood express the same, if not similar beliefs, they are inclined to amalgamate, if not to unite, and form an intermediary type." We thus find that symbols which differ from each other, such as the winged globe, the conical stone, or the wheel, have, after a time, become amalgamated with each other, producing one composite type. But even in the case of living creatures we find such an amalgamation. Thus Bancroft, in his *Native Races of the Pacific States*, referring to the totems in use among the Indians of North-West America, says : " When the descendant of a ' hawk ' carries off a wife from the ' salmon ' tribe a totem representing a fish with a hawk's head for a time keeps alive the occurrence, and finally becomes the deity." This shows how symbolical composite figures of various types have arisen amongst all peoples.

It has been held by many scholars that animal symbolism amongst the Semites has an astrological origin owing to the fact that the principal constellations seem to have a close resemblance to the forms of animals. The difficulty, however, in accepting this view is that, whilst it must certainly be admitted that astrology played an important part in the religion of Babylonia, its influence is comparatively late—certainly later than that to which we can trace back animal symbolism.

Again, it seems very likely that the form of many mythological monsters in Assyrian decorative art was determined by sound rather than by sight. M. Heuzey, in a paper on Musique Chaldéenne,[1] points out that in representations of the gates of heaven upon Babylonian seal cylinders, there are always lions above the doors; whilst on a seal in the Louvre there is a representation of Shamash, the sun-god, emerging from the eastern gate of Heaven; and below these gates are two lions with pivots on their backs. In another case we find on a Sumerian bas-relief the sound-case of a harp surmounted by a bull to symbolize the vibrant tone of the instrument.

Now, in a description of the doors of a Sumerian temple built by Gudea, patesi of Lagash, there occurs the following passage : " The doors of cedar-wood installed in the great gate-way were like the god of thunder thundering in the heavens. The bolt of the Temple E-Ninnu was like a raging hound, the pivots were like a lion . . . on the gadu placed above the doors (he) Gudea caused a young lion and a young panther to dwell." M. Heuzey regards this description as an explanation of the animal symbolism of Babylonia, and refers to a description of a musical instrument in a contemporary text, where its sound is compared to a bellowing bull. (Gudea Cyl. A. Col. xxviii, 17, Thureau Dangin, *Königsinschriften*, p. 120 f.)

The Babylonian temple was really a symbol of the heavenly dwelling of the god and the doors of Heaven were therefore represented by the doors of the temple, which were made of wood with the metal pivots on which they turned grinding in stone gate-sockets. It seems, therefore, that Babylonian animal symbolism is to be

---

[1] See *Revue d'Assyr.* ix, No. 3, 1912.

traced back to the grinding and groaning produced by the heavy temple doors when being opened or shut. These noises suggested the cries of the animals which were kept to guard the gateways, and after a time the animals were not merely associated with the gateways, but with the temples themselves. It may thus have been sound rather than sight which produced the animal symbolism so closely connected with the Babylonian temples and palaces.

Even a cursory inspection of some of the monster bulls, lions, and other winged figures found at Nineveh, and now adorning the British Museum, will convince the observer that they were designed to symbolize certain beliefs connected with the religion of Assyria. And it is very likely that some of these composite figures consisting of human-headed bulls and lions, were intended to represent symbolically the primitive belief that the deity was a higher type of animal possessed of human form and thus akin to both man and animal.

Primitive man regarded the bird which flies through the air as a symbol of the soul, and on Egyptian monuments the soul of the king is represented as a bird. The Arabs and Jews also represented the soul as a bird hovering around the body and screeching. In Ps. xi, 1, we read : "In the Lord put I my trust : how say ye to my soul, flee as a bird to your mountain."

Wings have always been the symbol of mind, of spirit, or of air. No more fitting symbol could be found for a rapid and resistless element than birds or their wings. From the remotest times we find that wings were added to human forms, and for the earliest suggestion of celestial beings of the winged human type we must look to the art works of Egypt and Assyria. In Egyptian art, Neith was represented with wings, and in the Old Testament God himself is described as walking on the wings of the wind (Ps. civ, 3). In all probability, therefore, the winged figures which guarded the portals of Assyrian palaces and temples were intended to symbolize the union

of spiritual wisdom with physical force—the natural
guardians of religion and government. The winged representations of the Assyrian monuments have had a profound
significance all the world over, and many scholars have
pointed out the close resemblance between some of these
symbolical figures and those seen by Ezekiel in his vision.
The four forms of the living creatures in Ezekiel—man,
lion, bull, eagle—were similar to those of the Assyrian
monuments, and it has been argued that the coincidences
are so close as to suggest that the symbols were derived
from Assyrian sculptures. We must bear in mind,
however, that many of these animal motives on Babylonian
and Assyrian representations, and particularly those of
a more conventionalized character, were not original at
all, but were derived from Elamite composite monsters,
although we have no definite information as to how far
Babylonia participated in the pre-historic culture of Elam.

Of the animals and birds which occupied an important
place in Semitic symbolism, one may refer particularly
to the following : The bull, though very rarely represented
on cylinder-seals and sculptures as a sacrificial victim, is
constantly represented as a symbol of strength and vitality.
The sheep, which was domesticated from the very earliest
times, played an important rôle in augury, seeing that the
markings on its liver were regarded as symbols in
Babylonian liver divination by means of which the omens
were deduced ; whilst the majesty of the lion and the
subtlety of the serpent caused them both to obtain an
important and prominent position in the heraldic and
mythological symbolism of Babylonia. The horse and the
ass, the gazelle, the dove, and the griffin were all of
symbolical significance ; whilst snakes and serpents were
often represented on boundary stones, vases, and cylinder-
seals. They were very numerous in Babylonia at the
earliest times, and it is of interest to note that Esarhaddon
says that the land of Bazu, which he conquered, swarmed
with snakes and serpents like grasshoppers.

We shall now proceed to consider the importance of these and other animals and birds, especially with reference to Biblical symbolism.

The bull was one of the principal visible forms by which the deity was worshipped in ancient Israel. But scholars are not at all agreed as to what aspect of the deity the bull was supposed to represent. Was it regarded as an image or a symbol of the national deity of Israel ? In order to decide this point, let us consider the origin of bull symbolism and how the Hebrews came to represent their deity under the form of a young bull.

One theory held by Maspero and Renan is that the Israelites became familiar with calf-worship in Egypt. This view is supported by the fact that we first hear of it immediately after the exodus, and that Jeroboam I, when driven into exile by Solomon, stayed in Egypt, where the bulls Apis and Mnevis were worshipped. Again, we are told in the Old Testament that the ancestors of Israel worshipped other gods, and that the worship of idols is to be traced back to Egypt. Thus Joshua (xxiv, 14) says to the people : " Put away the gods which your fathers served on the other side of the river and in Egypt ; and serve ye the Lord." Ezekiel (xx, 7–8) also speaks of the idols of Egypt which had had an evil influence on the people. The Egyptian form of worship contained a very considerable amount of religious symbolism and imagery, and a long residence of the Hebrews in Egypt may have affected them very considerably in their desire for a visible symbol of the deity. To the Egyptians the bull was the ideal conception of strength, and they therefore compared their most powerful gods to the strong bull.

Gramberg [1] supports the suggestion that the Hebrews borrowed their bull symbolism from Egypt, but he has a few interesting suggestions of his own in connexion with the matter. He points out that the city of On, where

---

[1] *Krit. Gesch. d. Religionsideen des Alten Testamentes* (1829), i, p. 444.

Mnevis was worshipped, was very near Goshen, and thus the Hebrews were influenced in their religious ideas by their environment. He argues that whilst the ritual connected with the ark was regarded as the public form of worship, there was also a private and domestic form of religious worship such as we shall see must also have existed in Palestine before the Israelites settled there. Jeroboam, seeing that there was no visible representation of the deity in the temple, thus came forward and declared as public and official a form of religion which the people had maintained privately in their own homes.

The theory that the Hebrews borrowed their bull-worship from Egypt is, however, opposed by most modern critical scholars. In the first place it is argued that Jeroboam wished to establish a rival seat of worship, but not a rival religion (1 Kings xii, 28),[1] and the fact that he described the calves as representing the god who brought Israel out of Egypt shows clearly that they were regarded as representatives of the God of Israel, and not of an Egyptian deity. Again, a people who had been enslaved in Egypt, where it had been subjected to such cruelty and oppression, would only be too glad to rid itself of any associations with the Egyptians or their culture, and it therefore does not seem plausible that once having obtained their freedom the Hebrews would have adopted in their form of worship a symbol by which the Egyptians represented their deity. Finally, we must note that it was not images which the Egyptians worshipped, but the living animal.

There is another possible explanation. Bull symbolism was a form of worship common to the principal Semitic religions, and existed in Babylonia, Northern Syria, and Palestine (before the settlement of the Hebrews). In Babylonia the bull was a symbol of strength, and the spirit which guarded the approach to public and private buildings

---

[1] He says distinctly : " It is too much for you to go up to Jerusalem : behold thy gods, O Israel, which brought thee up out of the land of Egypt."

was therefore supposed to have a bull-like form. Representations of bulls goring the enemy were placed on the
gates of walls and temples ; whilst at each side of the
entrance to a temple colossal figures of bulls made of metal
or stone were placed. These bulls, which were known as
kirubi, have been sometimes compared with the cherubim,
which were at the entrance to the Garden of Eden (Gen. iii,
24). The bull was represented in Babylonia as the son of
the storm-god, and was therefore also regarded as a
malevolent deity. We must bear in mind, however, that
the sacredness which the Semitic Babylonians attached to
the bull was probably due to Sumerian influences, and was
therefore of non-Semitic origin.

With reference to Northern Syria, the bull was the sacred
animal of Hadad. Jupiter Dolichenus, who was really
Hadad worshipped under another name, was represented
as standing on a bull with a thunderbolt (symbolizing his
character as a storm-god) in one hand, and a battle-axe in
another. On the Esarhaddon Stele of Zinjirli the Assyrian
king is also represented as standing on a bull.

We now come to the Canaanites. In the course of
excavations in Palestine numerous bulls' heads and small
statues of goddesses with horns on the head have been
found ; whilst on a Samaritan ostrakon, discovered in 1910,
was the name " Egelyo ", which means " calf of god ".
Many of these figures which have been found in tombs and
the ruins of private houses are very small—altogether too
small to have been used in public worship. And it has
therefore been suggested that they must have served as
domestic idols, and were probably used by the people for
private worship in their own homes.

They had also such names as Ashtoreth Karnaim,
which means " Astoreth of the two horns ", and Astarte
was represented as crowned with a bull's head. The
influence of the early inhabitants of Palestine upon Hebrew
culture and religious ideas must have been very great, and
it is therefore held by many scholars that bull worship

was learned by the Hebrews from the Canaanites. Many
of the scholars who hold this view argue that one of the
main causes which brought about the revolution by
which Jeroboam became king of Northern Israel, was the
attempt of Solomon to centralize the cultus at Jerusalem
and degrade the local sanctuaries. These efforts were very
unpopular with the masses of the people who still wished
to cling to the ancient faith of Israel, in which they could
continue to worship bull images at their own local
sanctuaries and in their private homes. Solomon's foreign
relations, and his marriage to the daughter of the Egyptian
king, which must have had considerable influence in
widening his religious outlook, resulted in the introduction
of foreign customs and forms of worship, which aroused
the opposition of the Ten Tribes, to whom all this appeared
to be a break with the past. In other words, despite the
relapses of Israel into idolatry in her early days she had
maintained a position of religious isolation. The strong
nationalist feeling of the tribes and their religious con-
servatism and sympathy with the worship of their ancestors,
caused them to sever their connexion with Solomon and
to set up images of their own such as their forefathers had
always worshipped. Duhm argues on these lines.[1] Vatke [2]
and Kuenen [3] argue that Jehovah was worshipped under
the form of a bull at all the important sanctuaries, including
Gilgal and Beersheba, Bethel and Dan, and that the worship
of bull images did not receive any opposition from the
religious leaders of the people. The form of worship which
existed at these sanctuaries from the early days of the
Judges shows that the bull was always regarded as an image
of the God of Israel. Furthermore, Vatke bases his
argument on the theory that the opposition to the making
of images which is contained in Exod. xx, 4, is a later
insertion, representing the view of a period long after Moses,

---

[1] *Theol. d. Propheten*, p. 47.
[2] *Biblische Theologie.*
[3] *Religion of Israel* (Engl. Transl.), vol. i.

when the character of Jehovah was regarded as being much more spiritualistic. On the other hand, S. A. Cooke thinks that the calves were not the images of Israel's God, but of a foreign deity. He thinks that the words of Moses : " Who is on the side of Jehovah unto me " (Exod. xxxii, 26), show that Jehovah was not the god worshipped in the golden calf, and the conflict was hardly between higher and lower forms of worship, but between Jehovah and a rival deity.

Now, assuming that the prohibition against the making of images contained in the Decalogue is a later addition— an easy form of argument which certainly does not appeal to the present writer—how far are the remaining arguments convincing for us to accept the suggestions based on them ? Surely the very words of Aaron to the people, " To-morrow is a feast to Jehovah " (Exod. xxxii, 5), show clearly that the bull which the people made was connected with the worship of the God of Israel, and not with any other deity. If another cultus had existed side by side with the worship of Jehovah, one would not have expected the people to make an image or symbol of another deity and worship it on a day sacred to him. The bull must, therefore, have been either an image or a symbol connected with Jehovah worship. Furthermore, the argument that some of the early prophets did not oppose the making of images, and that, therefore, the worship of the bull images of Jehovah must have been regarded by them as lawful, is also valueless. Did not Ahijah distinctly tell Jeroboam that he had done worse than all that were before him in making graven images ? Even if some scholars argue that the words put into the mouth of Ahijah bear evidence of a late date, " the fact remains that Jeroboam at the end of his reign had incurred the bitter enmity of the prophets."[1] Again, the fact that Elijah did not protest against this calf worship cannot be used as an argument to prove that he did not

Foakes Jackson, *Biblical History of the Hebrews*, p. 226.

object to it. In his day the great conflict was between the
religion of Israel and that of Baal, and under such circumstances the purification of Israel's ancestral faith from
corrupt symbolical representations could only be regarded
of secondary importance. Moreover, how are we to explain
the violent opposition to bull worship of Amos and Hosea ?
These prophets not only opposed the worship of the calves
as representations of the deity, but the whole spirit which
was at the basis of such practices. The worship of the
bull was to them not the disease in itself, but merely a
symptom of the disease, for it only represented the debased
spirit by which the religious outlook of the people was
characterized.

An analysis of the early religion of Mosaism shows
quite clearly that it embodied the conception of an image-
less worship. The account of Moses' anger when he learned
that the golden calf had been made, as well as the second
commandment of the Decalogue, show how strongly he
protested against any form of image worship. Furthermore,
the opposition of the Levites to bull worship both in the
wilderness, when they slaughtered its adherents, and in the
days of Jeroboam, when they deserted the Northern
Tribes (2 Chron. xi, 13), proves conclusively that right from
the Mosaic period there was a distinct aversion to any
representation of Jehovah by means of images.

But why is it necessary for us to accept so many out-of-
the-way theories in order to understand the simple facts
contained in the Old Testament? Surely the simplest
explanation is that the Hebrews regarded the bull not as an
image but as a *symbol* of Jehovah. Being an agricultural
race, to whom the bull was a symbol of strength and vitality,
they made use of it to represent their national deity.
Even if we accept the possibility that the Hebrews learned
their ideas of bull worship from their neighbours, it does
not necessarily imply that because to other Semitic peoples
the bull was an image of one of their deities, to the Hebrews
it must have been an image of Jehovah. We find in all

parts of the world that a synthesis is often produced by one religion appropriating the images and cults of another religion for its own worship ; whilst very often a higher and more spiritual religion seizes upon a symbol of a lower religion and imparts to this symbol a deeper meaning to correspond to its nature. So that even if the Hebrews learned and were influenced by the practices of their neighbours it may simply mean that they appropriated the bull for their own worship and used it for symbolizing their own deity. In the words of Tylor [1] : " An image may be to two votaries kneeling side by side before it, two utterly different things ; to the one it may be only a symbol, a portrait, a memento ; while to the other it is an intelligent and active being, by virtue of a life or spirit dwelling in it or acting through it."

How different was the Hebrew conception of their deity, even at the earliest times, from that of their neighbours ! There are no references to bull worship in the early patriarchal age. And a comparison between the religions of the peoples by whom the Hebrews were surrounded with the Decalogue and other portions of the early legislative codes of the Pentateuch, shows clearly that Mosaism had risen to a much higher spiritual and moral level. Jehovah was regarded as the only deity that Israel might worship, and his activity was not restricted to any particular region. He says distinctly to Jacob : " I shall guard thee wherever thou shalt go," and later He promises that He will make him into a great nation in Egypt.[2] In other words, the power of Jehovah was as manifest in Egypt as it was at Mount Sinai. Again, Jehovah was regarded as possessing an ethical character that was entirely lacking to other Semitic deities. If the Hebrews had conceived the godhead as being in the form of a bull they could not have used so many anthropomorphisms in speaking of Jehovah. And the very fact that their visible representation of the deity differed

[1] *Primitive Culture*, vol. ii, p. 169.
[2] Gen. xlvi, 3.

to so great an extent from their actual conception of him proves conclusively that it was merely by an association of ideas that the bull came to represent a symbol of their god and nothing more.

But, whilst we are discussing this question, there are two points which are specially worthy of note. If we accept the Old Testament account that the Hebrews had previously a much more spiritual religion without finding any necessity for a symbolical representation of the deity till after the exodus from Egypt, we find ourselves supported by a study of Comparative Religion. For, as we have already noted, man in his earliest stage does not feel the need for any images, and it is only in the second stage of his development that he begins to feel the necessity for such a form of worship.

Buddhism, although a much later religion, offers an analogy in this respect to the Religion of Israel. Early Buddhism knew nothing of image worship, which arose at a much later period,[1] probably four or five centuries after the death of the great teacher, for the early artists would never have dared to portray the bodily form of Buddha. Secondly, if we accept the existence of image worship in Ancient Israel, and assume that side by side with her worship of Jehovah there was a debased form of idolatry similar to that of her neighbours, which was legally sanctioned and permitted by her religious leaders and teachers, we are confronted with a much greater difficulty. For, under such circumstances, how are we to account for the *sudden* rise of the great spiritual and ethical teachings as taught by the prophets of the eighth century ?

It seems to the present writer, therefore, that the literal statements of the Old Testament are much more plausible than many of the modern critical explanations of them ; and our only conclusion can be that there was an attempt by the Hebrews after the Exodus and later in the days of

---

[1] A. Cunningham, *Mahbodha*, London, 1892, p. 53 f.

Jeroboam to introduce a symbolical representation of Jehovah, and, being an agricultural race, they selected the bull, which was everywhere regarded as a symbol of strength, in preference to other animals.

The lion was regarded amongst the ancient Semites as a symbol of sovereignty, strength, and courage ; whilst its fierceness and cruelty caused it to be used under the figure of a malignant enemy. As an emblem of power it was symbolical of the tribe of Judah (Gen. xlix, 9), and the figure of the lion was among the few which the Hebrews admitted in sculpture or cast metal. This may explain its symbolical meanings in the sculptures of the palace and temple of Solomon. Lions, with oxen and cherubim, adorned the bases of the brazen sea (1 Kings vii, 29). Nergal, as god of the burning sun, was symbolized amongst the Babylonians by a lion, and the animal was accepted by the Semites as a symbol of the hostile aspect of the sun-god. In Egyptian mythology the sun was supposed to pass through a tunnel, with a lion at each end. Goldziher [1] thinks that the symbolical connexion was due to the light colour, the mane, and the power and rage of the wild beast. Its hair, he thinks, represents the burning rays. In Joel i, 6, the powerful teeth of a lion are referred to as symbols of strength ; whilst in the Psalms the lion is often used as a symbol of the cruel and mighty (Ps. x, 9 ; xxxiv, 11 ; xxxv, 17).

The Oriental monarchs boasted of their successes as lion-hunters. Tukulti Nihib I (1275 B.C.) records that he slew 920 lions ; whilst Amenhotep III of Egypt boasts that he killed 102 lions in the first ten years of his reign. It was this which may have caused the lion to be regarded as a symbol of the king's enemies, and the power which the king of Lagash exercised over his enemies of the East and West can be seen from the symbols which compose the emblem of the ancient city. This consisted of an eagle with outspread wings clutching two lions facing in opposite directions. In the earliest period of Sumerian history we read of a king named Mesilim, who ruled over Kish, and to whom various southern cities owed allegiance. We have a votive mace-head from this reign, which is of particular interest. This weapon, which was sculptured by the king's orders with the object of being dedicated to a god, is decorated with figures of lions which seem to be pursuing and attacking one another. Each lion seizes the hind-leg and back of the one preceding it, and they thus form a chain around the object. Lions were also represented on seal cylinders as being in conflict with Gilgamesh, the Babylonian legendary hero, or his friend Eabani. Sometimes the lion was endowed with wings and the head of a man, and stationed at the entrance to the king's palace in order to prevent any evil spirit or demon from approaching. It was probably the belief that the lion never closes its eyes in sleep that caused it to be placed at the entrance to Assyrian and Egyptian temples; and it may be noted here that this type of spiritual vigilance is also found very frequently in Romanic and early Gothic architecture from the beginning of the ninth to the end of the thirteenth century. On account of its strength, it is frequently represented on the bas-reliefs of Assyrian palaces as being speared or stabbed.

The beauty of the gazelle is a favourite term of comparison with Oriental poets. In Prov. v, 19, we read that a wife is compared to " the loving hind and pleasant roe ". The modern Arab expresses the beauty of the woman he loves by comparing her to the black-eyed gazelle ; whilst the innocent fear and timidity which characterizes these beautiful animals is also referred to in the Bible (2 Sam. ii, 18 ; Isa. xiii, 14), and may well be compared to the bashfulness of a young girl. We can thus understand why on Phœnician gems the gazelle is figured along with the star as a symbol of Astarte.[1] The gazelles of Mecca were

---

[1] W. R. Smith, *Kinship and Marriage in Early Arabia*, p. 227.

probably connected with the cult of al Úzza, who is commonly identified with Aphrodite. Furthermore, gazelles occur as sacred symbols in South Arabia in connexion with Athtar-worship, and Robertson-Smith quotes an instance where a South Arabian tribe, finding a dead gazelle, washed it, wrapped it, and buried it, and the whole tribe mourned for seven days.[1]

Various characteristics of the serpent, such as the reptile's peculiar form and often its remarkable beauty, its mysterious and sometimes exceedingly rapid mode of progression, its staring gaze, its longevity, its habit of frequenting caves, ruins, and lonely places, its ability to renew its youth and beauty by the shedding of its skin, the insidious character of its attack, and its poisonous properties—all these have combined to make it one of the most admired and most dreaded of animals, and have given it a double repute for unrelenting hostility and hatred for mankind, as well as for wisdom and power to heal. The serpent possesses the power of lying for days upon the same spot as if asleep, yet eternally awake and with its eyes fixed on all who gaze at it. It can exist for long periods without food, and with no diminution of vigour. It is not surprising, therefore, that primitive man regarded it as a mysterious animal, swift as disaster, deliberate as retribution, incomprehensible as destiny.

The snake has often been regarded as a most friendly animal. This may be due to the fact that poisonous snakes rarely use their power against man except when they wish to avenge an insult or injury. It is believed by American Indians that a rattlesnake will not bite an Indian except in revenge,[2] and amongst the Zulus it is a crime to kill a venomous snake. In Egypt every house has a serpent which is regarded as its protector ; whilst in Armenia every village has its guardian serpent, to whom offerings are made. The snake plays a prominent part in

[1] *Rel. of the Semites*, p. 444.
[2] Emerson, *Indian Myths*.

the epic and popular traditions of India and in its architectural ornamentations. The cobra is still regarded as sacred in India. It is called the good snake, and although its poison is so deadly it is almost a crime to kill one. Offerings are made to it, and lights are burned before its shrines. The worship of this serpent is very closely connected with the worship of the sun, and it is thus intimately related to the orthodox Hindu religion.

The Arabs looked upon serpents as being supernatural, and we are told that Mohammed changed the name of a man called Hobab (snake) because it was " the name of a devil ", that is of a god.[1] But although serpent worship is by no means a rare phenomenon, it has often been confused with serpent symbolism. For example, we often find in India a sculpture of a cobra with three, five, or seven heads shadowing with its hood one of the deities. This does not prove serpent worship in the locality at all. The serpent was merely represented as an attendant upon the deity in order to symbolize his power. Similarly, the use of the snake in the snake dances of the North American Indians did not involve worship, but was probably due to the connexion of the serpent in folk-lore with springs and rain, and thus with agricultural fertility and bountiful harvest.

The serpent played a prominent part in religious art and symbolism, and many nations celebrated for wisdom have made it an accompaniment of their gods, heroes, and kings. With its tail in its mouth, together also with a disc, it is found amongst the most unrelated nations—Egypt, Persia, India, China, and Mexico. On account of its great vigour and spirit, it was looked upon in Egypt as an emblem of divine nature. The head-dress which the gods and goddesses and nearly all the kings are represented as wearing is formed of a serpent coiled round a disc—probably to emphasize deity and kingship. It is also found on

---

[1] *Kinship and Marriage in Early Arabia*, pp. 229–30.

the sacerdotal vestments of the priests. One may refer to Apophis, the serpent of the underworld and personification of evil, and the huge snake which was believed to live in the " mountain of sunrise ". In connexion with the latter, one may mention that serpent worship and symbolism was often combined with sun worship. In India the serpent was worshipped as the protector of the people who claimed solar descent, and the worship of the sun and serpent was everywhere conducted with the same rites and ceremonial. This combination is formed from the earliest times, and seems to have originated independently in areas quite remote from each other.

Amongst the Babylonians and Hebrews the serpent is connected with the tree of life. A very familiar example of the serpent in Babylonian mythology is a seal with two beings seated on either side of a tree, and a serpent behind one of them. This was once regarded by many scholars as being the Babylonian representation of the Hebrew account of the fall. Some of the Babylonian deities were intimately associated with the serpent, and we have representations in which the body of a god is formed from the coils of a serpent. On some seals a bearded god with the body of a serpent holds a branch in his hand. Although the meaning of this is not clear, the important part which the sacred tree occupied in Babylonian mythology leaves no room for doubt that this is symbolical. One may also refer to the stone vase of Sumerian times which Gudea patesi of Lagash dedicated to the God Nin-gish-zi-da for the prolongation of his life. The decoration on this vase is most elaborate. Two entwined serpents occupy the central part of the design ; whilst their tongues touch the edge of the vase near the spout. The serpents are flanked by two winged mythical creatures facing each other. These monsters are composite, having the body and head of a serpent, they are provided with claws and talons, whilst their headgear has a horned cap to symbolize their supernatural power.

Ea, the god of wisdom, was connected with the serpent, whilst the goddess Ishtar carried a staff wound with two snakes, similar to that represented on the vase of Gudea, to which we have just referred.[1] The staff, as we have already noted, was always a symbol of authority, and the snake wound round it would, of course, add to its symbolical import. Didorus Siculus informs us (11, 70) that in the temple of Marduk at Babylon there were very large serpents of silver. In the centre of each side of this temple there was a great gateway, and in Neriglissar's time there were eight bronze serpents—a pair of them near each entrance. The animal is referred to in various Babylonian myths. It was a serpent that plucked the wings of the eagle that was to carry Etana to heaven ; Gilgamesh lost the herb which was to renew life through a serpent ; whilst it plays quite a prominent part in the creation myth. There was a huge serpent surrounding the world, and another lay in the depths of the sea. This is reflected in Hebrew cosmogony also. On Egyptian, Hindu, and Persian monuments the universal orbit is symbolically represented by a serpent biting its own tail.

Some scholars, including Gunkel and Zimmern, argue that the Babylonian story of Marduk's victory over Tiamat—the dragon of the sea—has a parallel amongst the Hebrews, and they believe that traces of this can still be found in various mythological names in Hebrew, such as Rahab, Behemoth, and Leviathan. They identify the Leviathan of Job xl, 25, with the chaos-monster Tiamat, and Behemoth with his consort Kingu. A close examination of the passages in which these terms occur, and of others where there are references to a serpent at the bottom of the sea, shows that this theory has nothing to support it. If the serpent at the bottom of the sea, in Amos ix, 3, is to be identified with the Tiamat of Babylonian mythology which was to be cut in pieces, surely God would not have

[1] See Ward, *American Antiquarian*, p. 215, and Gressmann, *Altorientalische Texte u. Bilder*, ii, 92.

commanded it to bite Israel. Again, in Ps. lxxxvii, 4,
Rahab is a symbolical name of Egypt, whilst the plural,
Rehabim, in Ps. xl, 5, is used to represent false gods. In
Job xl, 25, Leviathan refers to the crocodile, and Behemoth,
in verse 15, to the hippopotamus, and in Isa. xxvii, 1, the
fleeing serpent and coiled serpent, which are coupled with
the dragon in the sea, are symbolical designations of world
powers. The Hebrew poets, especially, were fond of
using this old myth to symbolize the destruction of Israel's
enemies. As to the relation of the Hebrew to the
Babylonian conception of the cosmogony, the position has
been most clearly summed up by Driver, who says : " The
narrative of Gen. i comes at the end of a long process of
gradual elimination of heathen elements and of gradual
assimilation to the purer teachings of Israelitish theology
carried on under the spiritual influences of the religion of
Israel."

We are told in the Old Testament that the fiery serpent
which had been made by order of Moses and planted on the
top of a pole (Num. xxi, 6–9) was religiously preserved in
the chief sanctuary of the nation down to the time of
Hezekiah. Seeing that it had been the means of preserving
the people from the fiery poison of the snakes, incense
was burned before it. But as its continued existence seemed
to be a menace to the pure religion of Israel, it was thought
advisable in the time of Hezekiah to destroy it.

It has been suggested that the Nehushtan was actually
an image of the God of Israel, but this is simply incon-
ceivable, and finds no analogy elsewhere. If, on the other
hand, it represented some demon, it is difficult to see how
it could have been constructed by Moses. Many scholars
hold the view that the serpent was regarded by the ancient
Hebrews as a sacred animal, and that the brazen serpent
was therefore a symbol of the God of Israel during the early
days of the Hebrews, as the bull was during the period of
the monarchy.[1] They would compare with this the bronze

[1] See H. P. Smith, *Old Testament History*, p. 240 ; Baudissin, *Studien
zur Semitischen Religionsgeschichte*.

serpents which were set up in Babylonia at the entrance to
the buildings of which they were believed to act as divine
protectors, and they regard the brazen serpent as a symbol
similar to the human-headed bulls which stood at the
entrances to the Assyrian temples.

This also seems to the present writer to have little to
support it.   The serpent was revered by the Phœnicians
and Egyptians as a symbol of regeneration and the renewal
of life.   This was probably due to its swiftness and variety
of movements (in spite of its possessing no feet), and also
its longevity.   There are representations of a serpent on
Tyrian coins in connexion with altars and pillars ; whilst
Asklepios, the Greek serpent-god of healing, was identified
with Eshmun, a Phœnician god with similar functions.

Whilst we cannot enter here into any discussion as to a
possible explanation of the power attributed to the brazen
serpent in the Bible, it seems to the present writer that
analogies elsewhere suggest that it is based on the fact that
the serpent was regarded amongst the Hebrews as a symbol
of renewed energy and vigour.   In this connexion we may
note also the symbolical explanation which the Rabbis
attached to the passage.   According to their explanation,
the brazen serpent was placed high up on a pole to remind
the person bitten by a snake that the God of heaven was
the great healer of disease, and that it is to Him that the
people must look for a cure.   But as the people, eventually,
lost sight of this symbolical meaning, and worshipped the
serpent as the seat of healing instead of regarding it merely
as a symbol of renewed vigour, Hezekiah thought it
advisable to destroy it.

The horse was a symbol of war, and the ass a symbol of
peace.   Amongst the many passages in the Old Testament
where the horse is referred to, it is almost everywhere
mentioned as an adjunct of war.   In no instance was it
employed for the purposes of ordinary locomotion or
agriculture, if we except Isa. xxviii, 28, where we learn
that horses were employed in threshing.   The horse which

the Hebrews knew was not the same animal as the domesticated Arab steed that we speak of nowadays. It was a war-horse in all probability similar to the stalwart animal fitted for war purposes which is so frequently represented upon the Assyrian monuments. One may here quote the fine eulogium in the Book of Job (xxxix, 19–25):—

" Hast thou given the horse strength ? Hast thou clothed his neck with thunder ? Canst thou make him afraid as a grasshopper ? The glory of his nostrils is terror.

" He paweth in the valley, and rejoiceth in his strength : he goeth on to meet the armed men.

" He mocketh at fear and is not affrighted : neither turneth he back from the sword.

" The quiver rattleth against him, the glittering spear and the shield.

" He swalloweth the ground with fierceness and rage : neither believeth he that it is the sound of the trumpet.

" He saith among the trumpets, Ha, ha, and he smelleth the battle afar off, the thunder of the captains and the shouting."

The Egyptian armies were well equipped with horses, and it became the policy of the later kings of Judah to rely upon these for help (Isa. xxxi, 1). The chariot was also one of the recognized forces in war, and so " horses and chariots " is a regular metaphor used in the Bible. " Some trust in chariots and some in horses, but we will make mention of the name of the Lord our God " (Ps. xx, 7). One cannot fully understand the force of this and similar expressions without realizing the dread in which the chariot was held by the foot-soldiers. " Even the cavalry were much feared ; but the chariots were objects of almost superstitious fear, and the rushing sound of their wheels, the noise of the horses' hoofs, and the shaking of the ground as the prancing horses and jumping chariots (Nahum iii, 2) thundered along simply overwhelmed the foot-soldier with terror." Horses and chariots thus came to be used also as a means of representing Divine power (Ps. lxviii, 17 ; civ, 3). When God is angry He rides upon His horses and chariots of salvation (Hab. iii, 8), whilst Elijah is taken to heaven by a chariot of horses and fire. In the Assyrian sculptures we often see winged horses as symbols, which resemble very closely the pegasus of the Greeks. The winged horse was also a sacred symbol of the Carthaginians.

The ass plays a prominent part in scriptural narrative, and was as highly esteemed as the ox, the camel, or the goat. The king of Egypt presented Abraham with asses, and they are referred to as part of the possessions of Jacob and Job (Gen. xii, 16 ; Job i, 3). They must have been regarded as an important part of David's possessions, for we are told, in 1 Chron. xxvii, 30, the name of the special officer whom the king appointed to take charge of them. They were ridden by persons of the highest distinction, and white asses particularly were selected by persons of rank.

In Zech. ix, 9, the writer sees in recent events an earnest of complete Jewish independence. " Rejoice greatly, O daughter of Zion, shout, O daughter of Jerusalem, behold thy king cometh unto thee : He is just and having salvation ; lowly and riding upon an ass, and upon a colt, the foal of an ass. And I will cut off the chariot from Ephraim, and the horse from Jerusalem, and the battle bow shall be cut off, and he shall speak peace unto the Gentiles." The ass does not here symbolize humility, as has often been thought, but is really a mark of peace. If the king had been represented as a warrior, he would have been riding a war-horse surmounted with numerous armed men. But the king hoped for will be no military leader, but a prince of peace. It will be his aim to abolish the equipment of war from Israel itself ; and he will speak peace to the Gentiles. He is therefore represented as riding an ass. The ass has thus been described as " the beast of the peace-bringing Messiah, in contrast to the horse of the conqueror ". It is also of interest to note that in the stories of the Judges, who are held as deliverers, we are told that they rode upon asses—perhaps as a mark of dignity and peace. Abdon had forty sons and thirty grandsons who rode on seventy ass-colts (Judges xii, 13 ff.); similarly, Jair (Judges x, 3 ff.) had thirty sons who rode upon thirty ass-colts and possessed thirty cities.

The affection and fidelity of the dog made hardly any impression on the Semites, and is almost always referred to by them in terms of contempt. It is probably from this source that many derogatory expressions concerning this trusty companion of man have passed into the common speech of to-day. Job expresses his scornful feeling when he says : " Now they that are younger than I have me in derision, whose fathers I would have disdained to have set with the dogs of my flock." In the New Testament also dogs are pariah beasts outside the pale of human interests. The ancient Hebrews did not utilize the instinct of the dog for the pursuit of game, and the fact that it was ceremonially unclean and was the scavenger of Oriental cities caused it to be looked upon with aversion. The term " dog " was also used as a term of reproach and humility in speaking of oneself. " The Philistine said unto David, ' Am I a dog that thou comest to me with staves ? ' " (1 Sam. xvii, 43 ; see also 2 Sam. iii, 8 ; 2 Kings viii, 13 ; 1 Sam. xxiv, 14, etc.).

The wolf was used figuratively to denote persons of a cruel or persecuting spirit (Gen. xlix, 17), and is always a symbol of bloodthirstiness and cruelty. Those who persecute the truth are often compared to wolves (Ezek. xxii, 27), but the Messianic era will be a time when the wolf and the lamb shall feed together.

The unicorn (Heb. *reem*) is used in the Bible as a symbol of strength (Num. xxiii, 22 ; Deut. xxxiii, 17). The leopard is taken as a symbol of swiftness (Hab. i, 8), and its agility symbolizes Alexander's rapid conquests (Dan. vii, 6). The he-goat, as the leader of the flock (Prov. xxx, 31), symbolizes the rulers and rich, in contrast to the poor people. Ezekiel (xxxvii, 17) contrasts the weak flock (the poor) with their leaders, the rams and he-goats. In Dan. viii, 5, the Macedonian Empire is symbolized by an old he-goat.

In the Bible no bird is employed so largely in metaphor and symbol as the dove ; and doves and pigeons hold the same symbolical position amongst birds which sheep and lambs hold amongst animals. The plaintive, monotonous sounds of the dove, its strong flight (Ps. lv, 7), and gentleness are all referred to metaphorically in the Bible. The amativeness of the dove is referred to in the *Song of Solomon* (ii, 14; vi, 9), whilst its female beauty and faithfulness to its mate is taken in the Talmud as a symbol of conjugal fidelity. The Talmudic writers always contrasted the dove with the raven. The dove is mild, true, and loving ; but the raven is cunning and deceptive. It was probably these characteristics, together with its harmlessness and simplicity, which caused it to be regarded by the ancient Hebrews as a symbol of purity and innocence. In the sacrificial code the dove and the turtle-dove were the only birds admitted as sacrifices (Lev. v, 8 ; xii, 6, 8 ; xiv, 5, 22, etc.), and in Rabbinic literature it is taken as an image of the spirit of God (Rashi on Gen. i, 2 ; Sanh., 108b). In the Old Testament it is also a symbol of persecuted Israel (Ps. lxxiv, 19). The Babylonians also regarded the bird as a sacred symbol, and it was used for sacrifices and offerings. Eannatum invokes the wrath of Ninkharsag upon the men of Umma, and states that in his wisdom he has presented her with two doves as offerings. In Arabia we find a dove-idol in the Kaaba with doves around it, but it has been thought that this was an importation from Syria. In the Phœnician sanctuary of Eryx it received peculiar honour as the companion of Astarte.[1] The Jewish accusation against the Samaritans that they worshipped doves was probably based on this

[1] *Religion of the Semites*, p. 294.

superstition. On imperial coins of Cyprus there are representations of doves turned with their backs to each other on the roof of a temple. Again, on some stelæ in Libya we find two doves facing one another between the Bethel of a Cyprian Aphrodite. Lundy, in his *Monumental Christianity*, points out that the dove was often regarded as emblematic of the Holy Spirit. Adonis was called " the dove ", and at the ceremonies in honour of his resurrection the people described him as " the dove, the restorer of light ".[1]

The stork was regarded amongst all ancient Oriental races as a symbol of devoted maternal and filial affection. It is said to be unrivalled amongst birds for an affectionate and amiable disposition, and in Egypt it was looked upon as a symbol of a dutiful child. The Hebrew name " Chasidah " is connected with the word for " loving kindness ".

The glossy black plumage of the raven is compared in the Old Testament (Cant. v, 11) with the hair of the Shulamite's lover. In fact, the Hebrew word for raven, " oreb," is connected with an Arabic root which means " to be black ". The bird was always looked upon as a creature of ill-omen. This has been accounted for by the fact that this colour is always associated with death and misfortune, and that the bird lives generally in desolate places. In Isa. xxxiv, 11, the bird is used to symbolize destruction. But why was the raven expressly mentioned in the Old Testament as illustrating God's protecting love and goodness ? The answer to this is perhaps furnished by Jewish and Arabic writers, who tell strange stories of this bird and its cruelty to its young. They were told that owing to their featherless state young ravens are not acknowledged by their parents, and it was believed that after the eggs are hatched the bird cares nothing for its young until they are full-fledged. This explains the passage in Ps. cxlvii, 9, " who feedeth the

[1] *Calmet's Fragments*, vol. ii, pp. 21–2.

young ravens which cry." God who shows care
for young ravens after they have been driven out of the
nest by their parents shows similar care for all His creatures.

The "nesher", which is usually translated eagle, is the
term used by the Arabs in a modified form (nisr) for the
vulture. The term is also used of various species of the
true eagle. Its solicitude for its young, the swiftness of
its flight, its inaccessible nesting-places, and its longevity
and strength are all mentioned in the Bible. It was
probably because the bird is possessed of these
characteristics that it was taken by the ancient nations
as a divine symbol. In the vision of Ezekiel (i, 10) it
is mentioned in connexion with the throne of God, and
in the Talmud the eagle is referred to as king of birds.
The reference in Isaiah (xlvi, 11) to the "ravenous bird
from the East" is to Cyrus, probably because the
eagle was the emblem of Persia, its swiftness being used
to represent rapid inaccessible conquest.

In Deut. xxxii, 11, God is said to have taught Israel
as the eagle trains her young. This alludes to the fostering
care of the eagle for her young. When the eaglets are
old enough to fly, she stirs up her nest and compels the
young birds to fly to some neighbouring crag. Then she
flutters over them, teaching them to move their wings and
to sustain themselves by their movements. If she finds
them weary or unwilling she spreads her wings, takes her
brood upon her back, and soars with them aloft. The
eagle is said to be the only bird endowed with this instinct,
and the whole of her procedure is taken by the Hebrew
writers as suggestive of instructive lessons in relation
to the dealing of God.

The eagle formed part of the emblem of Lagash already
at the time of her first dynasty. It was a symbol of
royalty, and was the bird of the *summus deus*. In this
connexion, one may refer to the eagle on the shield of
Ningirsu, the eagle of Jupiter of the classical period, and
the eagle in the Mithraic mysteries. The wings of an

eagle were sometimes combined with the body of
a bull, or its head was joined to the body of
a lion, to produce some kind of composite majestic figure
which would terrify the spirits and demons. A figure
of this type is sometimes represented as striking down
a wild goat. The symbol of Ningirsu, the city god of
Lagash, was a lion-headed eagle. Seeing that it was
regarded as a royal bird, it is upon the wings of an eagle
that Etana seeks to ascend to heaven. The eagle-headed
or vulture-headed human figure is one of the most
prominent symbols on early Assyrian monuments. Usually,
it is represented as conquering a human-headed lion or
bull, and the victory of the eagle-headed figure over the
lion or bull may symbolize the superiority of intellect
over mere physical strength. We can thus see how it
came to represent a type of the supreme deity, and we can
perhaps connect this with the statement in the Zoroastrian
oracles preserved by Eusebius,[1] that " God is he that
has the head of a hawk ". Gesenius has suggested that
Nisroch, which is the Hebrew form of the name of an
Assyrian deity in whose temple Sennacherib was
worshipping when slain by his sons (Isa. xxxvii, 38), is
a lengthened form of Nesher. One may note here an
additional example of the Assyrian symbols which were
most probably borrowed by the Greeks, for the Gryphon of
Greek mythology which was connected with Apollo was,
in all probability, of Assyrian origin.

As the eagle is the symbol of victory, so the vulture
is the symbolical bird of prey in Mesopotamian art. And
on the famous " Vulture Stele " of early Sumerian times,
as well as on the bas-reliefs of Ashurbanipal's palace at

---

[1] See F. W. Madden, *History of Jewish Coinage*, p. 112. Herod,
King of Chalcis, was the brother of Herod Agrippa I. On some of the
coins from this period there is a representation of an eagle, and it has
been suggested that this was due to the attempt made to place a golden
eagle on the principal door of the Temple, and the eagle was therefore
placed on the coins previous to and after the sedition to which this
attempt gave rise.

Nineveh, to quote but two instances, there are representations of vultures carrying off the limbs and heads of fallen enemies. It is always represented as feeding on the bodies of the slain.

In later Christian art the Egyptian phœnix is represented as an eagle, and is the symbol of resurrection.

CHAPTER IV

SYMBOLISM OF NUMBERS

CHAPTER IV

SYMBOLISM OF NUMBERS

The exalted ideas which ancient thinkers entertained concerning the symbolic and mystic properties of numbers may be estimated from the uses to which they were made subservient. One is therefore tempted to suggest that, particularly in the case of much-used numbers, some symbolical meaning must lay hidden. A reference to some of the numbers used in Semitic literatures will show how often these are used in a loose sense, without attempting exactitude. Thus, in Hebrew " two " is used for a few. The widow of Zarephath, when Elijah asks her for bread, tells him she is " gathering two sticks " that she may cook the meal for herself and her son (1 Kings xvii, 12). " Five " is also used in this way. In Lev. xxvi, 8, the Israelites are told that " five of them shall chase a hundred ". When we come to Babylonia, we find that speculation upon the value of numbers held a very important place in their religious philosophy. The gods were designated by whole numbers, and the various kinds of inferior spirits by fractions.

Some scholars have suggested that in ancient times all numbers were sacred, and that there is a *mathematical* foundation for ancient Oriental religions. Furthermore, they attempt to account for the fact that certain numbers take precedence over others by the influence of some particular calendar system, the belief being that the symbolical importance of some numbers at least is due to the fact that the divine will is represented by the movement of stars and constellations, which are represented by numbers.[1]

[1] Hommel, *OLZ.*, May, 1907, and Jeremias, *The Old Testament in the Light of the Ancient East*, Engl. Transl., vol. i, p. 63.

But whether we accept one theory or another, a study of ancient Oriental Literatures is bound to lead us to the conclusion that there are some numbers at least which occur very frequently and were never intended to be taken in their literal sense by those who made use of them. This use of many numbers in a round sense can partly be explained by the fact that the notion of representative numbering is extremely common amongst Eastern nations who have a prejudice against counting their possessions accurately, and it thus also enters largely into many ancient systems of chronology.

Number, as defined by mathematics, is, of course, a purely abstract conception. But to man in the earliest stages of his civilization, primarily on account of the limitations of his intellect, it was regarded as entirely concrete. Primitive man could form no idea of an abstract number. Want of familiarity with the use of numbers, as well as lack of convenient means of comparison, must result in extreme indefiniteness of mental conception, as well as almost entire absence of exactness. If a tribe is engaged in trade or barter with its neighbours, an ability for reckoning will gradually develop amongst its members. Otherwise, this power will remain dormant, as there is so little in the life of the ordinary man to call for its exercise. As an example of the inability of primitive man to form an idea of an abstract number, one may note the following. In various primitive Asiatic languages, if a man wished to say " five " he would make use of the same word as when he wished to say " hand ", and in all probability when he said " five " his mental conception was really that of a hand consisting of five outstretched fingers. It was only after a time that the image which arose in his mind as a means of assistance for the comprehension of the number he wished to represent disappeared, and the abstract and concrete ideas which were associated with the number were slowly dissociated from each other, so that the number, instead of appearing

to him as a representation of a certain number of objects,
became an independent idea which he could recognize
without the assistance originally obtained from the
derivation of the word. In this connexion one
might compare the *memoria technica* selected by the
scholars of India for recording dates and numbers. Thus,
' Moon ' or ' Earth ' expressed one, there being but one
of each ; two might be called ' Eye ', ' Wing ', ' Arm ',
' Jaw ', as going in pairs ; for three they said ' Rama ',
' Fire ', or ' Quality ', there being considered to be three
Ramas, three kinds of fire, three qualities ; for four were
used ' Veda ', ' Age ', or ' Ocean ', there being four of each
recognized ; ' Season ' for six, because they recognized
six seasons ; ' Sun ' for twelve, because of its annual
denominations, or ' Zodiac ' from its twelve signs, etc.[1]

The one universal system of counting by primitive
man throughout all parts of the world seems to have been
the finger method. And it is of course a matter of common
observation that when children begin to count they turn
almost instinctively to their fingers as a means of assistance.

In this connexion there are a few references in post-
Biblical literature which are of special interest to us.
In *Yoma*, 22 *a, b*, there is a reference to the use of the
fingers for numbering, and there is also a trace of finger-
counting in the *Hekalot* (Jellinek, *Bet Hamedrash*, iii, 22,
No. 94). The five fingers are considered the appointed
ministers of the five senses (*Gershom b. Solomon*). There
is also a saying that each of the five fingers of God's right
hand has a special function.

Amongst primitive tribes who use their fingers and hands
in counting, it is found that, whilst the term used for
" hand " also expresses the number five, the number ten
is expressed by " both hands " and twenty by " man ".
Thus a traveller amongst the Watchandies[2] relates how he
once wished to ascertain the exact number of natives who

[1] Tylor, *Primitive Culture*, 1903, vol. i, p. 252.
[2] A. Oldfield, *Tr. Eth. Society of London*, vol. iii, p. 291.

had been slain on a certain occasion. The individual
from whom he made the inquiry began to think over the
names, assigning one of his fingers to each, until, after many
failures, he held up his hand three times in order to give
him to understand that fifteen was the answer to his
question.

The theory that man's primitive method of counting
was that of reckoning on his hand, helps us towards understanding the origin of numerals in general. For when
" five " is expressed, as in several languages of the Malay
family, by hand (*lima*), this is precisely the same as when
in the description of numbers by word, 2 is denoted by
" Wings ". We can thus see how at the root of all numbers
there are such metaphors as these, though they cannot
always be traced. Again, the Mexican names for the first
four numbers are obscure in etymology, but five is expressed
by *macuilli*, which means " hand-depicting ".[1] We are now
confronted with the question as to whether we can find
in the Semitic languages any philological connexion
between the words for " five " and " hand " or " to touch
with the hand ".

Now, in Hebrew and other Semitic languages, there
are a large number of triliteral stems which have no doubt
arisen from a biliteral base, called a root, since it formed
the starting-point for several triliteral modifications of
the same fundamental idea.

The most numerous examples of this type of word are
those in which the second or third consonants are identical,
or those in which the stem consists of one weak consonant
with two strong ones. One may quote as examples
דכך, דוך, דכא, דכה, all of which can be traced
back to the original idea of striking or breaking, and the
two consonants דך form the root common to all of

---

[1] Pott, *Zählmethode*, p. 46 ; also Rue in *Tr. Eth. Soc.*, vol. iv, p. 145.
It is of interest to note that Grimm, *Geschichte d. Deutschen Sprache*,
vol. i, par. 239, suggests that all numeral words have their origin in the
names of fingers.

them.[1] It is also of interest to note that Ball in an article
" Semitic and Sumerian " in the *Hilprecht Anniversary
Vol.*, pp. 50 f., has suggested that many of the present
triliteral forms in Hebrew have arisen from originally
biliteral forms which have been triliteralized by the prefix
שׂ in the sense of " to make ", and he quotes such
examples as שְׁקַל " to make light ", " to heave,"
" lift "; and so " to weigh ". שׁכב " to make act of
reclining " from root KAB = כפף " to bend down ", etc.
Furthermore, it has even been suggested that *all* triliteral
stems in Hebrew are derived from biliterals (König,
Lehrg. ii, 1, 370). The present writer ventures to suggest
that the hypothesis that many triliteral stems in Hebrew
have arisen from an original biliteral root by the addition
of a third consonant, will help us to explain the meaning
of many of these stems. A few examples will suffice.
The Oxford Hebrew Lexicon (BDB. p. 68) has no suggestion
to make for the root of אֵפֶר " ashes ", and in the case of
עָפָר " dust " it gives the root as dubious (p. 779).
One is tempted to suggest that both words are philologically connected with the root פרר " to break into
pieces ", and thus go back to an original stem פר
with the addition of א and ע respectively.[2] In the
Tell el Amarna letters " haparu " and " aparu " occur
as variant Assyrian words for " dust ".

Again, we have the verb רקק " to be thin ",
" slender " (BDB. p. 956) and פרק " to break into
pieces ", both no doubt from an original רק (cf. רֵק
"empty") with the addition of a third consonant. Similarly,
פרץ " to spread out or break forth " and רצץ " to crush
or break asunder " from a base רץ (cf. רוץ " to run "
perhaps in the sense of " spreading out one's legs ").
But there seem to be a number of triliteral stems which

---

[1] Gesenius-Kautsch, *Hebrew Grammar*, 30g.

[2] It is of interest to note that " dust " and " ashes " are actually
used interchangeably in the Old Testament. See chapter on symbolism
of Mourning Customs.

have arisen from a biliteral base, with the addition of ה
in preference to other consonants. Thus חדר " a chamber "
(BDB. p. 293) is connected with the verb חדר " to
enclose ", " surround." Might not these stems be again
connected with דור " circle ", " ball " (p. 189), which
actually means also in Aramaic and post-Biblical Hebrew
" to dwell ". So that חדר may have arisen from
דר with the addition of ה. Similarly, the base פר
may have given rise to פרה " to be fruitful ", and,
with the addition of ה, to חפר " to dig ". So
also שך may be the base for שכך " to cover ",
חשך " to darken " (cover the light), and חשך " to
withhold ".

On this analogy the present writer suggests that the root
of חמש " five " (which is said by BDB. to be unknown)
is connected with משש " to feel ", " grope ", " touch with
the hand ". So that in Hebrew as in many non-Semitic
languages " five " is expressed metaphorically by " to
touch with the hand ".

It is highly probable, and, in fact, almost certain, that
amongst the Ancient Hebrews there was a system of
numerical notation, although, unfortunately, no examples
have come down to us in the few Israelitish inscriptions
that have survived from ancient times. It seems that the
earliest system for the recording of numbers was founded
on the members of the body. The five fingers of the hand
gave the V of the Roman Notation,[1] and two of these
joined at their apexes gave X. The Egyptians sometimes
united the five in a star. In the Maccabean period we find
the letters of the Hebrew alphabet being used as numerical
symbols. Amongst the Rabbis there was a system of
notation in frequent use, the age of which it is impossible to
fix with absolute accuracy. By this the letters of the

---

[1] The familiar Roman Notation I, II, III, IV, V, VI, etc., suggests
quinary counting ; whilst the Greek πεμπάζειν to count by fives,
and a few kindred words hint at a remote antiquity in which the
ancestors of the Greeks counted on their fingers and so grouped their
units into fives. (Conant, *The Number Concept*, p. 168.)

Hebrew alphabet were used as numerals, from א to ט
for the units, from י to צ for the tens, and from ק to
the end of the alphabet with the help of the finals for the
hundreds.

Seeing that numbers are indicated by letters, a number
was also used to represent a name, the sum of whose letters
amounted to that number. An Old Testament instance is
" Eliezer ", the sum of the letters of whose name is 318,
the number of Abraham's servants when he went to
encounter Chedorlaomer. This estimation of names and
the method of representing them by numbers is called by
the Rabbis " Gematria ", a word that seems to have been
derived from the Greek " Geometreia ". In the Talmud
it becomes an elaborate system with modes and rules.
Whilst these methods were used for the interpretation of
the Bible with the most interesting results, they serve a
useful purpose as mnemonics, as may be seen in the
Massoretic notes at the end of each book in the Hebrew Bible.

But there was also another kind of symbolism of numbers,
known by the term " Gematria " (the term first occurs
amongst the thirty-two rules of R. Eliezer, the son of
R. Jose, the Galilean), which is a kind of cryptograph
giving, instead of the intended word, its numerical
value. In its simplest form it is thus a kind of arithmetical
equation.

Numbers played a most important part in Babylonia.
This was primarily due to two factors. In the first place,
the Babylonians made very considerable use of various
musical instruments in their religious services, as may be
seen from the constant references to these in Babylonian
texts (Frank, *Studien zur Bab. Religion*, pp. 229 ff.) ; whilst
secondly, building and constructing, especially for religious
purposes, led to a knowledge of solid geometry. As a result,
they soon learned that the laws of space and sound bear
a definite relationship to each other. Furthermore, the
formation of various kinds of crystals which Ea, the god
of art, placed at the bed of the earth, the harmony in

structure of man and animal, and above all the spacial
or temporal appearances in the heavens, led to the idea
that numbers are the most pregnant forms for the
expression of the nature and power of the deity.

This explains why everything in the life and religion of
the Babylonians was connected with numbers. In fact,
one may safely say that Babylonia was one of the oldest
homes of the science of mathematics, and that Pythagoras,
who is usually looked upon as the father of the symbolism
of numbers, was really the heir of a science which had its
origin in Southern Babylonia some 3,000 years ago. It
appears also that the Babylonians had a kind of onomantic
arithmetic in which the planets, the days of the week, and
the letters of the alphabet, as well as the Zodiacal signs,
were assimilated with certain numbers. Thus, by the use
of prescribed tables, arranged astrologically, according
to the aspects of the planets towards the twelve signs, the
adept could give all kinds of authoritative pronouncements
concerning the future. In fact, this was one of the
principles by which the Jewish Cabbalists were guided.
As the letters of the Hebrew language are numerals, and
the whole Bible is really composed of various combinations
of these numbers, they believed that by assigning to their
numerical value various difficult passages in the Bible, their
true meaning could be obtained. And the account informing
us how Elijah, after challenging the priests of Baal, constructed an altar of twelve stones corresponding to the
twelve tribes of Israel, was regarded as an instance of how
the symbolical value of numbers was taught in the Old
Testament itself.

A system of "Gematria" seems to have existed also
amongst the Babylonians and Assyrians, for when Sargon
speaks of the construction of the wall of Khorsabad, he
says that he made the measure of the wall *Dur Sharrukin*,
equivalent to the value of his name, which he reckons out
was 16,280 yards.[1]

---

[1] Hommel, *OLZ.*, 1907 pp. 225-8.

But even amongst the Greeks this form of " Gematria " existed. At Pergamum, which was one of the cities of the Apocalypse (Rev. ii, 12 ff.), inscribed stones have been found containing these " numerical riddles ", as they have often been called.[1] Furthermore, *graffiti* (wall scribblings), from Pompeii, dating from about A.D. 79, and containing, also, examples of the use of " Gematria ", were discovered and published some time ago ;[2] whilst a most difficult passage in Suetonius (*Nero*, 39) was explained by the discovery that the name " Nero " is there numerically resolved into " matricide ".[3] From these inscriptions we learn how the names of persons were often purposely concealed by resolving them into numbers. A few examples here will suffice. One of the *graffiti* at Pompeii reads : " I love her whose number is 545 " ; whilst another states, " Amerimnus thought upon his lady Harmonia for good. The number of her honourable name is 45." This now suggests to us that " Gematria " is the obvious method of solving the meanings underlying the apocalyptic numbers 616 and 666, and seeing that these numerical forms of riddles were not specifically Jewish or Semitic, but were common also amongst the Greeks, and as these numbers occur in a Greek book, we must attempt to solve their meanings by assigning to them the values assigned to the different letters of the Greek alphabet.

To the Pythagoreans number appeared as a kind of fundamental principle from which the whole objective world proceeds. It was the key to the understanding of all earthly and heavenly appearances. It was the origin of all things, and a knowledge of numbers was equivalent to a knowledge of God. The creation of the world was nothing more than the harmonious effect of a pure arrangement of

---

[1] See *Die Inschriften von Pergamon*, Nos. 333, 339, 587.
[2] By A. Sogliano ; see the extract in *Wochenschrift für klassische philologie*, 19 (1902), col. 52.
[3] F. Bücheler, *Rheinisches Museum für Philologie*, N.S., lxi, 1906, pp. 307 f.

numbers ; whilst the essence of all things in the moral and
spiritual world was accounted for by this numerical
explanation. In the world of ideas such things as love,
health, friendship, and justice were associated with certain
numbers. For example, " seven " was identified with
health, perhaps because seven as a complete number
suggested a complete and perfect state of life.[1] Justice
was represented by a square number probably suggested
by the old law of lex talionis, because the law of " eye for
eye ", " tooth for tooth " recalled to mind the composition
of a number of two equal factors ; whilst friendship and
love as a harmony best expressed by the octave was
symbolized by the number eight. How is it that the son
of a stone-cutter, as Pythagoras was, should have become
not only one of the most original figures in Greece, but in
all the world ? He was a scientist, a theologian, a guide
in untrodden paths in astronomy, and above all, as we
have already seen, a brilliant mathematician. Various
suggestions have been put forward, but the most plausible
one seems that he travelled considerably in the East, and
that the culture which he collected in his travels formed the
foundation-stones of his brilliant learning. We have no
evidence that he visited Babylonia, but we can say with
almost absolute certainty that he must have visited Egypt.
Herodotus speaks of the " Orphics and Bacchics " as
" Pythagoreans and Egyptians " ; whilst he even suggests
that the belief in the transmigration of souls, which was one
of the very foundation-stones of Pythagorean doctrines,
was of Egyptian origin.[2]

But we are also told that a large portion of Egyptian
philosophy and religion was constructed almost wholly
upon the science of numbers and that many things in nature
were explained on this principle alone. In his belief that
a secret virtue lay behind several numbers, Pythagoras

---

[1] Cf. Hebrew שָׁלוֹם, peace, welfare ; and שָׁלֵם complete, perfect.
[2] For further evidence that Pythagoras visited Egypt see Chaignet,
Pythagore et la Philosophie Pythagoricienne, vol. i, pp. 40, 48.

was followed by nearly all the philosophers of the Italic school. Plato designated his ideas later as ἀριθμοὶ νοητοὶ, and gave his pupils the opportunity of connecting his teachings with those of the Pythagoreans (Zeller, ii, 2nd ed., S. 430 ff.–S. 657). At a still later period we find that whilst Augustine, the distinguished Bishop of Hippo and one of the best known and most important of the fathers of the early Christian Church, attacked every form of superstition most bitterly, especially the science of astrology, he followed the footsteps of Plato and Pythagoras and attached the utmost importance to the symbolism of numbers. In the writings of Ambrosius and Augustine a most interesting example of this occurs in the explanation of John xxi, 1–11 (*Sancti Aureli Augustini Opera Omnia*, ed. Migne, iii, col. 1950 sqq.), with reference to the rich capture of 153 fishes. For Augustine this is not a chance number at all, but it has a symbolic meaning behind it. He reasons it out in the following manner : 10 is the symbol of law (e.g. the ten commandments), while 7 is the symbol of the spirit ; so that $10+7 = 17$ is the symbolical expression for holiness. Now, the number 153 is obtained by the addition of all numbers from 1 to 17 in arithmetical progression, for example $1+2+3+4 \ldots +15+16+17 = 153$; hence its symbolic nature. It was only after the Jews came into contact with Greek philosophy that the symbolism of numbers began to play a really important part in the Jewish interpretation of the Bible. Traces of Pythagorean influences exist in the oldest Jewish-Hellenistic work, the Septuagint. Thus the passage in Isa. xl, 26, " that bringeth out their host by number," is translated by the Septuagint " he that bringeth forth *his array* by number ".[1]

The symbolism of numbers is constantly referred to in the Talmuds and the Midrashim (see Nacham Krochmal, *More Nebuche Hazeman*, 4th ed., S. 202 f.) ; whilst the *Sefer Jezirah* is written in a Platonic-Pythagorean spirit (Zunz,

[1] R. R. Ottley, *Isaiah According to the Septuagint*, vol. i, p. 221.

Die Gottesdienstliche Vorträge der Juden, S. 165). Abraham Ibn Ezra was particularly fond of making use of the symbolism of numbers in his mathematical works ; [1] whilst the Cabbalists in their teachings of the symbolism of numbers were no doubt very considerably influenced by his works. It is of interest to note how profoundly much later philosophers have been influenced in their speculations by the Pythagorean doctrine of numbers. Thus Giordano Bruno and Auguste Comte attach enormous importance to the numbers three, four, and ten in their philosophy, and finally some of the greatest leaders of the modern school of nature philosophy have stated as one of their aphorisms that everything that is Real is absolutely nothing else than number.

In summing up the contributions which ancient and medieval scholars made on the subject, we are bound to admit that—whilst Pythagoras and Plato and the Cabbalists, in some portions of their enigmatic Cabbala, at least, went to the most absurd lengths and thus tended to bring discredit on the opinions which they held—many of their theories and suggestions are exceedingly valuable in helping us to gain some idea of the Oriental conception concerning the symbolism of numbers. It must be admitted that much of their work can only be regarded as learned trifling. Nay, at times it appears even worse than trifling, for it converts the Bible into an abracadabra, regarding it with respect to prophecy anent the future as but a juggler's book, which turns up different numbers according to the different throws of the dice. When necessity is not laid upon us to show the symbolical importance of a number, or how one number springs from another, the attempt should obviously never be made. Beyond, however, the limited range of numbers discussed in these pages, there are few numbers which can be set up as having any claim to symbolic importance in Semitic literatures. And it is satisfactory to note that in almost every instance

[1] W. Bacher, *Abraham Ibn Ezra als Grammatiker*, pp. 9 f.

which is adduced, history and Comparative Religion can be brought in to corroborate and regulate the deductions it seems warrantable to make.

THREE

Triads may be made to cover many a page. Land, air, and water in the macrocosm without; body, soul, and spirit in the world within. Oriental speculation tended to group all things under three heads. The heaven above, the earth beneath, the waters beneath the earth ; morning, noon, and evening ; the head, trunk, and legs of a body ; the source, stream, and mouth of a river—all have been regarded as testifying to the trinity which rules in natural things. And as three is the smallest number with a beginning, middle, and end, it came to represent a small, well-rounded total. A reference to a Bible Dictionary will show the frequency with which the number occurs in Biblical literature. In 1 Kings xvii, 21, we are told how Elijah stretched himself out over the child three times ; in 1 Chron. xxi, 12, David is given three things to choose from, either three years' famine, or three months to be destroyed before his foes, or for three days the sword of the Lord should destroy throughout the coasts of Israel. Daniel kneeled upon his knees and prayed three times a day (Dan. vi, 10). Pharaoh's butler dreamt of a vine-tree with three branches (Gen. xl, 10), and Joseph kept his brothers imprisoned for three days (Gen. xlii, 17) ; whilst Moses was hidden by his mother for three months (Exod. ii, 2). The Israelites are to ask Pharaoh to go for three days' journey in the wilderness (Exod. iii, 18), Canaan was cursed three times (Gen. ix, 25-7). The Israelites were to come to Jerusalem three times a year (Exod. xxiii, 17). Balaam blesses Israel three times (Num. xxiv, 10). Jonah was in the belly of the fish three days and three nights (Jonah i, 17). An examination of these passages is bound to lead to the conclusion that the number " three " is not used literally, but rhetorically, and symbolizes a small total. In Amos i, 3, we read : " For the three transgressions of Damascus, yea for the four I will not turn away the punishment thereof." Now many scholars used to regard these numbers literally, and understood that three transgressions had been committed by the Israelites, which might possibly have been pardoned by God, but that the fourth transgression was of such a terrible nature that all hope of pardon was now rendered impossible. This literal explanation seems hardly acceptable, and most modern scholars are agreed in explaining the two numbers symbolically. Three, as we shall see later, is symbolically used for " many " or " enough ", and represents a complete number ; four is therefore even more than enough, and so calls for punishment.

We can now understand why actions are so often repeated three times. Elijah poured water on the burnt offering three times (1 Kings xviii, 34). Elisha tells the King of Israel to perform three different actions, and afterwards Joash smites some arrows upon the ground three times, apparently for some magical purposes (2 Kings xiii, 18). After Samuel had been called three times, Eli recognized that it is the Divine Voice speaking to him. It seems obvious that the meaning of these passages can only be fully understood by explaining the number " three " to have the symbolical significance we have assigned to it. Furthermore, we often find words and phrases repeated three times. In Jer. vii, 4, the prophet says to the people, " Do not trust in false words saying ' The temple of the Lord, the temple of the Lord, the temple of the Lord are they '." Similarly, Isa. viii, 9, וָחֹתּוּ " and you shall be broken in pieces ", Isa. xxxiii, 10, עַתָּה "Now", Hos. ii, 19, 20, וְאֵרַשְׂתִּיךְ " And I shall betroth thee " ; " And I will betroth thee unto me for ever ; yea, I will betroth thee unto me in righteousness, and in judgment, and in lovingkindness, and in mercies. I will even betroth thee unto me in faithfulness."

One is reminded also of the passage in Jeremiah (xxii, 29), " O earth, earth, earth, hear the word of the Lord."
But perhaps the most interesting and best-known passages to illustrate our purpose are the following :—
" Holy, holy, holy, is the Lord of Hosts, all the earth is full of His glory " (Isa. vi, 3).
Evidently the threefold use of the word " Holy " is here (as we shall see also in other Semitic and non-Semitic languages) a circumlocution for the superlative. In the priestly benediction the name of God is thrice repeated (Num. vi, 24–6). " The Lord bless thee and keep thee. The Lord make His face to shine upon thee, and be gracious unto thee. The Lord lift up His countenance unto thee and give thee peace " ;[1] cf. also נֹקֵם (Nah. i, 2–3) and עַוָּה (Ezek. xxi, 32), the words in each case being repeated three times. When God makes a covenant with Abram He tells him to take a heifer three years old (Gen. xv, 8), possibly because, as Dillmann suggests, three was a sacred number, and therefore used symbolically in solemn affirmations and imprecations (see Driver's *Commentary on Genesis*, p. 176).

Babylonian.

An examination of the frequency with which the number three occurs in Babylonian literature suggests that here also the number had some symbolical or sacred significance. Let us first consider the triads. At the head of the Babylonian pantheon we have Anu Bel and Ea symbolizing the entire universe and personifying its three divisions— heaven, earth, and water.[2] It is the gods of this triad who

[1] One might compare with this the Shamash Hymn in Babylonian, which is also divided into three divisions :—
    May Ea rejoice over thee.
    May Damkina, the goddess of the ocean, enlighten thee with her countenance.
    May Marduk, the great overseer of the Igigi, raise thy head.
[2] We are no doubt justified in regarding the Biblical prohibition in Exod. xx, 4, against making an image of anything " in the heaven above, the earth beneath, or the waters beneath the earth ", as a reference to this triad.

fix the names of the months and who head the list of gods
invoked in the incantation texts. And when a king claims
his right to the Babylonian throne or prays that those who
deface his monuments may be severely punished, it is these
gods to whom he specially appeals in his prayers. When
the Babylonians wished to express in their cosmological
system the priority of Lakhmu and Lakhamu they represented them as the ancestors of this triad. It thus became
a model after which others were formed of a similar type.
By the side of the first triad we find another which
symbolized the influence of the astrological system in
Babylonia. Sin, the Moon-god, symbolized the hosts of
the heavens ; Shamash, the Sun-god, the beneficent power
of the sun ; and Ishtar, representing mother-earth,
symbolized the source of life and fertility. The remarkable
fact about this triad was that whilst to the Semite the Sun-
god was the lord and father of the gods and the moon was
either his female consort or an inferior and pale reflection
of the sun, in this triad Sin was the chief god and was
regarded as the father of the other two.[1]

These three gods were also the rulers of the Zodiac, and
as the first triad represented space, so they represented
time.[2]

In addition to the above-mentioned triads we have also
many minor ones such as Apsu, Tiamat, Mummu ; Ea,
Damkina, Marduk ; Ea, Marduk, Nabu ; and Shamash,
Adad, Ishtar. The three seasons of the year no doubt
corresponded to those triads. When the Babylonian
astrologers learned that the sun and planets move in certain
fixed orbits, they divided the ecliptic known as the " Path-
way of the sun " into three divisions and called each
after one of the deities of the first triad, which, as we have
already seen, symbolized the powers of the universe. The
formation of the Babylonian triads was an artificial scheme
and was no doubt the work of a theological school. The

[1] Sayce, *Hibbert Lectures*, 1887, pp. 155, 193.
[2] F. X. Kugler, *Entwicklung der Babylonischen Planetenkunde.*

Babylonian pantheon rested on a triad just as the orthodox theological system of Egypt rested on the Ennead. In fact, the Ennead has been regarded as a multiple of the triad. The important fact that we must note, therefore, is that the Babylonian triads were not trinities in any way. They were composed of divine persons who were partners and divided the universe between them. Each one was supreme in his own particular locality, and that portion of the universe over which their power extended was carefully arranged in groups of three.

We learn from a Babylonian record of the creation that the world was considered as a celestial and an earthly whole, and that each of these was divided into three regions. The celestial world consisted of (1) the waters of heaven, (2) the Zodiac, (3) the North heaven ; whilst the earthly world consisted of (1) the waters surrounding the earth, (2) the earth, (3) air. In the Magical texts the times chosen by the witches for their manifestations were the three divisions of the night—evening, midnight, and dawn. In order, therefore, to destroy their influence the incantations were recited and various symbolical acts were performed also on these three occasions. Similarly, the day was divided into three divisions (Straszmaier, *ZA.* iv, 190). The third day was most critical in the development of any disease.[1] A chafing dish stood at the bedside of a sick person for three days. At the reconstruction of a temple we read of three meal-offerings being brought for Ea, Shamash, and Marduk. For magical purposes three cords were tied round the neck of a sick person.[2] In the Ritual tablets we read of three sheep for Ea, Shamash, and Marduk, three altars for Ishtar, Shamash, and Nergal, and three loaves of wheaten flour.[3]

The repetition of an exorcism three times made it much

---

[1] Küchler, *Beitr. zur Kenntnis der ass.-bab. Medizin,* 42–3.
[2] K.B., vi, 1, 365.
[3] Zimmern, *Beit. Rit. Taf.,* Nos. 56, 4, 7.

more effective,[1] and sometimes certain words, particularly at the beginning of the adjuration, were repeated three times for emphasis. Greetings and blessings were often of a threefold nature. " To the king my Lord, to my Lord the king, to my Lord the king." The ritual amongst the Babylonians before going to battle is also of great interest. " When an enemy attacks the king and his land, the king shall go forth on the right wing of the army, and thou shalt sweep the earth clean and sprinkle pure water, and set three altars, one for Ishtar, one for Shamash, and one for Nergal, and offer each a loaf of wheaten meal, and make a mash of honey and butter, pouring in dates and . . . meal, and sacrifice three full-grown sheep."

In the Labartu series we are told of a ceremony for curing a man who is possessed of demons. The incantation which accompanies the ceremony is to be repeated three times, at dawn, mid-day, and evening, a figure of Labartu is to be put at the sick man's head for three days, and on the third day, as the day draws to its close, it is to be buried in the corner of the wall (Myhrman, *Die Labartu-Texte, ZA.*, xvi, 1903). A priest who prays for a sick man should say " Ea hath sent me, three times " (King, *Bab. Magic and Sorcery*, 58-9 ff.). In the Maklu series we are told of various incantations which are to be repeated three times over the threshold of a house and the evil foot will not approach the house of a man (K. 10333). A prayer for the cure of tooth-ache—Mix fermented drink, the plant *sakilbir*, and oil together, repeat the incantation three times and put it on the man's tooth (cf. Thompson, *Devils and Evil Spirits of Babylonia*, ii, 163). For rheumatism spin together hair from a dog and hair from a lion, thread three cornelians thereon, bind it on and he shall recover. If a man looks upon a corpse and the spirit seizes him, he must perform various religious rites, part of which is that he must eat a meal three times before Shamash, Ea, and Marduk, and

---

[1] Zimmern, *Beit. Rit. Taf.*, No. 11.

he must also set three " adagur-vessels " and three censers
of incense (Zimmern, *Beit. Rit. Taf.*, 52).

Egyptian.

Of Egyptian triads much has already been written. We
are immediately reminded of the Abydos triad of Osiris,
Isis, and Horus, and of the Theban triad consisting of
Amen-Ra, Mut, and Chonsu. But, according to some scholars,
it is Osiris, Cneph, and Phtha that form the true Egyptian
triad of deity—a triad which most nearly approached to
the trinities of India. " As Osiris was a title afterwards
applied to the sun, so Phtha was to the fire that issued from
the solar orb ; while Cneph was the mighty spirit that
pervaded and animated the whole world." [1]   With reference
to the Egyptian trinities, we are no doubt justified in
drawing an analogy between the Indian conception of a
trinity and that held by the deepest thinkers in Egypt.
As Barth points out,[2] " the Indian conception of a trinity is
not a cosmographic distribution of the deified forces of
nature, but a threefold evolution of the divine unity."

It is important to note, however, that the Egyptian
trinity was posterior to that of the Ennead, and was really
of artificial character, having been formed by the union of
foreign elements. For example : the trinity of Osiris, Isis,
and Horus (whose leading position in Egypt was similar to
that of Anu, Ea, and Bel in Babylonia) was formed by
transferring Nebhat and Anubis, the allies of Osiris, to his
enemy Set. In the same way the Theban trinity owed its
origin to the rise of the Theban Dynasties when Thebes
became the capital of Egypt. We can thus trace the growth
of the Egyptian trinity and the ideas and tendencies which
lay behind it. It was the culminating stage in the evolution
of the religious system which took its first start amongst
the priests of Heliopolis. First, creation by means of
generation, then the Ennead, and lastly the triad and trinity

[1] Maurice, *Indian Antiquities*, chap. ii of Dissertation at end of
vol. iv.
[2] A. Barth, *Religions of India*, translated by Wood, pp. 180-1.

—such were the stages in the gradual process of development. But scholars have attempted to trace other abstract ideas underlying the Egyptian Pantheon, and find references to a trinity composed of a generative, a destructive, and then preserving power ; whilst to denote the threefold deity a triangle was used by the ancient Egyptians.

The existence of a Phœnician triad (Baal Astarte, Esmoun, and Melcarth) and of a Palmyrian triad has been conjectured, but without sufficient reason. The existence of Carthaginian triads, however, is very much more probable.

Samaritan.

From the available Samaritan MSS. of the Bible it appears that the Samaritans were in the habit of arranging groups of three letters, each group being believed to represent one of God's mysterious names. And, furthermore, it is of interest to note that in the Samaritan Phylacteries, which have been published by Dr. Gaster,[1] where the letters are arranged to form all kinds of permutations and combinations, the square in the phylactery is so arranged as to be the result of two triangles. This was used for mystical purposes, the idea being that just as the writing diminished into the apex of an inverted triangle, so the illness would diminish. In connexion with the arrangement of the divine name into groups of three letters, might not the repetition of the Divine name, even in Biblical times, have had some symbolical or mystic significance ? In Ps. l, 1, and Joshua xxii, 22, God is called by three Divine names יהוה, אֵל, אֱלֹהִים.

Talmud.

In order to give the reaping of the Omer more publicity, many Rabbis suggested that the grain for the Omer must always be reaped by three persons, each with his own sickle

[1] *PSBA.*, vol. xxxix. I wish to acknowledge here my indebtedness to Dr. Gaster for his kindness in drawing my attention to this article.

and basket (*Menahoth*, vi, 1). The reaping was also carried out with much ceremony. Special messengers were sent by the *Beth Din*, who tied the heads of the stalks together. Then when the time for gathering came, the reapers asked permission to do so by repeating a formula three times, and we are distinctly told that this was done in order to impress upon the Bœthusians that the proper time for the gathering of the Omer had arrived (*Menahoth*, vi, 3). In the Rabbinical laws dealing with the ceremony of the Red Heifer (Num. xix), we are informed that after the priest who was to burn it had been made ritually unclean he was obliged to immerse in water. The priest then took some cedar wood, purple wool, and hyssop, showed it to those present, and said, " Here is cedar wood, here is hyssop, here is purple wool." This formula was repeated first by him and then by the congregation three times (*Parah*, iii, 7, 10), so as to emphasize the fact that every part of the ceremonial carried out by the priest was done with the consent and under the guidance of the congregation and not of his own accord.

In the Halizah ceremony, which arose from the Biblical command of the levirate marriage (Deut. xxv, 5–10), three small straps are attached to the front of the shoe. The widow repeats the following words after the presiding judge: " So shall it be done unto the man who will not build up his brother's house, and his name shall be called in Israel, ' The house of him that hath his shoe loosed.' " This last phrase is repeated by the widow and the assembly present three times, in order, as the Mishna says (*Jebamoth*, xii), to show that the removal of the shoe is the most important part of the ceremony.[1] We are also reminded of the three sayings ascribed to each of the five pupils of Rabban Johanan ben Zakkai (*Aboth*, ii, 14 ff.), the three sayings of the men of the Great Synagogue (*Aboth*, i, 1), and the three things on which the world stands (*Aboth*, i, 19).

---

[1] See *Jüdische Zeitschrift*, vol. ii, pp. 108 ff.

The evil spirit *Bath Chorin* which rests upon the hands at night is very strict. He will not depart until water is poured upon the hands three times. According to the Talmud a three-cornered house is immune from uncleanness in leprosy, and it has been suggested that this had some connexion with the frequent usage of the number three in magic. The following is a late Hebrew charm for killing an enemy: Take dust from the grave of a murdered man who has been slain with iron, and take water from three wells which are a considerable distance apart. Knead the dust with the water, make it into a cake and throw it into the house of thine enemy, saying, "As this lord of the dust was slain, so may . . . be slain" ("Folklore of Mossoul," *PSBA.*, 1906, p. 104). Even amongst modern Jews there is a superstition that in order to nullify the effects of an evil eye the mother should kiss the child three times, spitting after each kiss (*J. E. Sv., Superstition*).

Cabbala.

In the Cabbala there is a trinity of three great *Sephiroth* : Kether (the crown), Chochmah (wisdom), and Binah (understanding), all emanations of and synthesized in the "Infinite". The first Sephira, "Kether," was regarded as the omnipotent father of the universe. The second, "Chochmah," was the Logos or creative wisdom ; whilst the third, "Binah," was the heavenly intelligence which pervades, animates, and governs this boundless universe. The Cabbalists applied a mystic meaning in the case of the three holy men referred to by Ezekiel (xiv, 14), each of whom they said saw the creation, destruction, and restoration of the world. Noah saw the earth reduced to chaos and restored after the flood. Daniel saw Jerusalem (a world in miniature) entirely destroyed, and later in his days the temple was rebuilt ; whilst Job saw his house and family (which was also a small world to him) destroyed and then become prosperous.

Vedic Literature.

The number three is one of the most sacred numbers of the *Rig-Veda*; in i, 95, 3, there is a reference to a threefold division—earth, air, and heaven. We also read of three heavens and three earths; whilst in the fifth book we are told that three heavens, three rain-spaces, and three light-spaces are the places of the highest gods. The gods descend to the sacrifice three times a day—morning, noon, and night. " Even where the dual character of the gods is characteristic, three is applied, as it were, mechanically in their praise." " Thrice come to us to-day, three tigers are on your chariot, thrice by day you come and thrice by night. Thrice ye compass earth and through three distances ye come, three are the wheels of your threefold chariot." Then we have also reference to groups of three—Agni, Soma, and Gandharva, Aryaman, Mitra, and Varuna, Agni, Indra, and Sairtai; whilst a trinity of goddesses is formed by Saraswati, the white one, Lakshmi, the red one, and Pa, the black one.

According to the Hindu system of cosmogony there were three regions : Heaven, the atmosphere, and the earth.[1]

Amongst the Indians part of the ceremony for driving out demons from women is for the " Fairy Woman " to take three different coloured silk or cotton threads and tie knots in them.

Just as in the Babylonian cosmogony the world of Anshar is threatened by Tiamat and Kingu, so in the Avesta the worlds of light and darkness are placed in antithesis. Then from Pahlavi literature we learn that the combat completes itself in a series of ages each consisting of 3,000 years. The first 3,000 years form a period of spiritual creation; in the second Ahura Mazda creates three Amshaspands, each of which is accompanied by the triad Sun, Moon, and Tishtrya. In the third period of 3,000 years Ahriman appears, and in the fourth Zarathustra appears.

Three, again, and its square play an exceedingly

[1] See Monier-Williams, *Sanskr. Dict.*, and the Appendix to Thompson's translation of the *Bhagavad-Gita* sub. " Siddha ".

important part in the rites of the Greeks and Romans, and also of the Eastern branches of the Aryans. In ancestor worship the father, grandfather, and the great-grand-father are selected out of the whole lineage as "Tritopatores" or paternal triad ; whilst the sacredness of the number meets us as early as Homer, where a trinity of deities, Zeus, Athene, and Apollo, are addressed in a single supplication. Amongst the Greeks and Romans supreme power was constantly associated with the number " three ". We have this idea prominently emphasized in the Greek theogony when the three sons of Kronos—Zeus, Poseidon, Pluto — divided the universe amongst themselves, a division which played a very large and important part in Greek religious myths and partly corresponded to and partly influenced the development of ritual. Amongst the Greeks, as amongst ourselves, "three" was regarded as the determining or final number. The idea of excellency or completeness attached to it is manifest in a vast collection of words in which the term $\tau\rho\iota\varsigma$, " thrice," occurs as the prefix enhancing exceedingly the force of the word. In Greek literature we have also references to the Three Fates, Three Furies, Three Judges of Hell, Three-forked Spear of Poseidon, Three-headed dog of Pluto, Zeus' Three-forked Lightning, Apollo's tripod. The Three-eyed Zeus at Larissa was the oldest of the Grecian deities, whose triple eye indicated his sovereignty over earth, water, and air, the three forms of matter. In the Roman theatres the applause was thrice repeated, and it was customary, when bidding a last farewell to the corpse of a deceased friend, for the relative to repeat the word " vale " three times. Corineus went three times round the assembly at Misenus's funeral to purify them. In the festival called the Amburvalia the victim was to be led round the fields three times. In the sacrifices of Bacchus the priestesses were to go three times round the altar with dishevelled hair ; whilst three times was the effigy of a coy lover to be drawn round the altar to inspire him with love.

The Pythagoreans believed that all and everything is determined through triplicity. They regarded the triad as the most perfect form in the Universe, unless it were the tetrad or four, which to them was simply the triad more fully developed. They also believed in the principle of three worlds—the inferior, the superior, and supreme. The inferior contained bodies and magnitudes, next above was the superior world intended for superior powers, and finally the third world, which is supreme, was regarded as the abode of the one great deity.

In the Pythagorean ideas on Eschatology, as set forth in Plutarch's *De facie in orbe lunae*,[1] we are told that man is made up of three parts, νοῦς, ψυχή, σῶμα. Of these the first and highest, νοῦς, belongs to the sun; ψυχή, which ranks next, belongs to the moon; whilst σῶμα is purely terrestrial.

Corresponding to these three divisions are three classes of people, viz. those who, after a temporary sojourn on the moon, where they stay after death, are purified, and then admitted to the sun and the region of Aether; those who, on account of their piety, are very soon admitted to the moon, which is situated between the sun and atmosphere; and third, those who are confined to the lower parts of the atmosphere near the earth, and there are punished for their crimes in life.

Later Greek thinkers were influenced in their conception of the number by the importance assigned to it by the Pythagoreans. Aristotle says that the number three was taken from nature as an observation of its laws as the most proper to be used in sacrificing to the gods and other purifications (*de Caelo*, i, C. 5).

Both Socrates and Plato acknowledge three principles of things—god, idea, and matter.

But the importance of the number has continued down to modern times, and is so firmly incorporated into many of

[1] See Stewart, *Myths of Plato*, pp. 437–45.

our civil and religious ceremonies that its observance
has become an immovable item in the habits and customs
of the people. Public approbation of a toast or sentiment
is displayed at a banquet by the honour of three or three
times three acclamation.   We start our runners in a race
with " One, two, three ! "   One is reminded also of some
expressions of our poets :—

> Thrice noble Lord, let me entreat of you to pardon
> me.—*Shakespeare.*

> Thrice happy isles,
> Thrice happy men
> And sons of men, whom God hath thus advanced,
> Thrice happy if they know
> Their happiness, and persevere upright.—*Milton.*

There is also a German proverb worth noting in this
connexion :—

> Aller guten Dinge sind drei.

The constant recurrence of the number three, invested
everywhere as we have seen it to be with such importance
and solemnity, has been explained by scholars in various
ways.   Some think its importance is due to the smallness
of the number and its being an odd.   But surely one can
then see no reason why the unit should not have had a
prior claim to such pre-eminence.   Whatever may have
been the origin of the idea of triplicity, the fact that in
nature things usually require for their production the
co-operation of two factors was not overlooked.   Mahler
suggests that the symbolic importance of " three " arose
through the three ancestors of the Hebrew race—Abraham,
Isaac, and Jacob—and that these again are to be connected
with the ancient Egyptian idea of the division of the year
into three periods.   Furthermore, with their four wives,
Sarah, Rebekah, Rachel, and Leah, in all seven, they were
suggested by the idea of the seven planets.   He also connects
the twelve tribes which were descended from Jacob's
twelve children with the twelve Zodiacal signs.   But

SYMBOLISM OF NUMBERS

SYMBOLISM OF NUMBERS 113

perhaps Dr. D. Wilson [1] is correct when he suggests that the symbolism of three in being used to represent " many ", preserves the memorial of that stage of thought, when all beyond two was an idea of indefinite number.

Let us now consider whether a philological examination of the words for " three " in the various Semitic languages will help us to understand the symbolical usage of the number amongst the Semites. If we place side by side the words for " three " in Semitic, we have :—

Hebrew : שָׁלֹשׁ.
Aramaic : תְּלָתָא.
Arabic : *tlat.*
Assyrian : *shalashtu.*

The *Oxford Hebrew Lexicon* (BDB.), p. 1025, states that the meaning of the Hebrew root שׁלשׁ is unknown.

The present writer, however, ventures to suggest that the following explanation is most plausible. The interchange between שׁ and ת in Hebrew, Aramaic, and Arabic is very common, so that we could reduce these four stems to a common base, *tl*, which means in all the four languages " a mound " or " a heap " ; whilst the verb תָּלָה means " to pile up", " to heap up " (in a triangular form), " to hang ", " to suspend ". (Cf. Assyrian *tillu*, mound, Muss. Arnolt, *Assyrian Dictionary*, p. 1160.)

But, furthermore, the Sumerian word for " three ", *mesh*, which is made up of *me*, which means " to be called ", and *esh*, the plural ending of the imperfect of the verb, has the value of *maduti*, " many " [2] (CT. xii, 3), thus

---

[1] *Prehistoric Man.*

[2] Many Australian tribes, as well as the bushmen of South Africa, reckon three or anything beyond as " many " (Conant, *The Number Concept*, p. 28). There is an old English nursery-number rhyme which runs :—

One's none,
Two's some,
Three's many,
Four's a penny, etc.

The relation of singular, dual, and plural is shown pictorially in Egyptian hieroglyphics in the following way : If one is meant, the picture of an object is marked by a single line | , if two are meant by two lines | | , if three or an indefinite plural number by three lines | | | .

I

suggesting that in Sumerian " three " and " many " were
synonymous. Again, the Hebrew verb שָׁלֵשׁ " to repeat
a third time " has a corresponding verb in Assyrian
shalashu, represented by the ideogram PESH (S°),
which also represents the Assyrian verbs *napashu* and
rapashu, " to extend," thus suggesting that *shalashu*
may also have meant in Assyrian " to extend ". Seeing,
therefore, that the base of the word for " three " is used in
all the Semitic languages in the sense of " to extend " or
" to raise ", and that adjectives are repeated three times
in order to give them a superlative sense, we can now
understand that the Hebrew שָׁלִישׁ does not mean " third
man in a chariot ", but " one who has attained the highest
rank " (cf. Assyrian *telu*, sublime, lofty, Muss. Arnolt,
Assyrian Dictionary, p. 1161). This also suggests that the
Hebrew מְשֻׁלָּשׁ and מְשֻׁלֶּשֶׁת in Gen. xv, 8, should not be
translated as meaning a heifer " three years old ", but
rather " one that has reached its full growth and
development ".

Again, our connexion of the number with the verb " to
hang " or " to suspend " explains why the Egyptians and
Pythagoreans symbolized the number " three " by a
triangle.

FOUR

The number four no doubt derived its symbolical
importance in different parts of the world from the four
cardinal points of the compass. It thus came to denote
completeness, and the four directions North, South, East,
and West suggested the adoption of the number as a symbol
of the earth.[1] Nowadays one would prefer a circle to a
square in representing the world, but surely if any
significant number was to be employed, four would more
readily occur than any other. Isaiah speaks of the circle

---

[1] Cf. Hebrew expression אַרְבַּע כַּנְפוֹת הָאָרֶץ and Assyrian *arba
kippati*.

of the earth (Isa. xl, 22), and yet one feels that there is no contradiction in his speaking also of the four corners of the earth and the four winds of heaven. Ezekiel says to the wind : " Come from the four winds and breathe a breath upon these slain " (Ezek. xxxvii, 9). The cosmogony of Job seems to have corresponded with the same idea, for there is a fourfold division of the heavens (Job ix, 9)— Arcturus, Orion, Pleiades, and the chambers of the South. The world powers in the book of Daniel are four in number ; whilst the horns of the Gentiles which Zechariah beholds in a vision are also four (Zech. i, 18).

These passages can be readily understood by realizing the Hebrew conception of the earth. To the Hebrews the earth was a disc surrounded by an ocean ; whilst the heaven was a vault over-arching that ocean. The four ends of the earth corresponded to the four ends of the heaven, and so the winds come from the four corners of the earth and from the four ends of the heaven (Dan. vii, 2). As for the occurrence of four as representing completeness, one may refer to the following : the river of Eden parted into four heads so as to embrace the lands of the earth (Gen. ii, 10), Jepthah's daughter is bewailed for four days (Judges xi, 40), Nehemiah's enemies are sent to him four times (Neh. vi, 4), God sends four kinds of pestilence or four sore judgments (Ezek. xiv, 21). In Zech. i, 8 ff., four different coloured pairs of horses pass over the earth, each towards a cardinal point.[1] In Zech. vi, 1, are four chariots which come from between the two mountains drawn by four pairs of different coloured horses to the four cardinal points.

Blessings and curses which are meant to be diffused abroad have a fourfold character. So Balaam, in the doom he utters over the heathen nations, adopts a fourfold classification (Num. xxiv), and his last prophecy foretells the victorious supremacy of Israel over all its foes and the

[1] The four horses in the New Year races in Germany have also a cosmic meaning. (*Im Kampfe um Babel und Bibel*, Jeremias, 4th ed.

destruction of all the powers of the world. This prophecy
is divided into four different prophecies by the fourfold
repetition of the words : " And he took up his parable."
One is also reminded of the account of the victory of the
four kings against five (Gen. xiv, 8).

Babylonian.—The Babylonians assigned to the number
four a similar symbolical meaning. The world was divided
into four quarters, and even the oldest Babylonian kings,
such as Naram Sin, Dungi, and Bur Sin, as well as those
in later times who wished to express their world-wide
power as conquerors of the whole universe, call themselves
" King of the four quarters" (*shar kibratim arbaim*).[1] To
the Babylonians the four planets represented the chief
points of the sun's orbit, each of them bearing in a special
sense the solar character. Marduk was the spring or
morning sun, Ninib the mid-day or summer sun, Nebo the
autumn or evening sun, and Nergal the night or winter
sun. In the same way the four planets corresponded to the
moon's phases. The disc of the moon was divided into four
quarters, each representing another land. If all the four
sides were dark, it meant there would be darkness over all
the lands. If there was darkness on the left side it meant
there would be trouble in Elam. Four also represented the
gods as protectors on all sides, so in the *Tafel des Weres Die
Bösen Götter* (CT. xvi, pl. 4, 143 ff.) : Shamash in front of
me, Sin behind me, Nergal at my right, and Ninib at my
left (see Kugler, *Im Bannkreis Bibels*, 68 ff.). In King's
Bab. Magic and Sorcery, No. viii, 12–13, the following
passage occurs : Propitious be the favourable *Shidu* who
is before thee : may the *Lamassu* that goeth behind thee
be propitious : that which is on thy right hand increase
good fortune : that which is on thy left hand attain
favour.

In Mohammedanism there is a class of angels called

---

[1] The Zikkurat or temple tower was quadrilangular, with the four
corners towards the four cardinal points to symbolize the four quarters
over which the Babylonian kings held dominion.

" Throne bearers ", who are said to be at present four in number, but on the day of resurrection they will be strengthened by an additional four, who will then bear the throne of God above them (Klein, *Rel. of Islam*, 66 ; *Koran*, Surahs 40, 69). In Palestine belief in the evil eye is universal, and various methods are employed for removing its effects. If a European should pass the head of a native child in the presence of a nurse, the woman will take the child into a room, and then, collecting some dust in a shovel from each of the four corners, will throw it on the fire and exclaim : " Fie on thee, evil eye " (G. Robinson Lees, *Village Life in Palestine*).

In connexion with the Hebrew atonement system for cleansing the leper or the house in which leprosy has occurred, the *Talmud* on Leprosy (xii) enlarges on this in the following way. A round house, a three-cornered house, a house built on a ship or on a mast, or one built on four beams, do not receive uncleanness in leprosy. But if the house is square, even though it be built on four pillars, it receives uncleanness in leprosy.

Mohammedan traditions tell that Abraham was able to work magic, and that when he cut the birds in pieces in his sacrifice—a dove, a peacock, a raven, and a cock— he retained their heads only, then he mixed the flesh and feathers, laying them in four parts on four mountains. Then when he called to each by name they rejoined them- selves in their first shapes to their heads (*Koran*, Surah ii).

The Arabian analysis of female beauty was founded on the same principle, and made to consist of thirty-six (four × nine) excellencies. Four things in a woman should be black : the hair of the head, the eyebrows, the eyelashes, and the dark parts of the eyes ; four white : the com- plexion of the skin, the whites of the eyes, the teeth, and the legs ; four red : the tongue, the lips, the middle cheeks, and the gums ; four round : the head, the neck, the forearms, the ankles ; four long : the back, the fingers, the arms, and the legs ; four fine : the eyebrows, the nose, the lips, and the fingers ; four wide : the forehead, the eyes, the bosom, and the hips ; four thick : the lower part of the back, the thighs, the calves of the legs, and the knees ; four small : the ears, the breasts, the hands, and the feet ; in all thirty-six (see Lane, *Arabian Nights*, vol. i, p. 29).

To the Greeks the tetrad was the root principle of all things because it was the number of the elements.[1] Jupiter represented fire, Juno air, Pluto earth, and Nestis water. Similarly, the intelligible world was also believed to be made up of four elements. According to Plutarch,[2] the Pythagorean world consisted of a double quaternary. According to Philo-Judaeus, the quadrate number not only comprehends all—point, line, superficies, and body—but possesses other perfections, one of which is that the addition of all the numbers of which it is formed make up the number ten, which is so perfect that in counting we can go no farther, for the parts of four added together $1 + 2 + 3 + 4 = 10$.

Amongst the Hermesians, the number four, amplified into a cube, was the symbol of truth, because from whatever point of view it may be contemplated it is always the same. Four is to a large extent the sacred number of the New World, and the four world-quarters or directions are expressed by swastika-like symbols. In many parts smoke is offered to the four directions, and most ceremonial acts are repeated in sets of fours. The aboriginal savages of America had an attachment to the number four, for the Mexican priests were enjoined to burn incense before the image of the deity four times a day. They had a public celebration every four years, and forty days before the annual festival of *Quetzalcoatl*, the Mexican Mercury, a slave was fattened as a victim to be sacrificed at the festival. Furthermore, in order that Tlaloc, the god of rain, might be propitious and send a good harvest, four children were sacrificed to him on the summit of four

[1] Plut., *de Plac. Phil.*, p. 878.
[2] *De Anim. procr.*, 1027.

square pyramids.[1] It is also of interest to note that the tetragrammaton was regarded, even down to the seventeenth century, as a most powerful amulet.

How did four receive its symbolical significance ? Apart from the four cardinal points of the compass which, as we have already seen, had this influence in various parts of the world, it has been suggested that "four", like "seven", was regarded by the Semites as a divine title. The well-known city Arbela is written in cuneiform (alu)arba ilu, the number four being here a divine title ; whilst in Hos. x, 14, we read of Beth Arbel, " The House of Arbel," as though Arbel was a god. The symbolism of the numbers four and seven may be explained by the fact that the name of Sin, the moon-god, as written in cuneiform, is (god) number thirty—because of the thirty days of the lunar month. And Winckler has thus suggested that four and seven represent different phases of the moon-god—four, the four phases of the moon ; seven, the seven-day week as a lunar quarter.

SEVEN

In the case of the number seven, it would indeed be a work of supererogation to go over all the passages of the Bible where it occurs in order to make out that it has a deep significance. From the time when the seventh day received the special seal of heaven, down through the ages when circumcision came to be imperative after seven days, and the sprinklings of water and of blood were seven times performed, and the Passover and Feast of Weeks and the Feast of Tabernacles and the Sabbath Year and the year of Jubilee, all were arranged in harmony with the number seven, there was continual reference to the meaning of the symbol.

By the older school it was regarded as a symbol of God's covenant of grace (Bähr, Symbolik, vol. i, p. 187). The seven years of plenty and of famine in Egypt were

[1] Stephens, Travels in Yucatan.

accounted for in this way. So, also, they explained why
the command should have been given to Naaman to wash
seven times in the Jordan. The Syrian would know that
this connected his cleansing with Israel's God. Would he
or would he not own allegiance to the God of Israel ?
Would he by washing seven times acknowledge his cure to
be wholly from the Lord ? We know the result in his glad
confession: "Behold, I know that there is no god in all
the earth but in Israel." But how comes it, however, that
Noah sends forth the dove always at the end of seven days,
that Laban in Ur of the Chaldees should speak of the week
of Rachel, and even in the book of Job, in the land of Uz,
the sevenfold division of days is known and the weekly
sacrifices offered by Job ?   Many scholars have argued
that at least some of these passages—such as, for example,
the command to Naaman to wash seven times in the
Jordan, or the sevenfold sprinklings in Israel—are most
arbitrary. But, in view of the frequency with which this
number occurs, not only in the Old Testament, but also in
the literatures of other Oriental peoples, this seems hardly
likely.

Let us consider further Old Testament passages in which
the number seven occurs. The one who comes in contact
with a dead body is unclean for seven days (Num. xix, 11 ;
xii, 14). Purification from leprosy takes seven days
(Lev. xiii, 14 ff.) ; the young of an animal may not be
sacrificed before it is seven days old (Exod. xxii, 29 ;
Lev. xxii, 27). The feast celebrating the dedication of the
temple was held in the seventh month, "seven days and seven
days" (1 Kings viii, 2, 65). Job's friends sit by him seven days
and seven nights. Jacob works for Rachel for seven years (Gen.
xxix, 27). The first day of the seventh month is a solemn
sabbath, a memorial of blowing the trumpet (Lev. xxiii, 24).
The clean beasts were taken into the ark by sevens, the
others by twos (Gen. vii, 2). Seven steps led up to the
temple of Ezekiel (xl, 26). The period of mourning was
seven days (Gen. l, 10 ; 1 Sam. xxxi, 13 ; 1 Chron. x, 12 ;

also Sir. xxii, 13 ; Judith xvi, 24).[1] In Num. xxiii, 29,
Balaam offers seven bullocks and seven rams upon seven
altars. In connexion with the fall of Jericho (Joshua vi),
we are told that after seven priests had blown the trumpet
once daily for six days, and on the seventh day seven times,
Jericho fell. In Zech. iii, 9, we are told that before Joshua lies
a stone with seven eyes upon which God will engrave an
inscription. It is of interest to note that Babylonian
records often bear the sign of the seven planets, and in the
East these planets are frequently compared to eyes. For
this reason Nork and others have assumed that planets
are referred to here. One should also mention that Philo
(Jos., *Ant.* iii, 7, 7) explains the seven-branched candlestick (Exod. xxv, 31) as referring to the seven planets.

Arabic.—The *Koran* is said to have been revealed in
seven dialects (*Mishkat*, ii, ch. ii). The most common
explanation of this tradition is that by changing the
inflections of words the text of the Koran may be read
in the then existing " Seven dialects of Arabia ". There
are seven verses of the Koran in which the word " peace "
occurs. These verses are recited by Muslims when in
trouble or during sickness. In some places these seven
verses are written on paper and then the ink is washed off
and drunk as a charm against evil spirits. The
Mohammedans had their seven heavens and seven hells.
According to some, Paradise is in the seventh heaven ;
whilst according to others there are seven seas of light
above the seventh heaven ; then come an undefinable
number of separations of different substances, seven of
each kind, and then Paradise, which consists of seven stages
one above the other. Similarly, the seven hells are situated
beneath each other—the first for the reception of wicked
Mohammedans, the second for Christians, the third for
Jews, the fourth for Sabeans, the fifth for Magians, the

---

[1] We are told that Gilgamesh wept for his friend for six days and
seven nights (KB. vi, 1, 244 f.), thus taking this as a full period of
mourning amongst the Babylonians.

sixth for idolaters, and the seventh for hypocrites. They also believed in the existence of seven earths, and they assigned to the earth seven climates and to heaven seven spheres.

In the alchemy of the Arabs we meet with seven metals, seven stones, seven volatile bodies, seven natural and seven artificial salts, seven kinds of alum, seven chief chemical operations, etc. (see article by Bertholet in the *Revue des deux Mondes*, 1893, p. 557). The Mohammedans have various beliefs concerning the future destination of the souls of the dead, one of which is that they stay near the grave for seven days. An Arab often leaves a sum in his will to be spent in the sacrifice of a victim on his behalf. And on the day of Korban, each Arab family kills as many camels as there have been deaths in the family during the last twelve months, seven sheep being a substitute for one camel.[1] In the story of Seyf el-Mulook of the *Arabian Nights*, we are told that the Jinki's soul is in the crop of a sparrow, which is in a box, in another box, within seven boxes in seven chests in a coffer of marble. One of the Arab demons known as the *Kird* sat upon the shoulders of a man one day, and he became dumb, but after reading the pain away for seven days he recovered his speech. The Order of *Bakhtashiyah* use a mystic girdle as their symbol, which they put off and on seven times, repeating a certain formula. In the *Sword of Moses* [2] we read that in order to catch a lion by the ear, say number ninety-one, make seven knots in the fringe of your girdle, and repeat these words with each knot, and you will catch him. The Arabs have a tradition that if a child is very ill the mother should take seven flat loaves of bread and put them under its pillow (Zwemer, *Arabia*, 283). In Eastern magic the bones of a frog buried for seven days and then exhumed would automatically show themselves for either love or hatred ("Folklore of Mossoul", *PSBA.*, November, 1907, p. 287, No. 59).

[1] Burckhardt, *Notes on the Bedouins and Wahabis*, i, 99.
[2] Ed. Gaster, p. 41.

Talmud.—Hershon, in his *Talmudic Miscellany*, quotes the following as a cure for night blindness. Take a hair-rope, bind one end of it to the patient's leg and the other to a dog's, and then let children call out after him : " Old Man ! Dog ! Fool ! Cock ! " Then let him collect seven pieces of meat from seven houses and set them at the threshold to eat them. After that he must untie the rope, and say : " Blindness of N., son of N., leave N., son of N., and be brushed into the pupil of the eye of the dog."

The Cabbalists, who were influenced very considerably by Babylonian thought, set an archangel over each of the seven planets that governs the world on specific days of the week : Raphael, the sun ; Gabriel, the moon ; Chamael, Mars ; Michael, Mercury ; Zadkiel, Jupiter ; Annael, Venus ; Sabathiel or Kephziel, Saturn.[1] According to Clemens Alexandrinus, *Stromata*, 6, the seven spirits before the throne of God (Rev. i, 4) correspond to this view, and must be regarded as the planets.[2] The connexion between the days of the week and the planets amongst the Sabeans can be seen from the Nabatean book of El Makrisi (Chwolsohn, ii, 611). The Cabbalists believed in the existence of seven *Sephiroth*, which they denominated— strength, mercy, beauty, victory, glory, foundation, and kingdom. The benefits of these divine splendours were communicated by gradations and compared to ascending the steps of a ladder. They also believed in seven hells. In later Hebrew magic a person who wishes to cause anyone to perish must take clay from two river-banks, make an image with it, and then take seven stalks from seven date-trees, make a bow with horse-hair, stretch the bow, and shoot the stalks (J. E. s.v. Amulet, i, 548).

Babylonia.—The frequency with which the number seven occurs in Hebrew and Arabic has its parallels also in Babylonian literature. In the Deluge narrative the storm began to calm down after seven days,

---

[1] Kohut, *Angelologie im Talmud.*
[2] See A. Jeremias, *Babylonisches im Neuen Testament*, 1905.

and Ut Napishtim was then able to leave the ship. After seven days the dove was sent out. In the story of Adapa's contest with the south wind, we are told that the wings of the latter were broken and for seven days the south wind did not blow across the land. Jastrow [1] suggests that here " seven is to be interpreted as a round number, as in the Deluge story, and indicates a rather long, though indefinite, period ". In the Ashipu Ritual we read of seven altars, seven vessels of incense, seven cups of wine (Zimmern, *Beit. Rit. Taf.*, No. 26) ; whilst for exorcism seven loaves of pure dough are to be taken. After the flood Ut Napishtim presents an offering of seven × seven bowls as a sacrifice. In the Gilgamesh Epic Ut Napishtim attempts to heal the hero from his illness. As a result the latter falls into a heavy stupor in which he continues for six days and seven nights. In Babylonian medicine there are numerous references to the symbolism of seven. The seventh day of a disease is a most critical one. The patient must not eat certain foods on that day. As a means of releasing the demons of whom he is possessed seven knots are tied and seven grains of a *shi shi* plant are to be pounded (Küchler, *Beiträge z. Kenntnis d. ass.-bab. Medizin*). For colic seven kinds of plants are to be applied. Before the fight with Gilgamesh and Eabani, Humbaba is clothed with seven garments (KB. vi, p. 162, l. 40). Ninib's terrible weapon, Gishgashagimina, has seven heads. The fish which is represented as most frightful has seven fins. The Zikkurats, or temple towers, consisted of seven stages. Incantation formulæ are to be repeated seven times (Gray, *The Shamash Religious Texts*, pl. ix). The means for relieving a person suffering from headache is to bind knots twice seven times, perform the incantation of Eridu, and bind the head of the sick man. Gilgamesh is the seventh wooer of Ishtar. The goddess Labartu has seven names by which her numerous qualities are completely expressed. Seven

[1] RBA., 546.

different kinds of plants should be applied for the healing of cuts and bruises (Küchler, *Beiträge z. Kenntnis d. ass.-bab. Medizin*). Gudea celebrated the completion of the temple of Enninnu with a feast for seven days. For this period of time all law was abolished. The slave was equal to his master, the servant to her mistress, strong and weak rested side by side. The underworld being provided by seven gates is completely closed and therefore designated " The land of no return ". The ritual sprinklings in Hebrew legislation (Num. xix, 12 f.) have their parallel in Assyrian religious ceremonials. The Assyrian sorcerer is advised to make seven little winged figures to set before Nergal (Zimmern, *Beit. Rit. Taf.*, No. 54). In order to wash away the *rabisu* demon a long formula was to be repeated, of which the following is part : " May Marduk, eldest son of Eridu, sprinkle him with pure water, clean water, bright water, limpid water, with the water twice seven times." In an Assyrian text, which is part of the seventh tablet of the Shurpu Series, we are told that in order to remove a taboo, seven loaves of pure dough should be applied. Amongst the things required in connexion with the ceremony for the laying of ghosts are seven small loaves of roast corn. In an Assyrian exorcism for ophthalmia, black and white hair are to be woven together and seven knots tied therein.

Ishtar, in order to boast, recounts her seven names (Reisner, *Hymnen*, No. 56) :—

My first name I am Ishtar,
My second name conqueror of the lands,
My third the exalted who causes the heavens to
    shake and the earth to quake,
My fourth flaming fire,
My fifth Irnina,
My sixth one who is exalted by herself,
My seventh Mistress of E-ul-mash.

The seven-storied temple of Marduk, in Babylon, was called E-temen-an-ki, " House of the foundations of heaven and earth." In sympathetic magic seven knots, or 7×2 knots, were tied or untied. At the beginning of many of the Tell el Amarna letters, we often meet with the expression " At the feet of the King, my Lord, do I fall seven and seven times ". This sevenfold prostration was no doubt in order to show complete subjection to the king (cf. Gen. xxxiii, 3). The Babylonian tree of life, with its seven branches, may have symbolized the fullness of life. The mystic tree was represented with seven branches, each with seven leaves, and in the centre was a larger seven-leaved branch.

When the number seven is insufficient to express the complete thought required, then multiples of seven are used. Thus in the plastic art of Babylonia either seven or a multiple of seven was often used. The winged bulls at the entrance to Sargon's palace at Khorsabad had two rows of twenty-one (3×7) feathers on their wings.

Seeing that the hand was used more than any other part of the body for all kinds of actions, it came to be regarded as a symbol of power, and the hand of a certain being was used symbolically to denote the power exerted by him. In Egypt the sun was depicted with numerous rays each terminating in an open hand ; whilst among the Hebrews (Exod. xvi, 3) " the hand of God " is used figuratively for the power of God. The symbolical character of seven can also be seen most clearly from seal cylinders which have representations of a hand with seven fingers.

In order to understand the general meaning of the use of seven, we might take as an example the seven spirits. The Babylonians believed that they were surrounded by a number of evil spirits, which they depicted on monuments with human bodies and the heads of animals. The lions and bulls with heads of the form of human beings represented the same idea.[1] These spirits were almost

---

[1] Perrot & Chipiez, *History of Art in Chaldea and Assyria*, ii, 81.

innumerable, and performed their secret activities in groups. They attacked men in various ways, and were the causes of all sickness and disease, as may be seen from the following poem :—[1]

Fevers unto the man, against his head, hath drawn nigh,
Disease unto the man, against his life, hath drawn nigh,
An evil spirit against his neck hath drawn nigh,
An evil demon against his breast hath drawn nigh,
An evil ghost against his belly hath drawn nigh,
An evil devil against his hand hath drawn nigh,
An evil god against his foot hath drawn nigh,
These seven together have seized upon him,
His body like a consuming fire they devour.

Now the Babylonian incantation texts consist of formulæ and descriptions of symbolical actions to be used in order to gain control over these evil spirits. The methods employed for the purpose were many and varied. Sometimes an image of the demon was made and thrown into the fire, or nails were stuck into it, the belief being that just as the image was destroyed, so the object which it represented would be similarly destroyed.[2] Another method of gaining control over these spirits was to mention them by name, for once the name of the spirit that was performing these actions was known it was no difficult matter to obtain control over its activities. But with so large a number of demons it was obviously impossible to hit upon the one who was causing the evil at any given time. For this reason, instead of referring to each demon individually, reference was usually made against them as a group, and, seeing that seven was a complete number, they were referred to as a group of seven. An incantation text, which refers to this group of seven, gives a detailed description of their manifold natures and activities :—

[1] R. C. Thompson, *Devils and Evil Spirits of Babylonia*, ii, p. 29.
[2] C. Fossey, *La Magie Assyrienne*, Paris, 1902.

Seven are they, they are seven.
In the subterranean deep, they are seven.
Perched in the sky they are seven.
In a section of the subterranean deep they were reared,
They are neither male nor female.
They are destructive whirlwinds,
They have no wife, nor do they beget offspring.
Compassion and mercy they do not know.
Prayer and supplication they do not hear,
Horses bred on the mountain are they,
Hostile to Ea are they.
Powerful ones among the gods are they.
To work mischief in the street they settle themselves
   in the highway.
Evil are they, they are evil.
Seven are they, they are seven, seven, and again seven
   are they.

(Jastrow, RBA., p. 264.)

These seven spirits constantly appear in various forms
in the legends of other Semitic and many non-Semitic
peoples.[1]   The old Palestinian tradition of the unclean
spirit in all probability owes its origin to them (Luke xi, 24) ;
whilst in a Syriac charm, published by Professor Gollancz,[2]
these spirits are referred to as " seven accursed brothers ".
They even have power to bewitch the gods, and are able to
cause an eclipse of the moon ; whilst they are the
personification of every form of evil and wickedness.   They
appear in all sorts of imaginable places, at all times, and
under all conditions.   There is no place where they are
not to be found.   They were begotten in the mountain of the
sunset, and were reared in the hollow of the earth, and are
proclaimed on the top of the mountains.   It is clear that
the number seven cannot be taken literally, for, as a matter

---

[1] There may be some connexion between the seven Assyrian spirits
and the seven devas or " arch-demons of Zoroastrianism " (E.Bi.
col. 1073).

[2] H. Gollancz, *Selection of Charms.*

of fact, when these demons are actually enumerated, we find sometimes that there are only six ; whilst in other cases there are as many as fourteen. We are, therefore, justified in concluding that the number seven is here not to be taken literally, but symbolically, as representing a complete whole number. Assyrian inscriptions often begin with an enumeration of the principal gods of the pantheon, and the list ends with the words *il VII bi ilani rabuti,* the seven great gods. For example, the Bavian inscription reads: Ashur, Anu, Bel, Ea, Sin, Shamash, Adad, Marduk, Nabu (Ninib), Ishtar, *il VII bi ilani rabuti.* There are ten gods mentioned here, so that the number seven cannot refer to the names of the previously mentioned deities, but can only be taken as a symbolic round number in which all the gods of the pantheon are included.

In a hymn published by Craig (*Assyrian and Babylonian Religious Texts,* i, 55), the goddess Nana is described as excelling her seven brothers. In no other text is there any mention of the fact that Nana had seven brothers, and it is therefore plausible to suggest that the passage means that Nana excels *all* her brothers. Similarly, the temple, as the home of *all* the gods, was known as " the house of seven gods ". The penitent, praying that his innumerable sins may be forgiven, describes them as being seven times seven :—

My god, my sins are seven times seven, pardon my sins.
My goddess, my sins are seven times seven, pardon my sins.[1]

Furthermore, in another inscription (K. 3500) we read : *il sibitte ilani qarduti ina kakke-shun [u . . .] ku-un lish-kun.*[2] May the seven gods, the powerful gods, accomplish your defeat with their weapons. Here the verb *lishkun* is singular, although it should, of course, be in the plural, in agreement with its subject, the seven gods, and the only explanation

[1] See Zimmern, *Babylonische Busspsalmen,* p. 65.
[2] Winckler, *Altor. Forsch.,* ii, 10 f.

K

one can offer is that the seven gods are used collectively. This is, of course, what one would expect, for, as we have noted, the seven spirits are referred to in various texts as moving *in a group.*

Seven was sacred to Minerva, and was also consecrated to Mars, because he had seven attendants. It was a symbol of Osiris, because his body was said to have been divided into seven parts, according to some accounts, and twice seven according to others, by Typhon. It was sacred to Apollo, or the sun, because, being placed in the midst of the seven planets, they proceeded harmoniously together through the vast expanse, so that the poets represented Apollo as playing on a harp with seven strings.

But the use of the number seven has not been confined to any age or nation, as may be gathered from the seven vases in the temple of the sun near the ruins of Babian in Upper Egypt, the seven altars which burned continually before the God Mithras in many of his temples, the seven holy fanes of the Arabians, the seven bobuns of perfection exhibited in the religious code of the Hindoos, who also circumscribed the whole earth within the compass of seven peninsulas surrounded by seven seas.

In the *Rig Veda* the number also frequently occurs. Indra uses the expression " I am a seven slayer ", i.e. a slayer of many. Indra subdues seven fortresses. The expression " better than seven " means better than many. There is the seven-bottomed sea, and the custom by which the new bride according to Hindu law was compelled to take seven steps around the altar at the time of the wedding ceremony. We also have the group of seven stars called the " seven seers " (Latin, Septentriones), or the seven streams which in the *Rig Veda* and the Persian *Avesta* gave the name to the country. Indra has seven rays and seven friends. Proper names are made of " seven ", such as Saptagu, Saptavadhri. There are references to sevenfold song and seven kinds of music, and sometimes the numbers three and seven are associated together.

Thus, for example, Varuna rules seven streams and looks on three heavens, three earths (viii, 41, 9). Furthermore, the number seven is sometimes raised to three times its value; thus the soma-streams, the heavenly streams, and the rivers are all trebled and raised from seven to twenty-one. The seven secret places of Agni (i, 72, 6) are raised to thrice seven. Thrice seven cows (ix, 70, 1), opposed to seven cows (ix, 86, 53, 21), and in the tenth book we have references to thrice seven streams.

When we now come to the Upanishads, we find the same preference for the number seven—the seven breaths proceed from Brahma, the seven flames, the seven kinds of fuel, the seven oblations, the seven passages of the vital airs.[1] So also fire has seven wavy tongues—the black, the terrific, the thought-swift, the red, the purple, the scintillating, and the tongue of every shape divine ; while Vasivanara or Purusha, the spirit that permeates all living bodies, is said to have seven members, viz. the sky, the sun, the air, the ethereal expanse, the food-grains, the earth, and the sacrificial fire.

The Pythagoreans considered seven to be a religious number and perfect. It was believed that the custody of the world was in the seven planets, and it was from this that Pythagoras formed his doctrine of the spheres. The Pythagoreans also regarded the number as the *Vehiculum* of man's life. It is in accordance with this belief also that we find the life of a man divided into seven ages, thus bringing it into harmony with the Ptolemaic division of the life span in which the first four years are ruled by the moon, the succeeding ten years is the Mercury period, then is the period of Venus for eight years, then comes the period of the sun, followed by Mars and then Jupiter and Saturn. Hippocrates has a treatise on the number seven, which marks the most flourishing epoch of Greek history in

---

[1] Gough, *The Philosophy of the Upanishads and of Indian Metaphysics*, p. 105.

the popular belief in the efficacy of that number.[1]   He
tells us that the embryo takes shape after seven days
and proves itself a human being, and he deals with the
seven vocal signs of the Greek language.   Solon had already
considered the importance of the number seven in the
demarcation of the ages of man, but now the whole world—
the human soul, the human body, the winds, and the
seasons—all were to be stamped with the hall-mark of
seven.   The earth is compared with the human body, and
seven parts of the body and seven parts of the earth are
selected and arranged with one another.   Finally, one is
reminded of the seven-headed dragon in the legends of
India, Persia, Cambodia, Western Asia, East Africa, and
the Mediterranean area.[2]

Even in recent years a man's life was considered
to be greatly affected by the Septenary year, which
was believed to produce considerable changes in body and
mind.   But the most remarkable change in a person's life
was believed to take place at the 49th year (7×7), or at
the grand Climacteric, the 63rd year (7×9), which was
conceived to be fraught with peculiar fatality.

The question now arises as to how we are to explain the
origin of the symbolical character of seven amongst the
Semites.   It is held by Winckler, Jeremias, and Hommel[3]
that this symbolism arose through the sun, moon, and five
larger planets — Mars, Venus, Mercury, Jupiter, and
Saturn—being regarded as one single group.   This view
is connected with the astral-mythological theory first
put forward by Winckler, and supported by Jeremias
and many other scholars of distinction.   By astral-
mythology these scholars mean that all myths, legends,
and even many symbolisms, originated in the personification

---

[1] *Zur Pseud-Hippokratischen Schrift: Rheinisches Museum*, N.S.,
xlviii, 433.
[2] For further details concerning the Seven-headed Dragon, see the
chapter on the subject in Professor G. Elliot Smith's work, *The Evolution
of the Dragon.*
[3] *Aufsätze und Abhandlungen*, p. 373.

of the heavenly bodies. They argue, further, that the accounts in the Old Testament, not only of the patriarchs, but of even much more firmly established narratives, are merely the reflections of an astral-theology which originated and was developed in the priestly schools of Babylonia, and which made the phenomena of the heavens as the basis of its teachings. This theory has been applied not only to Semitic, but even to many non-Semitic peoples, and there is a society in Germany which, by means of its publications, issued under the title of *Mythologische Bibliothek*, applies this astral-theory to the myths and folk-tales of all nations. But the explanation offered by these scholars seems hardly applicable in this case. First, in the case of the Hebrews, there are only fairly definite references to two planets in the Old Testament, and it seems that previous to the Babylonian Exile the Hebrews had only a very limited and imperfect knowledge of astronomy, and were unacquainted with a group of seven planets such as has been suggested.[1] But even when we come to Babylonia we find that it was only Jupiter and Venus that were first clearly differentiated from the remaining planets.[2] Yet, in spite of this, the sacredness and symbolical character of seven seems to have impressed itself on the Hebrews during the very earliest period of their history, and can even be traced back, further, to the earliest period in the history of civilization. At the time of the First Dynasty of Babylon there are references in incantation texts to the symbolic meaning of the number, and if we go back to a still earlier period we find that Gudea's temple (E-pa) was known as " the house of seven divisions ", that a seven-day festival was celebrated on its completion, and that seven-fold offerings were sacrificed in honour of the event. We can thus trace the idea right back to the Sumerian period. Now, it seems hardly likely that at so early a period in

[1] Schiaparelli, *Astronomie im AT.*, 45 Anm. I, 117 f.
[2] Jastrow, *Aspects of Religious Belief and Practice in Bab. and Assyria*, p. 217.

the history of civilization man should have already
perceived the idea of uniting the sun, moon, and five planets
into one group. Again, if the sacredness of the number
seven in Babylonia had been brought about by the
importance attached to this group, one would have expected
that this group of planets would have played a much more
important part in the Babylonian pantheon. But, as a
matter of fact, the principal rôle is assigned to the sun, as
the creative force of nature. Ishtar also occupies a definite
individual position of her own, as the goddess of vegetation
and consort of Tammuz ; whilst Venus, also, has an
individual position of her own, sometimes as evening star
and sometimes as morning star. And it is of interest to
note, also, that whilst, as we have already seen, there is
no reference to a group of seven planets in Babylonian
literature, Saturn, Mercury, and Mars were often classed
together as a group of three before they were more sharply
differentiated from one another, probably on account of the
difficulty involved in observing their separate courses.[1]

We must also take note of the fact that amongst many
non-Semitic nations who had a seven-day week the
symbolism of the number arose through entirely different
reasons. Thus, in India (*Atharva Veda*) a week of seven
days was obtained by dividing into quarters the lunar
month of twenty-eight days ; whilst Roscher [2] has shown
that in Greece the seven-day week had no connexion whatever with the seven planets, but also originated through the
division of the month of twenty-eight days by four.

The belief that each of the seven planets ruled over a
different day of the week may have originated in Babylonia
after the symbolical nature of the number had already
impressed itself on the people ; but it was only at a very
much later time—about the first century B.C.—in
Alexandria that this belief actually gained currency.[3]   It

---

[1] Jastrow, *Aspects of Rel. Belief in Bab. and Assyria*, p. 222.
[2] *Die Hebdomadischen und Enneadischen Fristen und Wochen der
Aeltesten Griechen.*
[3] See Schurer, *ZNTW.*, vi, 17 ; and *ThLZ.*, 1906, No. 31.

seems, therefore, very plausible to suggest that amongst the
Semites the symbolical character of seven originated with
the division of the lunar month into quarters. That the
movements of the moon and its phases should have played
so important a part in the life of primitive man as to give
rise to the symbolism of the number in question seems
very likely. To man, in the earliest stages of civilization,
both sun and moon are the two most active powers
affecting his fortunes and welfare. The sun furnishes light
and heat, and in the agricultural stage of society is, of
course, all-important on account of the help it gives in
producing the fertility of the soil. But the services of the
moon were also of the utmost significance. Its assistance
as a guide by night, the help of its regular phases in the
measurement of the seasons, and, finally, its influence
in astrology on health and disease, wind and storms,
caused it to be looked upon as supremely important. In
fact, we are actually told in Gen. i, 14, that the lights in the
heavens were to be for " symbols and seasons ".[1] Now,
Semitic Symbolism is based on the belief that there is an
analogy between all activities in heaven and everything
which takes place on earth. The length of a lunation is
$29\frac{1}{2}$ days, and a quarter of this is $7\frac{3}{8}$ days. But as men
found it necessary to keep to the nearest number of whole
days, a period of seven days arose as being the nearest
equivalent to a quarter of a lunation. Seeing, therefore,
that the number seven was regarded as sacred in heaven,
it must also be held as sacred on earth. It is this explanation which has been offered by many scholars for the
origin of the sacred and symbolical character of the number.

Amongst the Babylonians, the 7th, 14th, 21st, and 28th
days of the week thus arose as specially marked-out days,
and in a Babylonian Calendar now in the British Museum [2]

[1] לְאֹתֹת וּלְמוֹעֲדִים.

[2] Rawlinson, *Cuneiform Inscriptions of W. Asia*, vol. iv, tab. 32, 33.
Sayce, *Records of the Past*, ser. I, vii, 157–8. Jastrow, *RBA.*,
pp. 376 ff.

we are told that these days are unlucky, and various things
are forbidden to be done on them.   The priest was forbidden
to utter any oracles, the king dare not attend to any matters
of state, whilst the doctor was forbidden to lay his hands
on a sick person.

These days were evidently chosen as corresponding to
the phases of the moon ; whilst besides these four days
the 19th day of the month (starting with the previous new
moon, it was the 49th day—7×7 from then) was also
singled out in the same way.   It is of interest to note,
however, that whilst these kinds of work, as well as many
others, were forbidden on those days, they were not
occasions on which the *whole* of the community was compelled to cease work, such as on the Hebrew sabbath, and
whilst the seventh day was to the Hebrews a day of joy
and pleasure, these days were most mournful occasions to
the Babylonians.   In spite of this difference, however,
many scholars trace the origin of the Hebrew sabbath to
Babylonia, and base this suggestion on the hypothesis that
the sacredness of the seventh day amongst the Hebrews also
arose through the phases of the moon, seeing that in
Hebrew literature Sabbath and New Moon are often
mentioned together (2 Kings iv, 23 ; Amos viii, 5 ; Hos.
ii, 13 ; Isa. i, 13) [1] ; whilst Jastrow goes as far as to say
that " the connexion between the Hebrew Sabbath and new
moon is obvious, and this being so it could not have been
originally celebrated every seventh day, but, at the most,
every 7th, 14th, 21st day after the new moon, and on the
day when the new moon made its appearance ".[2]

Now that we have seen how sacred and important a
part the number seven played amongst the Semites, let
us consider whether philology may be of help to us in
explaining the origin and meaning of its symbolism.   The
Hebrew for " seven " is שֶׁבַע, evidently connected with
the Assyrian *siba* (Muss. Arnolt, p. 744).   There is also

---

[1] Meinhold, *Sabbat und Woche im AT.*, Göttingen, 1905.
[2] See his article in *The American Journal of Theology*, ii, 314.

a Hebrew verb שָׂבַע " to be satisfied," " full," " complete," which is used in an abstract sense. Thus in Deut. xxxiii, 23, we read נַפְתָּלִי שְׂבַע רָצוֹן וּמָלֵא בִּרְכַּת יהוה " Naphtali is satisfied with favour and full of the blessing of the Lord." Here the verb שָׂבַע is actually parallel with the usual Hebrew verb for " to be full ". We often read of . . . having died " satisfied with days " (שְׂבַע יָמִים), in other words, having lived his complete life. But is it not curious that, already in Sumerian times, the number seven should have been associated with the idea of fullness or completeness ? For we have a tablet in the British Museum (K. 2054) in which we find amongst other equations that seven=kishshatu (totality, completeness), thus proving that the connexion between the two ideas goes back to the Sumerian period of Babylonian history.

Now that we have seen how the symbolism of seven arose, and have connected it with the idea of " completeness " or " fullness ", we can understand why it was used both in the Old Testament and New Testament in preference to any other number to express such ideas.

In Deut. xxviii, 7, we are told that God will make Israel's enemies who arise up against them to be smitten before them. They will go out unto them in one way, but they will flee in seven ways, i.e. in all directions.

In Gen. iv, 15, " Whoever slays Cain will be avenged sevenfold " ; in other words, he will be completely avenged. Similarly, Lev. xxvi, 18, " I shall punish you sevenfold (completely) for your sins " ; cf. also Isa. iv, 1 ; xi, 15; Judges xvi, 13 ; Ps. xii, 7; xxix.[1] Particularly, Prov. vi, 30, " If he is found (the thief) he shall pay sevenfold," and the meaning of sevenfold is actually expressed in the second half of the verse, i.e. " he shall give all the wealth of his house." For New Testament cf. Luke xvii, 4 ; Matt. xviii,

[1] See the author's article on Ps. xxix in The Expository Times, November, 1915.

21, etc., whilst the seven evil spirits (Mark xvi, 9 ;
Luke viii, 2) have been compared to the seven evil
spirits already referred to in Babylonia [1] (Zimmern,
KAT., 3rd ed., p. 462).

But another problem now presents itself. Can we explain
the connexion between the Hebrew words for " seven "
and " to be complete " with the word " to swear " (שָׁבַע
in the Niphal), all three of which seem philologically
connected ? At least in pre-massoretic times, before our
Hebrew text was pointed and the שׂ and שׁ were
distinguished, these three stems must certainly have been
often confused. Let us take one example from Gen. xxvi.
In verse 31 we read of the covenant made between the
servants of Isaac and those of Abimelech. Verse 31 reads :
" And they rose up early in the morning and they sware
one to another." In verse 33, however, we are told that
Isaac called the well which his servants had dug " Seven "
(שִׁבְעָה), therefore the name of the city is " Beer Sheba "
(Well of Seven) unto this day.

Now, in the first place, it is of interest to note that the
Septuagint scholars seem to have read שְׁבֻעָה (oath)
instead of שִׁבְעָה.[2] This, of course, seems more appropriate.
For if the men " sware " one to the other, one would expect
them to call the well " oath " or some similar name (not
seven). But, furthermore, the Vulgate, instead of reading
" Beer Sheba " (Well of Seven), reads Abundantia (plenty),
probably based on the Hebrew שָׂבַע. So that the three
stems " to complete," " seven," and " to swear " were
all confused.

Of course, they are all expressed by the same three
consonants (the interchange of שׂ and שׁ need not be taken
into account), so that such confusion could easily have
arisen.

---

[1] See also Nielsen, *Die altarabische Mondreligion*, 165.
[2] G. gives ὅρκος.

Again, whilst a connexion has already been shown between the ideas of " completeness " and " seven ", on further consideration we find that we can connect these with the taking of an oath.

In Babylonian incantation texts the names of the various gods of the pantheon are very often recited, the belief being that once the names of these gods are mentioned they will assist in preventing the evil spirits from carrying out their mischievous performances. Very often even Heaven and Earth are called in as witnesses, and we very frequently meet with the expression : " By Heaven be ye exorcised ! By Earth be ye exorcised ! " In other words, " all celestial and earthly powers are thus called in against the invisible foes, who will thus be spellbound." [1]

In the Old Testament we also find Heaven and Earth called upon as witnesses to a compact (Deut. xxxi, 28): " Gather unto me all the elders of your tribes and your affairs, that I may speak these words in their ears, *and call heaven and earth to record against them.*" Also Deut. xxxii, 1 : " Give ear, O Heavens, and I will speak, and let the Earth hear the words of my mouth " ; cf. also Isa. i, 2 ; Ps. l, 4, etc. So that, seeing that in oaths, compacts, and incantations, " heaven and earth," or, in other words, all the forces of nature, were called upon to act as witnesses, we can understand that the stem expressing completeness or fullness should be identical with that which is used for " swearing " or " taking an oath ".

It is of interest to note that amongst the Greeks it was also customary to call upon many gods of the pantheon to act as witnesses to a treaty, and about the time of Alexander it became usual to end up a long list of deities with the formula τοὺς θεούς πάντας καὶ πάσας (all the gods), meaning thereby that all the gods had thus been invoked as witnesses to the treaty.

[1] R. C. Thompson, *The Devils and Evil Spirits of Babylonia*, vol. ii, Introduction, p. xxvii.

TEN

An examination of the numerous passages in which the
number ten occurs in Old Testament literature shows that
it is to be treated as an independent and distinct symbol.
Some of the older scholars regarded it as signifying " the
perfection of divine order ",[1] but one is rather inclined to
suggest that we must look for the symbolical meaning of
ten in Hebrew and Assyrian to what we find running
throughout all languages. There seems no use made of this
number in the Bible but what can be accounted for by
the commonest usage amongst man. A decimal system
of numeration everywhere prevails. After the first nine
digits come the teens, then twenty, thirty, forty, to the
hundreds ; then thousands, myriads, and millions. The
very word " digit " implies the theory on the subject that
is probably correct. Meaning a finger, it reminds us of the
primitive form of calculation in which the fingers played an
important part. Amongst the Hebrews we read of this
from the very earliest times. The pleading of Abraham
will suggest itself. First for fifty, then for fifty lacking
five, then forty, thirty, twenty, and ten. In the measurement of Noah's ark and the division of time connected with
the flood, we discover the same familiar decimal system.
The length of the ark was 300 cubits, its breadth 50, and
its height 30 (Gen. vi, 15). For forty days and nights the
rain descended (Gen. vii, 12), and after 150 days the water
had abated (Gen. vii, 24). We may expect, therefore, the
same laws to hold in regard to the scriptural use of ten that
obtain in other languages. It is employed as a round
number, and to express " indefinite magnitude " some
power of ten, one thousand, or a myriad is used. Who, for
instance, would treat otherwise Jacob's indignant remon-
strance : " Your father hath deceived me and changed my
wages ten times " (Gen. xxxi, 7) ? Or let us compare the
passage in Num. xiv, 22 : " all those men which have seen

[1] Bullinger, *Numbers in Scripture*, p. 243.

my glory and my miracles which I did in Egypt have tempted me these ten times." Or "How should one chase a thousand, and two put ten thousand to flight?" (Deut. xxxii, 30). But this symbolism led naturally to the use of ten and its compounds as denoting perfection. Thus, in the second commandment of the Decalogue we are told that though God visits the sins of the fathers upon the children to the third and fourth generation, He showeth kindness to thousands of them that love Him and keep His commandments. Thus expressing the belief that to all generations His mercies would be shown. Similarly, Deut. xxiii, 4 : "An Ammonite or Moabite shall not enter in the congregation of the Lord ; even to their tenth generation shall they not enter into the congregation of the Lord for ever." And lest any other construction of the passage should be considered possible than the one suggested, we find the interpretation given in Neh. xiii, 1 : "On that day they read in the book of Moses, and therein was found written that the Ammonite and Moabite shall not come into the congregation of the Lord for ever."

It is in the same way that the tithes in Israel are seen to be significant. Though but a tenth, they were given in token of the whole being the Lord's. Under this feeling, doubtless, Abram gives tithes to Melchizedek as the priest of the most High, and Jacob made his vow at Bethel regarding his giving a tenth to God. So, too, we understand why ten plagues should have descended upon Egypt in token of the outpouring of God's wrath, why ten words should have summarized the entire law, and why the number ten should have been the measure in every way of the sanctuary, for ten cubits broad and long and high was the Holy of Holies in Israel. One can further see the round sense of " ten " from the following passages :—" Ten women shall bake your bread in one oven " (Lev. xxvi, 26). Elkanah says to Hannah : " Am I not better to thee than ten sons ? " (1 Sam. i, 8). " You have put me to shame these ten times " (Job xix, 3). Cf. also Isa. vi, 13 ; Amos

v, 3 ; Zech. viii, 23 ; Eccles. vii, 19, and in the New
Testament, Matt. xxv, 1 ; Luke xv, 8 ; Rev. ii, 10.

Talmud.—But is not the suggestion that ten symbolized
" indefinite magnitude " further supported by the Mishna
and Gemara ?   In Aboth v we read that there were ten
generations from Adam to Noah to make known to us how
long-suffering God is, for all the generations continued
provoking Him to anger until He brought upon them the
waters of the flood. Similarly, we are told that when God
created the world He purposely used ten expressions in
order that the wicked may receive greater punishment for
destroying the world and the righteous greater reward for
maintaining it. The Cabbalists drew a parallel between the
ten fingers and the ten *sephiroth*. On account of this the
priests deliver their benediction with outstretched fingers,
and for this reason a man should not stretch out his fingers
except in prayer (Zohar iii, 145*a*).

Assyrian. — The Babylonians attached very great
importance to the number ten, not only in their numerical
system, but also in their symbolical expressions. The
numbers symbolizing many of the most important gods of
the pantheon are multiples of ten. Shamash is represented
by 20, Sin by 30, Ea by 40, Bel by 50, Anu by 60 ;
whilst in K. 170, Nusku, the fire-god, is represented by
the sign ⟨ , which has the value of ten. The sign for god
followed by the sign for ten (▶⊁⟨) represents the total
symbol of the great gods.

Although we have no direct evidence for deciding when
the payment of tithes became a fixed institution in
Babylonia, there are very frequent references to it in the
archives of Babylonian temples, and particularly in the
later Babylonian period. In any case, Babylonia abounded
in temples far earlier than the time of Moses, and it is very
likely, therefore, that the payment of tithes began in those
early times. Furthermore, it is of interest to note that
amongst a large number of inscriptions unearthed at
Nippur in 1889, written in old Babylonian characters and

of a period not later than 2000 B.C., there were a number of business documents referring to the registry of tithes.

The decad was the great number of the Pythagoreans, because it comprehends all arithmetical and harmonical proportions. It was called " Cosmos " or " World " because they regarded it as comprehending all numbers, just as the world comprehends all forms. It formed the boundary and extent of every created thing. There is nothing beyond it. If one wishes to count a greater number than it contains, one must recommence with unity and go on till one is again stopped by the decad and unity once more recurs.[1] Its harmonical properties were due to the fact that it was produced by the addition of the first four numbers $(1 + 2 + 3 + 4 = 10)$. Furthermore, half of ten being five, the middle number, if we take the next superior and the next inferior numbers, six and four, their sum will be ten, the next two in similar progression, seven and three, will also make ten, and so on throughout, the integers eight and two, nine and one, produce the same result.

The symbolism of " ten " has been accounted for in many ways. As we have already noted, according to some scholars its symbolic importance arose because it is the basis of the decimal system, according to others because it is the sum of the two numbers three and seven, themselves symbolical.

Thureau Dangin [2] has shown that the metric system, of which the Assyrians and Babylonians made use, rested entirely on a fixed standard of measurement, that of the arm's length.

However, a philological analysis of the terms for " ten " in Hebrew and Babylonian will help us to understand its

---

[1] Cf. the Hebrew for eleven עַשְׁתֵּי עָשָׂר. Some scholars connect the form עַשְׁתֵּי with the verb עָשַׁת " to think ", thus suggesting that when one wishes to count further than ten the ten figures are to be retained in one's imagination and one recommences with unity.

[2] " Le système métrique Assyro-Babylonien," in the *Revue Numismatique*, Paris, 1910.

symbolical usage. The Hebrew word for " ten " עֶשֶׂר is
given in the *Oxford Hebrew Lexicon* under y, p. 796, and
the suggestion is made that it is to be connected with the
Arabic word for " kinsman " or " tribe ", or " collection ".
But is it not more plausible to connect it with the root
שׂרֵר " to act as a prince ", " rule " (p. 979), and to compare
it with the Assyrian *shararu* " to rise in splendour ", the
y being a later addition to the biliteral stem שׂר ?   This
suggestion seems to be borne out by Assyrian in the
following way : The sign ⊨≡ representing five in Assyrian,
is also the ideogram for *nadu* " to raise," " exalt," *tani
attu* " exaltation," " majesty " (see Brünnow, *Classified
List of Cuneiform Ideographs*, 3980). The symbol represents kingly majesty, something above the earth, and it
may have obtained its importance from the five planets.

Furthermore, the Babylonian sign for ten also represents
the following ideas : *Shaku* high, *liu* strong, *idlu* a hero,
kabru big, *kishshatu* totality.   Seeing, therefore, that in
Assyrian the ideogram for " ten " also represents such
ideas as exalted, strong, high, we can understand why
the Hebrew terms for " prince " and " ten " should be
philologically connected, and why the same number and
its multiples should thus have been used to symbolize
greatness, exaltation, and magnitude.

FORTY

The number forty occurs very frequently in Semitic
literatures, and seems to have been used by all the Semitic
nations, as well as by many non-Semitic peoples, as a round
number.

Hebrew.—In the Deluge narrative we read that the rain
lasted forty days (Gen. vii, 4, 12, 17), and an equal number
of days were required for the embalming of Jacob
(Gen. l, 3).   Both Moses and Elijah were without food for
forty days (Exod. xxiv, 18 ; 1 Kings xix, 8). The spies
spent forty days in Canaan (Num. xiii, 25).   Both Isaac

and Esau married when they were forty years of age (Gen. xxv, 20 ; xxvi, 34). Ezekiel had to lay on his right side for forty days to represent the forty years of the sins of Judah. Goliath challenged the Israelitish army for forty days (1 Sam. xvii, 16), and in Ezek. xxix, 11–13, there is a prediction that Egypt will suffer from desolation for forty years. Ben-Hadad sent Elisha a gift of " forty camels burden " (2 Kings viii, 9). Solomon had forty stalls of horses (1 Kings v, 6), and in the temple, as described by Ezekiel (Ezek. xli, 2), the side-courts were forty cubits long. Forty stripes were inflicted on certain evildoers (Deut. xxv, 3). Forty days were required for purification after the birth of a male and eighty after the birth of a female (Lev. xii, 2–5). David reigned forty years (2 Sam. v, 4). Finally, it is interesting to note the frequency with which the number occurs in the Book of Judges. A few instances will suffice : (Judges iii, 11) " And the land had rest forty years. And Othniel, the son of Kenaz, died." (Judges v, 31) The Song of Deborah ends with the words " And the land had rest forty years ". (Judges viii, 28) " The country was in quietness forty years in the days of Gideon." (Judges xiii, 1) " And the children of Israel did evil again in the sight of the Lord, and the Lord delivered them into the hand of the Philistines forty years."

Multiples of Forty are also frequent in the Old Testament. The army of Barak consisted of forty thousand men (Judges v, 8). The same number of Syrian footmen were killed by David (1 Chron. xix, 18). In Solomon's temple there were four hundred pomegranates for the two networks (1 Kings vii, 42). In Gen. xv, 13, God told Abraham that his descendants will be oppressed for four hundred years in a strange land. Moses lived 120 years (40×3).

How are we to account for the frequency with which this number and its multiples occur and their symbolical usage ? According to some scholars this was due to the fact that the national consciousness of Israel was impressed by the forty years of wilderness wandering. In any case a period of forty years was used to represent a generation. In Num. xiv, 29–43, we read that the whole generation who murmured would wander about for forty years in the wilderness until they all died (cf. Ps. xcv, 10).

In 1 Kings, vi, 1, we are informed that Solomon built his temple in the 480th year after the Exodus. One is therefore tempted to suggest that this period of 480 years is a round number made up of twelve generations, each of forty years. But this is actually borne out in the following manner : In 1 Chron. v, 29–40, there is a long genealogical table from Amram, the father of Moses, to Jehozadak. Furthermore, in 1 Kings iv, 1–4, we are told that Zadok the priest lived at the time of Solomon, so that one would expect twelve generations from Amram to Zadok, and this is what we actually find in the genealogical list referred to above, thus :—

Amram	Uzzi
Aaron	Zerahiah
Eleazar	Meraioth
Phineas	Amariah
Abishua	Ahitub
Bukki	Zadok

Now we are told in 1 Chron. v, 41, that Jehozadak lived at the time when the Hebrews were driven into exile by Nebuchadrezzar, so that the period from Ahimaaz, the son of Zadok, to the Babylonian exile also consisted of twelve generations lasting 480 years, thus :—

Ahimaaz	Zadok
Azariah	Shallum
Johanan	Hilkiah
Azariah	Azariah
Amariah	Seraiah
Ahitub	Jehozadak

We thus see how the time from the Exodus, when the Israelites formed themselves into a nation, till the Babylonian exile was divided into two periods, each consisting of twelve generations and spread over 480 (12 × 40) years.[1]

But there are other considerations which may account for the symbolical importance of the number forty : amongst the Semites as amongst some non-Semitic races, especially the Greeks, the fortieth year was regarded as the height or acme of a man's life. This may explain why in Acts vii, 23, Moses is said to have been forty years of age when he first realized his duty to his people (" And seeing one of them suffer wrong he defended him that was oppressed, and smote the Egyptian," cf. Exod. ii, 11), why Isaac and Esau married at the same age—evidently meaning that they had then attained their full manhood—and why Caleb was forty years of age when he was sent as a spy (Joshua xiv, 7).

Mohammed received his call as a prophet at the age of 40, and in the Koran, xlvi, the following passage occurs : " We have prescribed for man kindness towards his parents. His mother bore him with trouble, and brought him forth with trouble, and the bearing of him and the weaning of him is thirty months, until when he reaches puberty, and reaches forty years, he says : ' Lord ! Stir me up, that I may be thankful for thy favours wherewith thou hast favoured me and my parents.' "

We can also now understand why we are suddenly informed in the Old Testament that Moses was 80 years of age when he stood before Pharaoh (Exod. vii, 7), for his life of 120 years may be divided up into three generations. It seems that until his fortieth year he was preparing himself for his call. The period of his exile amongst the Midianites and of his prophetic course can be regarded as another generation, so that when he reached the eightieth year of his life—his full manhood—his first public act was to free his people. And he then led them to the end of their desert wanderings for forty years. One may compare with

<hr/>

[1] Ernst Bertheau, *Kurzgefaszten exegetischen Handbuch zum Richterbuch*, 2 Aufl., S. xvi ; also *Das Himmelsjahr als Grundelement der altorientalischen Chronologie, ZDMG.*, vol. lx.

this the lives of Hillel and Johanan b. Zakkai, which have also, by tradition, been divided up into three periods of forty years each.

Babylonians.—When we come to Babylonian literature we find that there are again numerous references to the number forty. We have already seen that the Babylonian deities were represented by various numbers, and Ea, the Babylonian water-god, was represented by forty. The question now arises whether this has any connexion with the rain and wintery seasons which were believed to be embodied in the Pleiades, and which disappear in the light of the sun for about forty days and are heliacally abolished at the beginning of Spring. According to some scholars forty, as the number of the Pleiades, came to represent want and privation. This explains the forty years during which the Israelites wandered in the wilderness and the forty days during which Elijah wandered in the desert.[1] Winckler (*Gesch. Isr.*, ii, S. 83 f.) has even suggested that the period of forty days between the resurrection of Jesus and His ascent to heaven (Acts i, 3) can also be explained in the same manner. In the Babylonian astrological texts there are references to the forty days during which the evil spirits rage (*kima Utukkish* 40 *ume undalli*, K. 1551, and see also Craig, *Astr.-Astron. Texts*, p. 39) ; whilst for forty days after childbirth both mother and child were ritually unclean. Even at the very earliest period of Babylonian history, for example, during the reign of Gudea, we find that this number is of considerable significance in connexion with the sacrifices to the goddess Bau.

Mandæans. — The genuine descendants of the Babylonians are the present-day Mandæans, whose religion is a conglomeration of original Semitic, old Persian, Jewish, and Greek elements. The main characteristic of their religion is a water-cult, consisting of a kind of baptism. According to Zimmern, it seems that this religion has still

---

[1] KAT., 3rd ed., p. 389.

preserved traces of the old Babylonian Ea cult (Schrader, KAT., 3rd ed., p. 359). A woman after having given birth to a child is ritually unclean for forty days, and must then purify herself by a kind of ritual purification in water (W. Brandt, *Die Mandäische Religion*). Furthermore, according to the Mandæans, the soul had to appear forty days after death for judgment. We also read in Mandæan traditions of men who reached 120 (40 × 3) years of age. There are forty commandments which every Mandæan priest must learn by heart.[1]

Jews.—According to one Jewish tradition, the periods of Hillel's life are parallel to those of Moses (*Sifre, Deut.*). Both lived to the age of 120 years. Hillel went to Palestine at the age of 40, spent forty years in study, and passed the last forty years of his life as the spiritual head of Israel. The tradition that he went to Palestine at the age of 40 probably arose in order to suggest that he was then in the prime of his manhood. A tradition has been preserved (*Suk.*, 28a) that he had eighty disciples.

The life of Johanan b. Zakkai was also divided into three periods of forty years each. He spent his first forty years following a mercantile pursuit, the second forty years in study, and the third as teacher (*Talmud Rosh ha-shanah*, 30b). According to tradition, when Akiba was forty years of age and the father of a large family dependent upon him, he commenced to attend the Academy of his native town, Lydda (*Abot de-Rabbi Nathan*). He learned Torah for forty years, and then served Israel for forty years.

Zadok, who was a Tanna of priestly descent, lived at the time of the dissolution of the Jewish state and is said to have fasted for forty years to prevent the destruction of the temple. As a result of this, however, he became so weak that Johanan b. Zakkai appealed for him to Titus, who had him treated by a physician (*Git.*, 56b ;

---

[1] See, further, Kessler's article in Herzog's *Realenc.*, vii, 146 ff.

Lam. R., i, 5). In order to be ritually fit for use, the *Mikwah* or ritual bath must contain forty seahs, which the Rabbis estimated was sufficient to cover entirely the body of the average-sized man (*Mik.*, ii, 1). A woman who marries after forty cannot bear children (*Baba Bathra*, 119B). In *Shab.*, 69a, we are told that there are forty principal labours which are forbidden on the Sabbath Day. The Sanhedrin left the temple just forty years before it was destroyed (*Shab.*, 15a). After a period of drought lasting forty days it is permissible to declare a public fast. Each stone which was carried into the Jordan weighed forty measures (Joshua vi ; *Sotah*, 34). The fortieth year is the age of reason (*Ab.* v, 26). R. Isaac B. Joseph learned a decision with reference to the Passover offering from R. Abahu forty times till he knew it thoroughly (*Pesachim*, 72a). Samuel learned from Rab the following point in Jewish ritual, forty times : " If a woman says I am ritually unclean for marriage and gives a reason for her statement, even if she afterwards denies this, her first statement is believed " (*Kethuboth*, 22a, b). Raba said : " One has not done one's duty if one postpones the meal celebrating the Purim festival for some other occasion." This he repeated forty times for emphasis (*Megilla*, 7b). It appears that, according to Jewish tradition, until the fortieth day after pregnancy there is no definite decision as to whether the child will be a male or a female, because we are told in the *Bab. Talmud* (*Berachoth*, 60a) that there is time from the third to the fortieth day to pray that the future child shall be a male. A small bottle of wine which has been standing for forty days is a cure for the sting of a wasp (*Shab.*, 109b). In *Nidda* iii, 7, we are told that the male embryo develops in forty-one days and the female in eighty-one.[1] This addition of one to the round number forty and its multiple eighty is merely in order to complete the

---

[1] Roscher, *Enneadische Studien*, S. 80–1, shows that the same belief existed in ancient Greece.

number in full. Similar instances occur in the literatures of other nations. We have only to think of the story of *A Thousand and One Nights* in Arabic literature. It seems clear from the above instances quoted from the Talmud that forty is there used as a round number to express the idea of completeness much more fully and effectively than seven.

Arabs.—In Arabic literature forty also plays an exceedingly important part. Let us commence with some Arabic sayings and proverbs : Whilst the soul of the irreligious man wanders for forty days before it comes to its resting-place, in the case of the religious man his punishment for his sins on earth is completed in seven days (Wolff, *Muham. Eschatologie*, S. 65). The *Koran* ought to be read through in forty days (*Cod. Lips*, 383, Vollers). The prayers of a drunkard are not heard for forty days. A person should eat meat at least once every forty days. A sack of flour preserves itself on the surface of water for forty days (*Thousand and One Nights*). The one who takes part in public prayer in a mosque for forty days is certain to be immune from degeneracy and hell (*Cod. Lips*, 383, V.). The one who attempts to speculate in food prices by storing up food for forty nights, severs thereby his connexion with Allah for ever. An old Arabic proverb says that to exact blood vengeance even after forty years is still too soon. In *Cod. Lips*, 383, V., there is a command that every Muslim should learn at least forty of Mohammed's sayings by heart ; and in the same Codex we are told that those sinners who recite in hell the passage from the *Koran* i, 10–11, "Praise to Allah, lord of the world," will be immune from the punishment which they would otherwise have to undergo for forty years. Heaven and earth weep at the death of a religious man for forty days (*MS.* 383, Vollers, Leipzig). A beggar who possesses forty Dirhem is to be considered brazen-faced and refused all charity. Allah will enlighten the heart of the one who eats pure food for forty days, and will cause the sources of wisdom to flow from his heart to his tongue. One ought not to allow a period of more than forty days to pass without shaving, trimming one's beard, or cutting one's nails. An old Mohammedan tradition says that forty of the prophet's precepts should be collected and made use of. The one who becomes intoxicated with wine is to receive forty to eighty lashes, according to Islamic law (*Cod. Lips*, 383, V.). Similarly, one who accuses a respectable woman of immorality, and cannot produce four witnesses to bear out his charge, is to receive 40 × 2 lashes (*Koran* xxiv, 4–9). The one who leads a blind man forty paces will certainly enter Paradise. No one is to be taxed who has less than forty sheep ; whilst for every forty sheep a man possesses he must give one to the poor (383, V.). The command in Lev. xii that a woman who gives birth to a male child must be regarded as ritually unclean for a period of forty days has its parallel amongst the Arabs and many other Semitic and non-Semitic nations. In Upper Egypt the period of impurity is also forty days, and after this period the woman must bathe herself in forty bowls of water if she has given birth to a male child, but thirty bowls of water will suffice if she has given birth to a female. Goldziher (*Globus*, lxxxiii, S. 304) quotes a superstition amongst the Arabs that if a man is jealous of his wife, but is at the same time forbearing, then Allah sends a bird which places itself by the door of his house and waits for forty days, during which time it whispers to the man that God is Himself jealous and loves those who are jealous. It takes three periods, each consisting of forty days, for the embryo to develop (*Koran* xxii, 5 ; xxxix, 8). The same thought is expressed in the Talmud, on which this Arabic saying is probably dependent. One is reminded, of course, of the story of *Ali-Baba and the Forty Thieves*. Furthermore, one should add that in the story of *A Thousand and One Nights* there are continual references to the number forty and its half.

The Islamic tradition that Mohammed was forty years

old when he received his call as a Prophet is, as we have
already seen, no doubt due to the belief that a man reaches
his acme at the age of forty, and his general temperament
and characteristics begin to show themselves at this
period (see article by Sprenger, *ZDMG*, 1859, p. 124).
The forty days of wind and storm play a most important
part in the Arabic Calendar. Many proverbs and verses
refer to the appearance and disappearance of the Pleiades.
It is of interest to note that, whilst in the Biblical account
of the Deluge we are told that the waters reached a height
of 15 cubits (Gen. vii, 20), according to some Moslem traditions their height was 40 cubits. There is an old tradition
which says that God showed Adam all the generations
of mankind that were to succeed him. He thus learned
that David's life would be a very short one, and, as a result
of his prayers and entreaties, God diminished Adam's life
by forty years and gave them to David. There are about
sixty Arabic inscriptions known as *Arbaïnat* (forty).[1] Most
of these deal with the history of a period of forty years.
There is a certain Islamic order known as the *Khalwati*,
whose adherents spend forty days annually in solitary
confinement and fasting from sunrise to sunset (Goldziher,
Revue de l'histoire de Religion, xxxvii, p. 323). The
prophet is said to have had forty followers, and at Ramleh
there are large underground caves which are said to form
their sepulchres (Goldziher, *Globus*, lxxi).

In Islamic eschatology 40 plays a very important
part. When the revival of the dead will take place, the
creatures who will be aroused from their graves will have
to spend 40 years in repentance, during which they will
have neither food nor drink, nor will they even be able
to sit down (Wolff, *Muham. Eschat.*, S. 115). The dead
will have to suffer for 40 years in the heat of hell-fire
(Wolff, p. 156). The Egyptian Arabs perform various

[1] See article in *Zeitschrift d. Vereins für Volkskunde*, 1907 (xvii), S. 187,
and the reference it contains to the work of Lidzbarski on the subject.
One may compare with these the *sebaïat* (sevens), which confine
themselves to seven years.

ceremonies by the graveside of a dead relative on the
40th day after burial. Lepsius (*Chron. d. Ægypter*, 15)
points out that in Syria the graves of Seth, Abel, and
Noah are still to be seen, and their length is stated by the
inhabitants to be 40 yards. It has been suggested that
the huge size of these graves may have some connexion
with the belief that in early times all men were of huge
stature; cf. especially the *Nephilim* referred to in Gen. vi, 4,
who were regarded as giants of enormous height.

When the end of a man's life is approaching, and he has
but another 40 days to live, there falls a leaf from a certain
mystic tree into the lap of Azriel, the angel of death,
under whose supervision the man is now placed and whom
God commands to take his soul. The period of mourning
for a dead relative is 40 days (Wolff, 76 f.). The beginning
of hell-fire carries on each of its four sides 40 years of
wandering (Vollers, 383). The smoke which will rise
into heaven on the day of resurrection will cover the earth
for 40 days (Koran, xliv).[1]

Amongst various races in the East, the 40th day after
burial is the most important one, and various religious
ceremonies and rites are then performed. In Sarajevo
it is customary to go to the grave of a dead relative on
the 3rd, 7th, and 40th day after burial, light a candle
there, and pray for his soul. The Moslems of Bosnia
hold a meal for the dead on the 7th and 40th days after
burial (Sartori, *D. Speisung d. Toten*, 1903, S. 33). The
inhabitants of Northern Nubia mourn for their relatives
40 days. On the 40th day they hold a feast, distribute
alms to the poor, and divide the testator's estate (*Globus*,
lxxvi, 338 f.). The sound of the trumpet at the period of
resurrection will last 40 years (Wolff, S. 93). The Temple
in Jerusalem will be rebuilt 40 years after the Kaaba.
Just as the number 40 occurs very frequently, so 20 as
a fraction, and also multiples of 40, are very frequently
met with in Arabic literature. Adam lay as a mere

[1] See Sale's translation with notes, 1876, p. 402.

SYMBOLISM OF NUMBERS   155

lump of clay for 80 (2 × 40) years, then after a hundred and
twenty (3 × 40) years Allah gave him human form and
breathed into him the human soul (Wunsche, *Schöpfung
und Sündenfall*, S. 7). Mohammed told Fatima that
a prophet's influence lasts half as long as that of his
predecessor. Whilst Jesus prophesied for 40 years, he
would only prophesy for 20 (*ZDMG.*, 1859, S. 171). On
the day of resurrection the dead will form themselves
into 120 (3 × 40) rows (Wolff, S. 121). The Hukub consists
of 4,000 years, each of these has four thousand months,
and each month is of four thousand days (Wolff, 173 f.).
Some of the *Arbaïnat* deal not only with a period of 40
years, but sometimes also with a period of 4 × 40 years.
In Paradise everyone will spend with his spouse a period
of 80 (40 × 2) years.

The use of forty and its multiples in order to represent
a complete number when seven was insufficient, was first
made by the Semites in connexion with measurements
of length, breadth, and time. It was then used in connexion
with magic and all kinds of belief in popular medicine.[1]
From this usage amongst the Jews it spread to the Greeks,
by whom the number was also used in connexion with
their prescriptions for all kinds of diseases.[2] Trace of
this practice may be seen in the word " quarantine ",
which is connected with the Latin (quadraginta) and
Italian (quaranta) terms for " forty ", and really means
a space of forty days, referring originally to the forty days
which a merchant coming from an infected port stayed
on shipboard for clearing himself. With this is connected
also the expression " fare la quarantine " to keep Lent
or fast forty days, or to keep forty days from company,
especially if one came from an infected place.

With reference to the use of the number amongst the
ancient Hebrews in connexion with ritual purity, especially
that required after childbirth, it is worthy of note that

---

[1] Traces of this are to be found in the *Bab. Talmud, Shabbath*, 109b.
[2] See Roscher, *Hebdomadenlehren*, S. 72 ff.

similar beliefs are to be found all the world over. Amongst all primitive peoples childbirth is regarded as a very important crisis in human life, and special measures are taken for the protection of mother and child. In fact, women after childbirth, and their offspring, are more or less tabooed all the world over. In the island of Delos no woman was allowed to be confined lest its sacred soil should be polluted. It is believed in Malay that mother and child are attacked by exceedingly dangerous spirits. For this reason the mother, for a period of about forty days after labour, has to mount daily a platform, upon which she is subjected to intense heat from a fire for a considerable period. Amongst the Bulgars, birth is followed by a vigorous taboo, which lasts forty days. In Cairo the period of impurity after childbirth is not more than forty days.

We can thus understand the Hebrew law in Lev. xii, which commands that the mother is to be excluded from the social cultus for a period which varies according to the sex of the child. In the case of a male child the period of impurity extends for forty days, divided into two stages of decreasing stringency, seven and thirty-three days respectively. In the case of a female child each of these stages is twice as long, making eighty days in all. It is obvious that after having been used in connexion with physical purification the number should also have been applied in connexion with fasting and repentance, which are forms of moral and spiritual purification. This explains why Moses fasted forty days and forty nights before God appeared to him on Mount Sinai, why Elijah went without food or drink for the same period till he reached Horeb (1 Kings xix, 8), and the many cases of fasting and prayer for forty days in later Hebrew and Semitic literatures.

CHAPTER V

SYMBOLICAL REPRESENTATIONS OF THE BABYLONIAN-ASSYRIAN PANTHEON

CHAPTER V

SYMBOLICAL REPRESENTATIONS OF THE BABYLONIAN-ASSYRIAN PANTHEON

Our knowledge of Babylonian and Assyrian symbolism, and especially of the symbolical representations of the gods of their pantheon, is derived chiefly from a study of cylinder seals, boundary stones, and the monoliths of Assyrian kings. The seal was a most important article in early primitive society, and its purpose was mainly to prevent any theft from taking place without detection. It was thus to the people of the ancient world what locks and keys are to us, and Herodotus (i, 195) tells us that in his time, every person in Babylonia carried about a seal as well as a walking stick. For example, if a man wished to leave his house and goods for some time, without having anyone to guard them, he would stick plasters of mud on the door, and then impress them with his seal, so that the seal would have to be broken by anyone wishing to enter the house, and robbery could thus be detected if not actually prevented.

Now, the scenes and emblems of the gods depicted on many seals throw very considerable light on our knowledge of the symbolism of the Babylonians, as well as on their religious and theological ideas. Thus, on a seal now in the British Museum, dating from the time of Shar Gani-Sharri and Naram Sin, kings of Agade, there are representations of Gilgamesh and Eabani. Sometimes there are representations of gods with heroes near by. On one seal now in the Metropolitan Museum, New York, Shamash, the sun-god, is represented by a horn-capped deity. He is seated on a stool, is wearing a long mantle, and rays of light proceed from his shoulders. There is a star in front of him and a crescent behind him. Near him are two

heroes, ready to kill a lion.   One of them has his left foot
on the lion's head, and is holding its tail with his left
hand ; whilst the other has a hatchet with which he is
ready to kill it.

On some seals, the gods are associated with serpents,
and the body of a god is represented as being formed from
the coils of a serpent.   Again, we find some famous
Babylonian legends, such as the story of Etana's attempt
to ascend to heaven on the wings of an eagle, symbolically
represented on such seal cylinders.   There is a seal cylinder
now in the Metropolitan Museum, New York, in which
we have a symbolical representation of the manner in
which the dragon, who was the very symbol of chaos,
is conquered by Bel-Merodach, the incarnation of order.

These seal cylinders were employed by the Assyrians
from the very earliest period of their history right down
to the time of the Persians, who in turn adopted
them also.

One may here refer also to the sacred tree, which is
constantly represented on Assyrian seals, and above which
there is often a representation of Ashur with his winged disc.

Boundary stones or kudurrus form a very interesting
class of objects from which our knowledge of Babylonian
symbolism is derived, for the emblems which are scattered
about on the seal cylinders are collected together in groups
on the boundary stones, and we are thus provided with
data which assist us in associating the gods of the pantheon
with their respective symbols.   These boundary stones
were first introduced into Babylonia during the period
of the Kassites, with the object of marking the limits
of private property, and they contain texts referring to
property conveyancing and land tenure.   They were
sacred to the god Ninib, who was known as *bel kudurre,*
" lord of boundary stones."   One of the most important
characteristics of these boundary stones are the symbols
sculptured either on top or on one of the sides.   For
a long time there was considerable discussion as to what

these symbols were intended to represent. According to some scholars, they were supposed to represent the signs of the zodiac. This view was first put forward by Oppert (*Documents Juridiques*) and was adopted by Epping, Strassmaier, and Hommel.[1] Other scholars regarded these symbols as representing certain powers, to whom the owners of the land appealed in connexion with their property ; whilst others again regarded them as representing the gods who are invoked in the inscriptions.

But now, as a result of discoveries made by the French expedition at Susa, numerous new boundary stones have been discovered, and from the information which they contain, we are no longer in doubt that these symbols are representations of certain gods, and it is worthy of note that on one of these stones from Susa (MDP. i, fig. 379) the names of the gods are actually written on the symbols.

A very fine specimen of a boundary stone is that of Nebuchadrezzar I,[2] which was discovered at Nippur. The whole of one side of this kudurru has a huge serpent around it. In the first of the six registers into which it is divided, there is a crescent symbolizing Sin, a disc for Shamash, and a star for Ishtar. The next register consists of a row of three emblems representing Anu Bel and Ea (or perhaps Ashur). Then come the symbols of Marduk and Nebo, and in the next row is the symbol of Ninib, a horse's head on a seat surmounted by an arch—in all probability one of the earliest representations of the horse in Babylonian art—and an eagle on the top of a column. In the fifth row is the goddess Gula, seated on a throne with a dog near by and a scorpion-man ; whilst in the last row we have a calf with a thunderbolt on top, representing the storm-god Adad, a tortoise, which often occurs on kudurrus and seal cylinders as an alternative emblem for Ea, a scorpion, and a lamp which is the usual symbol of the fire-god Nusku.

---

[1] *Aufsätze und Abhandlungen*, 1900.
[2] *New Boundary Stone of Nebuchadrezzar I*, W. J. Hinke.

There are another two boundary stones of great interest. One from the reign of the Kassite king Nazi-Maruttash (c. 1320 B.C.), and another from the period of Marduk-baliddin, king of Babylon (c. 1170 B.C.). Both boundary stones were found at Susa, and are now in the Louvre. The first contains the following symbolical representations :—

Row   I. Shrines with tiaras symbolizing Anu and Enlil.
Row   II. Shrine with goat-fish and ram's head representing Ea, also shrine with symbol of Ninlil.
Row III. Spear-head representing Marduk, mace with two lion-heads representing Ninib, mace with vulture's head for Zamama, and mace with lion's head for Nergal.
Row   IV. Bird on a pole representing Papsukal, lightning-fork on back of an ox for Adad or Ramman.

On another side is a crescent symbolizing Sin, a solar disc for Shamash, an eight-pointed star for Ishtar, the goddess Gula sitting on a shrine with a dog at her feet, a scorpion for Ishkara, and a lamp for Nusku. At the end of the inscription nineteen gods are named, and called upon to curse anyone who destroys or defaces it.

In the case of the boundary stone of Marduk-baliddin, forty-seven gods and goddesses are mentioned in all in connexion with the curses at the close of the inscription. The symbols are similar to those represented on the other boundary stones, but some additional gods are added, including Tammuz, his sister Geshtin-Anna, and the two Kassite gods Shukamuna and Shumalia.

One of the monuments which have helped us very considerably in the identification of these emblems is the rock-relief of Sennacherib, near Bavian. The monument refers to twelve gods, and also contains twelve emblems, and Jensen has noted that not only is the number of gods equivalent to the number of symbols, but that the order of sequence is the same. Thus the fifth in the list of deities is Sin, the moon-god ; whilst the fifth in the list of emblems is a crescent. Now, we are certain that Sin was represented by a crescent, for we constantly find on kudurrus and cylinder seals that the crescent accompanies the emblems of the sun and Venus, and forms with them the heavenly triad. Adad is seventh in the list of gods ; whilst the thunderbolt, which we may also definitely say was his symbol, is seventh in the list of emblems. Again, Ishtar occupies the eleventh position in the list of names, and the star, her symbol, occupies the same place in the list of emblems. The twelve gods of this list have thus been identified and arranged according to their symbols in the following manner :—Ashur, Anu, and Bel are symbolized by a horned turban ; Ea by a column with a ram's head ; Sin by a crescent ; Shamash by a winged disc ; Adad by a thunderbolt ; Marduk by a column with a pineapple top ; Nabu by a simple column ; Ishtar by a star ; the Igigi by seven dots. The tenth in the list, which we have omitted, is a column with two bulls' heads—very likely a symbol of Ninib.

Having now traced in bare outline the main sources by means of which scholars have succeeded in identifying the emblems on various monuments and inscriptions with the gods whom they represent, we shall proceed to discuss in detail the symbolisms of the principal gods of the Babylonian-Assyrian pantheon, and the manner in which they are represented in Literature and Art.

Ishtar

Just as Baal was originally a title applied to different deities, and after a time gradually clung to certain ones as a proper name, so Ishtar was, evidently, originally a title applied to many local goddesses both in Babylonia and Assyria, until the goddess probably lost her other name (if she had one) and came to be known by this title alone. Now, originally, Ishtar was worshipped in Assyria at three different shrines—Ashur, Nineveh, and Arbela— as one deity. In the course of time, however, the Ishtars of these different shrines grew into different divinities. The great variety of aspects assumed by deities bearing the name of Ishtar amongst the Semites is explained by W. Robertson Smith (*Religion of the Semites*, pp. 56–8), who shows how, as the organization of society advanced, the matriarchate gave way to a patriarchate, and so the old polyandrous mother-goddess became the wife of a god, and when a monarchy arose, a queen.

In discussing, therefore, the symbols by which Ishtar is represented, it is of importance to note first of all the different forms under which this goddess was worshipped. She was regarded as the symbol of creation. The Assyrians symbolized this trait of her character by representing her with breasts exposed and carrying a child on her left arm sucking her breast. Numerous figures with representations of such a nature have been found in various Babylonian temples, and it has been suggested that these figures were deposited by the Babylonian women in the temples of Ishtar in order that she may grant them her aid in childbirth. These figures really represent her as the mother and nurse of mankind. Every feminine phenomenon of the Babylonian pantheon is fundamentally embodied in her. She is the mother of the gods and mother-goddess, and is therefore prayed to in hymns as " helper " and " heavenly midwife ".

In the sixth tablet of the Gilgamesh Epic this trait of her character is well represented. The goddess is attracted to the hero by his achievements and pleads for his love. As the goddess of fertility she promises him abundance of possessions if only he will be her husband and grant her his love as a gift. But in spite of all her entreaties he refuses her advances, and recalls to mind the sad fate incurred by her previous lovers. The whole myth is symbolical. Uruk, where the scene of this story is laid, was a centre of sun-worship, and Gilgamesh is really a solar deity. Ishtar is, of course, the mother-goddess, so that the union of Gilgamesh and Ishtar would represent the union of sun and earth, by means of which the earth is fertilized and made fruitful. But Ishtar, who produces life, is unable to maintain it, hence the decay of vegetable and animal life symbolized by the sad fate incurred by her previous lovers. The story of Ishtar's descent to the domain of Ereshkigal in search of her lover Tammuz symbolized the change of seasons when bright and fruitful summer passes away and gives place to cold, barren winter. Before the goddess can enter this domain she must pass through seven gates, and as she passes through each gate she hands a portion of her clothing to the guardian until she appears in her sister's presence quite nude. The myth represents the decay of vegetation after the summer season. Tammuz, the sun-god, who was cut off in the flower of his youth and taken to another world, represented the vegetation of spring cut off by the destructive storms of winter. Ishtar's descent to Hades and the gradual loss of her clothing represents the gradual passing away of summer, replaced by barren winter. So long as Ishtar remains in the nether world all life and pro-ductivity on earth ceases. We are told that all sexual desire, and therefore all life, has now ended in man and beast. " Since Ishtar is gone to the land of no-return, the bull cares not for the cow, the ass cares not for the jenny, the man cares not for the maid in the market."

Ea now creates a messenger Aṣushu-namir (his rising is brilliant). He sprinkles the water of life on Ishtar and leads her out of prison, and in passing from one gate to another each portion of her clothing is returned to her. Water was always regarded as a symbol of purification, and the sprinkling of the " waters of life " represents her purification from the diseases from which she has suffered during her confinement. The release of the goddess and the return of her clothing as she passes back through each gate represents the return of the summer season with all its life and vegetation.

In the Gilgamesh Epic we are told that Ishtar assigns partners to public maidens at Uruk, the city of her abode. She is called *Kadishtu*, " the sacred prostitute," and the maidens who attended on her, acting as priestesses, symbolically represented the marriage union. The obscene rites which were connected with the worship of the goddess in Babylonia, and are described in detail by Herodotus (i, 199), were regarded merely as symbolical representations of her character as the goddess of the sexual passions and the mother of parturition. It is for this reason that she was symbolically represented on seal cylinders as absolutely naked, with what is distinctively female particularly emphasized.[1]

The temple at Nineveh which Ishtar inhabited was most beautifully adorned. It was repaired in the time of Ashurnasirpal II, and Ashurbanipal added a most elaborate altar. We are also informed that it contained a bed of some costly wood to give rest to her divinity. It seems very probable that this was in some symbolical manner connected with the obscene rites which formed part of the worship of Ishtar, and that on public feasts the image of the goddess reclined on this divan as the Roman gods reclined at their lecisternia.

The prophet Ezekiel, in describing the part played by women in the deterioration of faith and morals, informs us how, on turning to one of the most frequented entrances to the temple, he saw there the women weeping for Tammuz. Furthermore, the prophet tells us that he saw this vision in the sixth month of the year. Why was Elul (September) selected as the month on which this ceremony of mourning for Tammuz took place ? The reason is quite clear. Tammuz, as we have already noted, symbolized the fructifying sun at the height of his glory in the heavens

---

[1] **Ward,** *Seal Cylinders of Western Asia,* chap. xxvi, also **Heuzey,** *Origines Orientales de l'art,* p. 11.

in the month of July. In September the supremacy of the sun is at an end. The days are shorter and the nights are longer, so that the sun may be said to have succumbed to the powers of darkness. Therefore, when Tammuz was exiled to the land of darkness—the underworld—it was believed that Ishtar descended thither to try and bring him back before his doom was irrevocable. This also explains why Elul was known to the Babylonians as the month of the " Mission of Ishtar ". The weeping for Tammuz, therefore, symbolized, in the first instance, an expression of sadness for the departure of the beauty and richness of summer. But this nature myth was not merely a symbol of the phenomena of the outer world, but also a parable of the passions of human life, and thus there arose these acts of sexual vice that were associated with this and many similar religious ceremonies, and formed so obnoxious a feature of ancient Semitic religions.

It is of interest to note how the belief in these particular traits of the character of Ishtar survived throughout the ages. In various details the representations of the goddess were transformed to new and changing conditions. But she always seemed to represent the great female principle in nature, arousing the passions, acting as the mother of mankind, and governing the laws of vegetation. The *Mater magna* of Asia Minor and the sacred statue of Kybele, which the Romans brought from Phrygia with the hope of saving the empire from its doom, were merely different symbolical representations of the loving mother-goddess Ishtar.[1]

It was only natural that as the goddess of fertility and mother-goddess she should be represented as showing pity as a father or mother, and she was therefore appealed to in distress. Furthermore, Ishtar of Nineveh stood in special relationship to the people of Nineveh. She was known as " the Lady of Nineveh ", and Nineveh was

[1] Cumont *Les Religions Orientales parmi les Peuples Romains*, Paris, 1908.

known as " the City Beloved of Ishtar ". She must,
therefore, show her affection for her city by acting as its
protector in war time, and it was probably in this manner
that her character as a warrior goddess developed.

The goddess is also represented as appearing at the
summer solstice, and punishing those who offend her with
terrible disease. It is this which may also have caused
her character to develop into a fierce war deity. As
a war goddess she leads on her armies in battle. She is
described as " the powerful one amongst the goddesses ",
" the one who is girded for battle ", " the warlike Ishtar ",
etc., and in an old Babylonian hymn she is also described
as the one who gives help in war and battle.[1] Ashurbanipal,
who was particularly devoted to her cult, recounts how
she appeared to him in a dream previous to one of his
battles with the Elamites. " Ishtar who dwells in Arbela
entered, she had quivers hanging on her right and left
sides, and she held a bow in her hand with a sharp sword
drawn." Esarhaddon, in the Zinjirli inscription, boasts
that she lends her weapons to her favourite king. The
relief of Shamashreshusur shows very clearly her warlike
character. On her head is a crown of feathers, her right
hand is raised ; whilst in her left hand she holds the top
end of a bow fixed in the ground. Fortunately, all doubt
as to whom the figure represents is removed by the
inscription ṣalam Ishtar (image of Ishtar) underneath.

Now, in the Oxford Hebrew Lexicon (BDB., p. 905) the
root of the Hebrew for " bow " (קֶשֶׁת) is given as unknown.
A possible root, קוּשׁ, with an unknown meaning is
suggested, but this seems hardly plausible. The Hebrew
קֶשֶׁת, like other segholates, goes back to an original
monosyllabic form, קַשְׁת (cf. מֶלֶךְ, מַלְךְ, etc.). Furthermore, the Hebrew for " votary " קְדֵשָׁה may also go
back to an original קְדֵשְׁת. The final ה or ת is only,

---

[1] KB. iii, p. 112.

of course, a feminine suffix, and the present writer therefore suggests that both קְדֵשָׁה and קֶשֶׁת have arisen from an original stem קְדֵשׁ and that the form קֶשֶׁת is merely due to assimilation of the ד and שׁ.

We have many such instances of assimilation in Hebrew (see Gesenius-Kautzsch, *Hebrew Grammar*, par. 19), and in the case of a loss of a ד such as we have here, one may mention as a most common example in Hebrew the word for " one ", אֶחָד, which becomes in the feminine אַחַת for an original אַחַדְתְּ (par. 96). For the assimilation of a ד into a שׁ in Assyrian, one may quote the Assyrian *ana eshshuti* (anew) for *ana edshuti* (from *edeshu*, to renew).

Are we not justified, therefore, in regarding the philological connexion between the Hebrew words for " votary " and " bow " as showing how the characters of Ishtar as the goddess of love and the passions, and also the goddess of war and the bow, have developed from one another ?

In the astrological system Ishtar was identified with Venus, and thus came to be regarded as a symbol of light. She is described as " the shining torch of heaven ", " light of all dwellings ", " illuminator of heaven and earth ", etc. This trait of her character caused her to be represented by the symbol of a star of various shapes. On the bas-relief of Bavian, the Sargon Stele, and the rock inscription of Nahr el Kelb, the star is cross-shaped. On the Nabu-pal-iddin inscription she is symbolized by an eight-rayed star, and by a sixteen-rayed star on the Esarhaddon Stele from Zinjirli. On Phœnician gems the gazelle is figured along with the star and dove as symbols of Astarte.[1]

In the astrological system of the Babylonians every month was associated with a different deity. The sixth month was associated with Ishtar, thus symbolizing her

---

[1] W. Robertson Smith, *Kinship and Marriage in Early Arabia,* 1903, pp. 227, 304.

period of six months on earth and six months in the lower world.

As the goddess of light, it was natural that she should have been symbolically represented as possessing some of the attributes of Shamash the sun-god. She is, therefore, described as judging the cause of man with justice and righteousness.

The lion is the characteristic animal of Ishtar, and she is sometimes represented as standing on two lions. In the Rich collection the goddess is represented by a female figure in a flounced garment sitting on a seat ornamented with lions, with a lion also under her feet. In front of her are a crescent and star. It is, of course, possible that she herself was symbolized by a lion. In this connexion it is of interest to note that from the images of the gods in the temple of the Suti, a people living to the east of Babylonia, we learn that there was a goddess known as " Ishtar the lions ". This suggests that to these people the lion had some symbolical connexion with Ishtar.

But these symbols of a lion and dove, etc., can perhaps be explained in a different way. At the time of Mohammed the Arabs had three goddesses whom they regarded as daughters of Allah. One of these, al Ŭzza, seems to have been worshipped by the Arabs under the form of the planet Venus, and the Syrian Fathers Ephraem and Isaac, of Antioch, tell us of rites connected with her worship which resemble very closely those of Ishtar at Babylon. We are informed that the goddess was an adulteress and a polyandrous patroness of unmarried love. When one thinks of the golden gazelles and the dove idol in the Kaaba, one is tempted to connect the pre-Islamic goddess at Mecca with Ishtar, who was represented by the symbol of a dove and a gazelle. Again, the gazelle or antelope were so closely associated with the worship of the mother-goddess in Arabia that women were often compared by Arabians to antelopes. Robertson Smith [1] has also shown

[1] *Kinship and Marriage in Early Arabia*, 1903, pp. 145 ff.

how Arabic society has passed through a polyandrous
stage, and in his *Religion of the Semites* (p. 56) he suggests
that Ishtar of Erech reflects this state of society. In the
Gilgamesh Epic she is said to cohabit promiscuously with
whomsoever her fancy dictated, and the eagle, the lion,
and the horse are mentioned amongst her husbands.
When, therefore, Ishtar is represented by a female figure
sitting on one or two lions, this may simply be a symbolical
means of representing the goddess together with her
husband.

Ishtar was also represented under the symbol of a cow.
On a small tablet from Sippar, dating back to the period
of Hammurabi, are several cylindrical seals. One of these
is most interesting. Two priests raise their hands in
prayer towards Ishtar, whom one recognizes by the manner
in which she holds her hands on her breasts. She has
a crown on her head. In the background is a cow with
a suckling calf. This probably symbolized Ishtar as the
goddess of fertility. In this connexion, however, it is
perhaps worthy of note that Cumont thinks that every
god was regarded as a bull and every goddess as a cow,
in so far as they bear lunar character.[1]

BAU

Hommel connects the name Bau with " bohu " of
Gen. i, and suggests that this goddess was a symbol
of the watery depths of the Universe. But this philological
connexion is inadmissible. Bau was regarded as the
daughter of Anu, the god of the upper regions, and her
ship was therefore known as the " Ship of brilliant
offspring ". It is also of interest to note that in incantation
texts she is called the mother of Ea, the water deity. It
is possible, therefore, that she originally represented the
waters of the upper regions, just as Ea represented those
of the lower ones. At the time of Gudea she assumed

Die Mysterien des Mithra, 89.

great importance, and her festival, which was held on
New Year's Day, was the occasion of a symbolical marriage
between the goddess and Ningirsu, with whose cult she was
connected.   Ningirsu is represented as offering wedding
presents to Bau.   As the great mother-goddess from whom
mankind received the flocks and herds, and who provided
the agricultural labourer with his harvest, the heifer was
her symbol.   As a matter of fact, she resembles, in many
respects, Aruru, the goddess who assisted in the creation
of " the seed of man ", which springs forth from her bosom
like " the wild cow with its young ".   Sayce [1] suggests
that originally Bau was merely a spirit in the form of
a heifer, and shows that the ship of Bau was called " the
ship of the holy cow ".   On the boundary stone of Nazi-
Maruttash the symbol of Bau is a bird.

SHAMASH

The chief centres at which the sun-god was worshipped in
Babylonia were Larsa, Sippar, Cuthah, and Ur.   At the two
former centres he was known as " Ut "(day) or " Babbar "
(shining one), but after a time Shamash, the Semitic form
of his name, became the accepted one throughout Babylonia.
As darkness is always associated with wickedness and
wrong-doing, the piercing rays of the sun which penetrate
the darkest places and banish crime and injustice, caused
Shamash to be regarded as witness of all that passes
on earth.

Thy terrible brilliancy overwhelms the land ;
As for those that speak with the tongue in all countries,
Thou knowest their plans, their walk thou observest. [2]

Similarly, the Hebrews represented the sun as an eye,
and as possessing the attributes of an eye.   In Job iii, 9 ;
xli, 10 we read of " the eyelids of the dawn ".   In
Joshua xv, 7, there is a reference to a city known as

---

[1] *Gifford Lectures*, p. 365, n. 2.
[2] C. D. Gray, *The Shamash Religious Texts*, p. 15, ll. 48–50.

En Shemesh (eye of the sun) ; whilst it has been suggested that Anamelekh (2 Kings xvii, 31), who was worshipped at Sepharvaim, one of the Babylonian centres of sun worship, means eye of the sun-god Melech.[1] The Parsees call the sun " the eye of Ahura Mazda " (Yacna, i, 35 ; iii, 49) ; and even in Shakespeare we read that the sun with one eye vieweth all the world (King Henry VI, pt. i, 1, 4).

Shamash was regarded in Babylonia as the great source of justice, the king of judgment, and judge of the whole world. The Babylonian kings address him as daian shame irṣiti (judge of heaven and earth). The beneficent rays of his light bring order upon earth and symbolize justice. He is, therefore, constantly appealed to in hymns to deliver the weak from the strong and punish the evildoer. His word is law, and he is even known as " Lord of law " ; whilst he is sometimes associated with Ramman, and together they are described as " Divine Lords of Justice ". We can thus understand why at the head of the monument on which is inscribed the famous code of Hammurabi, the great king is represented as receiving his laws from Shamash—the paramount god of law.

The wicked judge thou makest to behold bondage.
Him who receives a bribe, who does not guide aright,
    thou makest to bear sin.
He who receives not a bribe, who has regard for the weak,
Shall be well-pleasing to Shamash ; he shall prolong his life.
The judge, the arbiter, who gives righteous judgment
Shall complete a palace, a princely abode, for his dwelling-
    place.
He who gives money for a boundary, the worthless fellow,
    what does he profit ?
He brings about deception for gain, and changes weights.
He who gives money for distant boundaries and gains in
    return one shekel for three,
Shall be well-pleasing to Shamash; he shall prolong his life.[2]

[1] Mövers, Die Phönizier, 1, 411.
[2] Shamash Religious Texts, p. 17, ll. 41–50.

As the judge of mankind, Shamash is usually represented seated, whilst his worshippers are bringing an offering, and they are followed by some of their attendants, who are also bringing some offerings with them. On the monument of Hammurabi the god is sitting on a throne. He has a long beard and is wearing a four-horned turban. On each side of his shoulders there are solar rays. He has a ring and staff in his hand, whilst under his feet there are hills. Hammurabi stands in front of the god receiving the law at his hands.

On the Stele of Nabu-apal-iddin, which was found by Rassam at Sippar, the god is also very clearly represented. He is seated on a throne, and is dressed in a long cloak with a five-horned turban. He holds in his right hand a sceptre and ring. Two priests and a worshipper are approaching him. In front is an altar upon which stands the sun disc which is held with ropes by Malik and Bunene, the two messengers of the sun god, who appear to be directing its course. The body of a serpent seems to be forming a canopy over the head of Shamash, and to be covering his back.

This scene is represented on a marble tablet which lay in a terra-cotta box covered over with a lid. The inscription accompanying the representation reads, " Image of Shamash, the great lord dwelling in Ebabbara situated in Sippar." A lower inscription, near the god's turban, reads : *Agu Shamash mushshi agu Shamash*. The meaning of the word *mushshi* is unknown, and has given rise to a great deal of discussion. Hilprecht [1] translates the inscription " tiara of Shamash, make the tiara of Shamash bright " (*mashu* = *namaru*, to be bright), and regards it as an instruction to the artist. Seeing that the sun-god was the source of all light, his crown should therefore be represented as sending forth rays of light. Prinz [2] suggests that *mushshi* has some connexion with the word

---

[1] *Explorations in Bible Lands during the Nineteenth Century*, p. 271.
[2] *Altorientalische Symbolik*, p. 76.

for serpent, thus referring to the serpent which forms the canopy of the god. But in this representation the serpent is probably the storm-cloud which rises out of the ocean and covers the throne of the sun reaching to the pillars which support the heavens. One might compare with this, Job xxvi, 9, 11 :—

He closeth in the face of his throne, and spreadeth his cloud upon it.
The pillars of heaven tremble and are astonished at his rebuke.

The pillars of heaven were believed to tremble at a storm, just as the pillars of the earth tremble in an earthquake. Malik and Bunene are often represented in Babylonian religious literature as the attendants of Shamash, and together with the latter they form a triad, the centre for whose worship was Sippar.

Such a representation of the sun-god as the one of Nabu-apal-iddin may perhaps be connected with the " Hammanim ", which are referred to in the Bible as images of idols, and were most probably introduced amongst the Hebrews from some foreign cult during the seventh century. In the Old Testament the Israelites are commanded to destroy these, together with the " masseboth " and " asherim ". On a Palmyrene altar there is an inscription (A.D. 48) which states that this " Hammana " and this altar were dedicated to the sun-god. The " Hammana " may have been a sun-disc as amongst the Babylonians ; or, perhaps, as is suggested by Rabbinic commentators,[1] a kind of obelisk which, of course, would have been introduced from Egypt. On the other hand, Robertson Smith suggests that the Hammanim were a kind of metal candelabra, such as are represented fairly often on Assyrian reliefs.[2]

In 2 Kings xxiii, 11, we read how Josiah put down the priests that burned incense to the sun, and that he took away the horses that the kings of Judah had given to

---

[1] *Mechilta, Yithro, Par.* 5 (on xx, 2).
[2] *Religion of the Semites*, 488 f.

the sun, and burned the chariots of the sun with fire. It seems that the chariot and horses which were placed at the entrance to the temple had been dedicated by some of the kings of Judah. This idea was probably introduced from Babylon, for at the entrance to the temple of Shamash at Sippar there was a chariot and, in all probability, horses. From references in Babylonian texts it seems that sacrifices were actually made to the chariot. On one tablet we are informed that on the 13th of Iyyar, in the fourteenth year of Nabopolassar, a white sheep was sacrificed to it; whilst we are also informed of a whole list of furniture consisting of articles of gold and silver which belonged to the chariot. When Ezekiel describes the twenty-five men at Jerusalem worshipping the sun [1] he refers to certain symbolical customs worthy of consideration. We are informed that during the ceremony they placed "the branch to their nose". The meaning of this symbolism is very doubtful, but there was a Persian ceremony in which the priests with their faces covered over with a veil used to hold a bunch of twigs in their hand during worship. Amongst the furniture belonging to the chariot of the sun at Sippar 2 *nurmu* are mentioned, and as *nurmu* probably means a fig-tree, the passage may mean that in the worship of the sun two branches of a fig-tree belonging to his chariot were held up before the face. What symbolic connexion there exists between the sun and the fig-tree it is difficult to suggest, but Frazer [2] quotes many instances amongst primitive peoples where the sun as a male god fertilizing the earth is conceived as descending into a tree. The natives of Timorlaut, Babbar, and the Leti Islands in the Indian Archipelago, worship the sun as the chief male god who fertilizes the earth, and they also believe that he descends into a sacred fig-tree.

Just as the moon was regarded in Babylonian imagery as sailing along the heavens in a barque, so the sun was looked

---

[1] See Ezek. viii, 16.
[2] *Folk Lore in the Old Testament*, vol. ii, p. 55.

upon as a warrior who travels in a chariot across the skies. He is represented as leaving his bridal chamber in the morning, running his course during the day, and then returning home to his bride in the evening. Aia, his wife, was even described in one hymn as coming out to meet him with joy :—

May Aia, thy beloved wife, gladly come to meet thee!
May thy rest-giving heart rest!
May the (glory) of thy Godhead dwell with thee!
O warrior, hero, sun-god, may they glorify thee!
O Lord of E-bara, may he direct thy straight path!
O sun-god, make thy path straight, a straight road for thy
   beams to go.[1]

In Ps. xix, 6, the sun is described as a bridegroom coming out of his bridal chamber and rejoicing as a mighty man to run a race. Similarly, in the Egyptian religion Ra was regarded as sailing in a barque across the sky. Cumont in his *Mysterien des Mithra* shows the same idea existing in the Mithra Cult. The sun rises in the morning and purifies the earth, then he drives across the ocean in his chariot. It was this belief which no doubt gave rise to the representation of Shamash by a disc. In MDP. i, 168, Kudurru I, there is a representation of a disc undoubtedly representing Shamash. The symbol on the boundary stone of Nazi Maruttash is described as *niphu namriru sha daiani rabi (ilu) Shamash* (MDP. ii, col. iv). The disc by which Shamash was represented appears in various forms. In Layard's *Monuments of Nineveh* (plate lix) there is a representation of a king seated on a throne receiving his vizir, who is followed by his attendants, and above them are the sacred emblems—the sun, the moon, and the planets. The sun is here represented by a disc with a smaller one inside. On the Bavian relief the symbol is provided with wings. Ball suggests a connexion between the Egyptian winged disc and that representing Shamash. One is

[1] G. Bertin, *Revue d'Assyriologie*, vol. i, p. 157, translated by Pinches, *Trans. Soc. Bib. Arch.*, vol. viii, p. 167.

reminded of Hebrew imagery also. In Joel ii, 2, there is a reference to the dawn spreading out its wings over the mountains. In Persian there is an expression " bird of the dawn ", the sun being thus compared to a bird. The rising sun is said to spread out his wings ; whilst the setting sun is spoken of as dropping his wings.

The sun was symbolized by a revolving wheel or disc by non-Semitic peoples also. It is a popular Armenian idea that the sun has the shape of a watermill ; it revolves and moves forward. As drops of water sputter from the mill-wheel so sunbeams shoot out from the spokes of the sun-wheel. In the old Mexican picture-books the sun is represented as a wheel with many colours.[1]

The idea of continuous motion may perhaps be contained in the names for the sun in all the Semitic languages. The Hebrew Shemesh may be connected with the Aramaic *shamesh* " to serve ", and *shumshemena,* an ant ; whilst the Hebrew for " dawn " is connected by Goldziher with *shachar* " to seek " in the sense of the movement of one who is looking for an object he has lost. In the Midrash the course of the sun is compared to a ship with 365 ropes (the number of the days of the solar year). In Greek mythology when Herakles sailed across the Okeanos, he used as a barque a golden bowl which he received as a present from Helios.

There are some seal cylinders on which a god with a horned head-dress is standing beside a gate and holding it with his two hands, apparently either in the act of opening or shutting it.[2] Menant (*Cyl. de la Chaldée,* p. 125) suggests that these were the gates of the abode of the dead through which Ishtar had to pass on her way to Hades. As the route to Hades was supposed to be the same for all souls, he regards this form of representation as showing how the soul passes through one of these gates and its

---

[1] See J. Grimm, *Deutsche Mythologie,* ⁴, ii, 585, and W. Simpson, *The Buddhist Praying Wheel,* pp. 87 sqq.
[2] See Smith, *Chaldean Account of Genesis,* p. 159.

submission to a deity standing within the gates. But the difficulty in accepting this explanation is that there is no representation of a deceased person, or of what can be described as the soul of the dead. There is a porter at the gate and a bearded god with a horned cap and rays proceeding from his shoulders. The god also seems to be raising his feet on to some kind of prominence—most probably a hill. In one hand he is usually holding what Menant describes as a branch, but what is most probably a weapon. Except for the handle it seems to be notched along the whole length. Ward's description of the whole scene is probably the correct one. The deity represented is Shamash, who has spent the night in the chambers under the earth. The sun-god, entering on his daily course, had to pass through the doors of the east, which were unlocked for him. The porter, therefore, now opens the gate to let him out for his day's course. He then climbs over the mountains whilst on his course, till he sets in the west. This idea was also represented clearly in a hymn :—

Sun-god, in the foundation of heaven thou dawnest,
And the bolt of the high heavens thou openest,
The door of heaven opens.

He rises from between the mountains of Nizir or of Elam in the east or he climbs up their sides. In his hand he has a weapon of war. Amongst Orientals the sun was not only worshipped as a deity, but also personified. In Ps. xxiv, 7–10, the gates are commanded to lift up their heads, so that the king of glory can pass through : " Lift up your heads, O ye gates, lift them up ye everlasting doors, and the king of glory shall come in. Who is this king of glory ? The Lord of Hosts, he is the King of Glory." Ward suggests that this idea may have been adopted from an old hymn to the sun.

Sometimes the god seems to be lifting himself up with his hands on to a mountain. After a time, however, instead of representing a mountain, a mere foot-stool was represented ;

whilst the weapon which the god carried also varied very considerably. One figure which Ward[1] describes is of particular interest. The sun-god is standing between two gates. His foot is lifted on to a mountain and he holds a sword in his hand. Above each gate there seems to be a small representation of a lion; whilst at the side are two guardians. It is also of interest to note that in old Babylonian legal documents there are references to the " saw " of Shamash, and by this was probably meant the " jagged key " with which he locks and unlocks the gates of heaven.

The point in connexion with our present discussion, however, is that these hills or mountains may not necessarily be part of a representation of Shamash, but may possibly have represented some other deity also. Amongst the Semites the deity was represented as a nobleman dwelling in his palace. Professor Petrie has even shown that the features and routine of the Egyptian temples were similar to those carried on in large households. The Assyrian and Hebrew words for temple, " Ekallu," really mean large house. Now, one of the most noticeable characteristics of the Babylonian temples is their enormous height. In Gen. xi, 4, we read that the people assembled in Babylonia (Valley of Shinar) and said: " Let us build a city and tower that shall reach to heaven." This truly represented the Babylonian conception of a temple. It was to be above all a " high " place, and there is a symbolic reason to account for this. Jensen[2] has shown that the Babylonians regarded the earth as a huge mountain. In fact, the earth was actually called E-kur, " Mountain House." Later, they began to identify one particular part of the earth, a mountain peak preferably, as the dwelling of the god, so that the temples which were built

---

[1] *The Seal Cylinders of Western Asia*, p. 87.
[2] *Die Kosmologie der Babylonier*, pp. 185–95. See also Herzfeld's monograph *Samarra* (Leipzig, 1908) for the minarets attached to the Mohammedan mosques.

later were known as " mountain houses ". The height
of the temple which formed the dwelling-place of the god
thus symbolized the mountain which had formed his
original home. From various references in the Old
Testament we also learn that amongst the neighbours
of the Hebrews the regular seats of religious worship were
situated on natural heights, which were often shaded by
the foliage of trees. Jeremiah xvii, 2, referring to the sin
of Israel, says : " Their children remember their altars
and their ' asherim ' by the green trees and upon the high
hills." Also in Deut. xii, 2, the Israelites are commanded
to destroy all the places, wherein the nations which they
shall possess serve their gods, upon the high mountains,
and upon the hills, and under every green tree. Again,
amongst the Semites mountains are referred to in connexion
with theophanies, and are places of idolatrous worship
(Isa. lxv, 7, etc.).

We can thus understand the symbolic idea that suggested
the zikkurats in Babylonia, the high places in Canaan, and
the sacred temple mount in Israel. Bearing the explanation
of this symbolism in mind, one can now offer, also, various
interpretations as to the symbolic meaning of the gates
on representations of the sun-god. The human-headed
lions and bulls at the entrances to Assyrian temples were
intended to protect them against the approach of demons.
Images of divinities and figures at doors and gates intended
to repel evil influences are found amongst many peoples.
Similarly, images of different deities, with all kinds of
invocations, were buried under the threshold of Assyrian
houses in order to keep enemies away from the house.
Also, in Palestine, various cup-markings, which were
intended as religious symbols, have been discovered
at the entrances to cave dwellings. These cup-markings
were symbols of a small deity worshipped by the
Aborigines.[1] In Babylonia and Assyria, gates of cities,

---

[1] See *ZATW.*, 1908, pp. 271 ff.

palaces, etc., were dedicated to a god, and each part of a house-doorway was associated with one of the great divinities. Therefore, the gates on the symbols of Shamash may have been intended to represent nothing more than the approach to a temple, which, as we have already seen, was always constructed similar to a large house. And the scenes on the seal cylinders described above would thus represent the home of the sun-god and not the rising sun.

Various other suggestions have been made as to the meaning of these gates symbols. Neubauer suggests that the name Sheariah (gate of God, 1 Chron. viii, 38; ix, 44) proves that there was a gate divinity amongst the Semites, and finds further support for this suggestion in the name " Tirathites " (1 Chron. ii, 55), which has been philologically connected with a probable locality in Judah bearing the name " Tirah " (a gate). But the fact that a man bore the name " Gate of Yah ", or that a town had the name of " Two Gates ", or that Babylon was called " Gate of God ", cannot in any way prove that the gate itself became a deity. As a matter of fact, the association of the gate with a deity would argue against its being identified with a god. In the Old Testament there are numerous references to gates as places at which courts of justice were held and disputes were decided (Gen. xxiii, 10, 18 ; Deut. xvi, 18, etc.). The reason for this custom is obvious, for the gates were places of great concourse, and courts held there would thus be easily accessible to all people. Priest and prophet often proclaimed their warnings at the gate.

From 1 Kings xxii, 10 ; 2 Chron. xviii, 9, etc., it appears that there was some particular place in the gates on which the judges sat on chairs. Nehemiah actually calls a particular gate " Counsel gate ". Even in later times one of the Sanhedrin assembled at the eastern gate. Now, seeing that Shamash was the god of justice, it seems plausible to suggest that the gates with which he is associated on these cylinders symbolically represent his abode.

In Babylonian mythology, the two solar gods, Tammuz and Gishzida, were said to be stationed at the gates of heaven. These two gods symbolized the phases of the sun on its approach to the summer solstice. It has been suggested that the two porters at the gate of Shamash symbolically represent these two deities.

Shamash, like other gods of vegetation, is often represented amidst some scenes connected with agriculture. Sometimes there is a representation of a bearded god with wheat or barley radiating from his shoulders and holding some ears of wheat in his hand.

The pure light of the sun became a symbol of beauty ; whilst amongst the Hebrews and Babylonians there are many poetical expressions which were intended to show the constant regularity with which the sun makes his journey across the heavens. The sun thus came to be regarded also as a symbol of constancy (Ps. lxxii, 5, 17 ; lxxxix, 36). In a Babylonian hymn to Shamash we read : [1]

Thou marchest across the heavens regularly,
To . . . the earth thou comest day by day.
The flood, the sea, the mountains, the earth, the heavens,
Like a [. . .] regularly thou traversest day by day.

NINGIRSU

Ningirsu, in some respects, is identical with the solar god Ninib, and as he was patron of Lagash and presided over its agricultural activity, he was known as " the god of the Corn-heap ". As such he is symbolically represented by a lion with a bough in its front claws. Sometimes he is also represented, like Ramman, with a sceptre consisting of the boughs of a tree (Janneau, *Une dynastie chaldéene, les rois d'Ur*, 35, fig. xi). In an old hymn he was also identified with Tammuz. He was

---

[1] *Shamash Religious Texts*, p. 13.

specially associated with the number fifty, and his temple in Lagash was known as " The house of fifty ". Gudea called the ship of Ningirsu *Kar-nuna-tu-udda*, " The ship of one that rises out of the dam of the deep," representing the sun as rising out of the deep. His most common symbol was an eagle, which very often also has a lion's head. On the silver vase of Entemena there are four lion-headed eagles, two of which seem to be seizing a lion with each talon. The lion may perhaps represent Bau, the mother-goddess of Lagash. The whole representation would, therefore, stand for Bau and Ningirsu. On some of the monuments of Lagash there is a representation of a lion-headed eagle seizing two lions. Sometimes Ningirsu is represented either as a goat or as a male figure sitting on a goat. On a seal cylinder from about the time of the dynasty of Ur there is such a representation (Weber, *Amtliche Berichte aus den Konigl. Kunstsammlungen*, xxxiv, 157). On one figure Ningirsu is represented with his wife Bau sitting on his knees and his arm affectionately around her (Sarzec-Heuzey, *Découvertes en Chaldée*, pl. xxxiv, 5). Ningirsu is represented as the protecting deity of Lagash on the Vulture Stele (Heuzey-Thureau-Dangin, *Stèle des Vautours*, pl. i). He holds an axe in his right hand, and his enemies whom he has caught are struggling about in a net which he holds in his left hand. Many of the important gods of the pantheon, such as Ea, Sin, and Marduk are similarly represented by a net.

Seeing that Ningirsu was a solar deity connected with agriculture and vegetation, it was only natural that he should be regarded as bestowing the "waters of life" on mankind. To the Semites running water was symbolical of life,[1] and the god, as giver of life, is therefore represented as pouring out water from a jar or vase. We have also representations of a male figure seated on a throne with

---

[1] Cf. Hebrew מַיִם חַיִּים " living water ".

a small vase of water in his right hand. At times the god is represented as pouring out water from a vase which he holds in his hand, and on one tablet there is even a " plant of life " growing out of a jar from which the god pours the water (Genouillac, *Inventaire des tablettes de Tello*, iii, 2, pl. i, 5963). Sometimes the god is referred to as being provided with horns. At times he is also symbolically represented by a club. On Kudurru IX (MDP. i, 178) there is a representation of a lion with a club, which Hommel regards as symbolizing Nergal.

NERGAL

Nergal, like Ninib, was a god of war and pestilence, and Cuthah was his sacred city. He represented the sun at midday, and the summer solstice, whose heat brought fever and pestilence to the inhabitants of Babylonia. It is important to note, however, that as a war-god he does not symbolize the powerful deity who assists his worshippers to destroy their enemies, but represents rather the fever and pestilence which accompany war.[1] This trait of his character is represented by his name, *Lugal-gira* " raging king ". He wanders about at night with his terrible weapons, which consist of all kinds of dreadful diseases, and battles with mankind, capturing as many victims as possible and imprisoning them in the confines of his gloomy domains. On account of this aspect of his character, he is referred to as " Lord of weapons ". Tigleth Pileser I says he received in his hands the powerful weapons and exalted bows of Adar and Nergal (KB. i, 38). In the Tell el Amarna tablets plague is called " the hand of Nergal ".

Being the god who was the cause of death, it was only natural that he should next develop into a " Lord of the Lower Regions ", where the dead were condemned to a miserable imprisonment in a region full of horror. He

---

[1] Jensen, *Kosmologie*, pp. 481 sq.

was thus described as being of a cruel and forbidding aspect, and the lion is, therefore, one of the most common symbols by which he is represented. The lion is also found as the animal of Apollo on the Lycian monuments, and it was probably regarded by many Semitic peoples as a symbol of the summer heat. There is an astronomical text which reads : " On the 18th of Tammuz, Nergal descends into the underworld, and on the 28th of Kislev he ascends again. Shamash and Nergal are one."[1] The sun is represented as the underworld, because in his light the stars disappear. On the other hand, the moon on account of her constant renewal, represented resurrection, and therefore the upper world.

NUSKU

Nusku was originally a solar deity, and thus came to be regarded also as a fire-god. He was often identified with Nabu, the god of wisdom. This can be seen from the sceptre which formed part of his ideogram. Shalmaneser II on his obelisk (KB. i, 130) describes him as " the bearer of the brilliant sceptre " (*Nashi hatti elliti*). Ashurnasirpal, in his monolith, employs a similar expression with reference to him. But, as a fire-god, it was only natural that he should be identified with Gibil. He was also described as " son of Anu ", the god of the heavens, in order to express metaphorically the divine origin of fire. As a means of purification fire played an important part in the incantation ritual. But it was also the means by which the offerings on the altar were consumed and brought to the gods. In a hymn to Nusku, we read :—

O Nusku, consumer, overpowering the enemy,
No table is spread in the temple without thee.
The great gods do not inhale the incense without thee.
Shamash, the judge, expects no judgment without thee.

This is the reason why Nusku was also known as " messenger of the gods ".

[1] See *KAT.*, 3rd ed., 388.

It was only natural that a fire-god should be symbolically represented by a lamp such as is found on various boundary stones. On the Kudurru of Nebuchadrezzar I the lamp seems to be on a kind of pole. On the Kudurru of Nazi Maruttash it has also an inscription of identification (MDP. ii, 90, col. iv, 18 f.), which reads (*ilu*) *Bil-Gi iz-zu shibru sha ilu Nusku* (powerful Gibil, instrument of Nusku).

ARURU

Aruru, the goddess who is represented in the epic of Gilgamesh as having created man out of a lump of clay, is symbolically represented on the boundary stone of Nazi Maruttash by a bird perched upon a rod. An explanation of the symbol is difficult, but this may have been intended to represent her inferior character as messenger of the gods.

NABU

The most important attribute of Nabu was that of wisdom, and he embodied in his person all the wisdom of the gods. His name Nabu designated him also as a " proclaimer ", and he was called " god of the stylus ". On boundary stones his symbol is usually the stylus of the scribe. As the god of wisdom and writing he instructs Ashurbanipal to collect the literary remains of the past. The worship of Nabu became most popular at the time of Adad Nirari IV (810–782 B.C.), and an inscription which was placed on a statue of the god actually ends with the words: " O posterity, trust in Nabu, trust in no other god." But it was by the Neo-Babylonian kings whose names, like Nabu-Kudur-Usur, Nabu-Naid, contained his name as one of the elements, that he was held in special esteem, and was constantly invoked as the patron of art and literature and the one who opened the ear to understanding. In this connexion one is reminded of an oracle which purports to come from Nabu and is uttered by a

woman named Baya.   The oracle ends with the words :
" I am Nabu, lord of the writing tablet, glorify me."

On one stele from the time of Tiglath Pileser III (KB. iv,
p. 102, l. 3) he is described as " the one who holds the bright
tablet, the carrier of the tablet of fate of the gods ".[1] This
merely expressed metaphorically his duties as the scribe
of the gods who recorded their decisions upon the tablets
of fate on which they inscribed the destinies of individuals.
But it has also been suggested that this represented his
character as an intermediary, and that the god whose orders
he carried out originally was Ea.   This is very likely, for
Nabu was originally a water-god, like Ea.   The epithets
bestowed upon both gods in various texts are exceedingly
similar, and as the god of wisdom he is constantly referred
to as the " son of Ea ", and is also regarded as the revealer
of the art of writing.   This accounts for his being described
in historical texts as (ilu) tashmitum, god of revelation.
His symbol was a staff.   This can be interpreted as representing either the stylus of a writer or a ruler's sceptre ;
whilst his temple at Babylon was known as E-pad-ka-
lama-suma, " The house of him who gives the sceptre of
the world."   On the Nahr el Kelb rock inscription and the
Bavian relief the symbol is represented by one vertical
line, but on the Esarhaddon Stele and the Sargon Stele there
are two parallel lines of equal length.   In the later
Assyrian inscriptions he is referred to as holding a sceptre,
which must have been intended to symbolize his power as
a ruler.

Every New Year's Day Nabu paid a visit to his father,
Marduk.   His statue was carried in procession along the
streets leading to Marduk's temple, and Marduk also accompanied him on part of his journey back.   By this the close
union between Marduk and Nabu was symbolized.   But
this ceremony had also another symbolical meaning.   The
great gods were all believed to assemble in a special chapel
on this occasion, where they decreed the fate of humanity

---

[1] *Sabit kan duppi elli nashi dup shimat ilani.*

for the new year. Marduk as the head of the pantheon was believed to preside over the assembly ; whilst Nabu as the intermediary and scribe amongst the gods sat by his side and recorded their decisions.

NINIB

Ninib was originally a solar deity, and, like Marduk, who was also at first a solar deity, he is described as the firstborn of Ea. As the former solar god of Nippur, he absorbed the duties of other solar deities until his name became a kind of general designation for sun-god. Jensen, in his *Kosmologie* (pp. 457–75), has shown that he particularly represented the morning sun, and thus came to symbolize the approach of the summer season which brings about the revival of nature. The sun was also regarded as a god of healing, and such expressions as " Light of heaven and earth ", by which he is described, represent his beneficent character as a solar deity. When one wishes to appeal against the power of the demons, it is to Ninib that this appeal is to be made. Furthermore, his consort Gula represented the earth as the source of vegetation and thus symbolized the great female principle ; whilst the union of sun and earth, by which all nature is revived, was symbolically represented by the myth in which both deities celebrate a marriage ceremony on New Year's Day.[1] But the powerful rays of the sun, particularly in a country like Babylonia, might also be destructive, and so Ninib was looked upon also as a powerful destructive force, whose help was invaluable in warfare. The Assyrian kings constantly emphasized his strength as a warrior, and ascribed their successes in their hunting expeditions and military campaigns to the mighty weapons which he placed in their hands, and the assistance with which he favoured them. Tiglath Pileser I, Ashur Nasir Pal, Shamshi Ramman, and Nebuchadrezzar I were particularly

---

[1] Cf. Ps. xix, in which the sun is described as a bridegroom coming forth from his bridal chamber.

fond of referring to these qualities of the god, and of invoking his aid in such expeditions. In the astrological system he is identified with Saturn, who has many of the attributes of Nergal, the great Babylonian war-god. And in many old myths his most common title is " warrior ".[1] The weapons of Ninib are very numerous, and in one inscription twenty-two weapons are actually assigned to him, each one having a series of ornamental names, such as " Destroyer of the Lord ", " Victor in battle ", " The one cutting off necks ", " The wide net of hostile hands ". In the *Annals of Ashurbanipal* (col. ix, 84 f., KB. ii, p. 226) he is called " The Spear " ; whilst in Shurpu (iv, 75) he is described as " Lord of the weapons ". It was only natural that the Assyrians should have regarded the great war-god who helped them in their hunting expeditions as the king of beasts, and should therefore have represented his symbol by the heads of two lions. This symbol is particularly common on boundary stones ; and on the Kudurru of Melishihu (MDP. i and ii), for example, it consists of a winged lion with a tail of feathers. According to Luschan and Hommel, the two lions' heads on a pole of the Bavian inscription are also symbols of the same god. At one period Zamama was identified with Ninib, and both gods were represented by the head of a vulture (MDP. i, 168).

Sin

The moon-god, Sin, was known by various names and designations, chief amongst which was that of En-zu, " Lord of knowledge." In fact, Sin may be a contraction of an original Si-in, which, in turn, may again be equivalent to the form En-zu inverted.[2] His knowledge and wisdom lay in reading the signs of the heavens, and in the astrological system of the Babylonians he even took precedence over Shamash, the sun-god, and was known as " the father of the gods ". He is described in hymns as " merciful father " and

---

[1] Hrozny, *Sumerisch-Babylonische Mythen von dem Gotte Nin-rag.*
[2] Combe, *Histoire du Culte de Sin*, pp. 1–16.

as " lord of fate " (*bel purusse*). We are told in the annals of Ashurbanipal that the priest reads by night on the disc of the full moon what Nabu has written on it, thus representing the character of the god as an oracle. His importance was symbolized by the way in which he was represented on seal cylinders as an old man with a long flowing beard, said to be of the colour of lapis lazuli. The symbolic colour of the moon was probably regarded as green because she was looked upon as the goddess of resurrection, the moon on account of her constant renewal representing the resurrection of the dead. She was described as *inbu sha ina ramanishu ibbanu*, fruit which produces itself from itself. On seal cylinders Sin is represented with a cap on his head, on which are the horns of the moon. This was no doubt due to the appearance of a " horn " which the moon suggests at a certain phase. The horn was regarded as the crown of Sin, and thus came to symbolize his power. As a result of this the horn became amongst the Assyrians a general symbol of divinity, and we can thus understand why the Assyrian kings, in order to symbolize their power, so often adorned themselves with a horned crown. Sin is described as " the bearer of the exalted horns " (KB. iv, 102, *nashi qarne siruti*) ; whilst many of the Babylonian and Assyrian kings are represented as wearing rounded caps with parallel horns encircling them from behind. Hittite deities wore caps ornamented with several horns, and Phœnician goddesses were usually represented as having the horns of a cow like Ashtoreth Karnaim (" of the two horns "). In the Egyptian religion Hathor, Ra, and Cneph were all depicted with horns, and part of the head-dress of an Egyptian king consisted of horns. Also on the stele of Zinjirli (Luschan, *Ausgrabungen in Sendschirli*, Tab. vi) Hadad has horns upon his head. Similarly, in Hebrew literature the word " horn " is equivalent to power. " To break the horns " of a people signifies defeat, " to raise the horns " means pride, victory. Balaam described God as having horns like a wild ox

(Num. xxiii, 22) ; whilst the tribe of Joseph is said to have horns like those of a unicorn, with which it will push people (Deut. xxxiii, 17). In paintings Moses was represented with horns. This is usually explained by the passage in Exod. xxxiv, 29, where we are told that the skin of his face shone (literally, sent forth horns). The expression is taken here to mean " sent forth beams of light ", but it has been suggested that there may be a textual error. The legend no doubt grew through the translation of the Vulgate " quod cornuta esset facies sua ". Similarly Cernunnos, whom the Gauls worshipped as god of the underworld, Agni of the Indians, and Yama in Buddhist mythology, were represented with horns. One can multiply this symbolism from the religions of many ancient peoples.[1] It seems fairly certain that in many instances the horns worn by the gods were really relics of their earlier animal form, and that the horn became a symbol of power because man noted how the horned animal made use of its horns as a destructive force. But in many cases, however, this symbolism probably arose through the crescent moon bearing a resemblance to a pair of horns.[2] The moon's crescent apparently also suggested the sight of a sailing barque, and the moon-god is therefore described in various Sumerian hymns as sailing along the heavens in a ship. In one of these hymns we read :—

Father Nannar, in thy passing on high, in thy sovereign
    glory !
O barque, sailing on high along the heaven in thy sovereign
    glory !
Father Nannar, as thou sailest along the resplendent road,
Father Nannar, when, like a barque on the floods, thou
    sailest along !

---

[1] In one of the legends of Alexander the Great he is made to say, " I know that thou hast made the horns to grow upon my head, that I may crush the rich of the earth " (Kampers, *Hist. Jahrb. der Görresgesellsch.*, xix, 434 ff.).

[2] Scheftelowitz, *Archiv für Religionswissenschaft*, xv, 461 ff.

Sin was often represented by a crescent as his symbol. This may be seen on the boundary stone of Nabu aplu Iddin, the rock inscription of Nahr el Kelb and the Sargon stele, etc. The moon's "horn" suggested also the appearance of a heifer (cf. *Talmud Babli, Rosh Hashanah*, 22B), where the moon is compared to a heifer), and as Anu was the god of the heavens the relationship between Anu and Sin was symbolized by describing Sin as "the heifer of Anu". He is also often described as a powerful bull (*buru ekdu*), and in one of the hymns addressed to him there runs a passage : "Oh strong bull, great of horns, perfect in form, with long flowing beard of the colour of lapis-lazuli."

The importance of Sin in the astrological system was symbolized by the formation of a triad—Sin, Shamash, Ishtar. Sin was given first place as representing the hosts of heaven, and the most common sign with which his name is written is that which represents the number "thirty", because in astrological reports all months were assumed to have thirty days. Ishtar, as the daughter of the moon, was, therefore, written with the number fifteen, and Shamash with twenty.

MARDUK

The ideographs "bur umu" which compose the name of Marduk, mean "child of day". This in itself would suggest that Marduk was originally a solar deity. But "buru" also means a young bull, and seeing that in ancient times the bull was regarded as symbolizing the power residing in the sun, it forms an appropriate component for the ideograph representing a solar god. There are many representations of the god which include a figure of a bull. Thus Ward describes one monument where a god is represented as sitting with one bull under his feet, another above his hand, and a third behind him.[1] Jeremias attempts to explain this symbolism by means of his astral theory.

---

[1] *Seal Cylinders of Western Asia*, p. 116, fig. 327.

Marduk, originally a solar deity, was brought into prominence by the dynasty of Hammurabi, which originated in Sippar, the home of sun-worship. In the astrological system Jupiter is identified with Marduk. The ideogram for Jupiter, which means " Bull of the Sun ", is explained by Hommel as " Furrow of Heaven " (meaning furrow ploughed by bull of the sun). In various Eastern religions the king is represented as a husbandman cultivating the land and bringing forth the harvest. Nebuchadrezzar describes himself as husbandman of Babylon, and the Emperor of China draws a furrow every year with a yellow plough. When Marduk is pictured as standing or sitting on a bull the symbol, therefore, really represents the king and his plough.

As a solar god Marduk was, like Shamash, the judge of mankind, and in religious texts he is therefore also described as a ruler. He controls the destinies of man, protects the weak from the strong, and even guides the counsels of the gods. We have a monument with a clear representation of the god, from the time of Marduk Nadin Shum (c. 900 B.C.). He has a crown of feathers on his head, holds a spear in his right hand and a staff and ring in his left hand, all of which symbolize his power and authority ; whilst the serpent which lies at his feet is the symbol with which he is identified. His astral character is shown by the star-shaped targets which cover the long cloak in which he is clad.[1] On Assyrian monuments all the gods are represented as having a staff and ring, but in early Babylonian monuments the only other god who is also represented with staff and ring is Shamash. In considering some early Babylonian monuments, particularly those from the first dynasty of Babylon, which contain a representation of a deity having a staff and ring without any inscription, it becomes exceedingly difficult, therefore, to decide whether it is

---

[1] Weissbach, *Babylonische Miscellen*, 16, fig. 1 ; Gressmann, *Texte und Bilder zum AT.*, ii, 59, Abb. 96.

Marduk or Shamash who is intended. Marduk also symbolized the sun of spring, which brings about the growth of vegetation and the revival of nature, so that in the story of Ishtar's descent to Hades, he is represented as filling with new life what appeared to be dead. When the great Babylonian king Hammurabi ascended the throne and succeeded in uniting North and South Babylonia under his rule, he made Babylon his capital city and Marduk its god, the head of the pantheon. Marduk is now, therefore, represented as a warrior who by reason of his supreme power holds sway over the other gods. This explains why his symbol is also a spear and sometimes a scimitar, which is so often found on Babylonian art belonging to the period of Hammurabi and the rise of Babylon. The god is usually represented as holding the scimitar downwards, though it occasionally rests on his shoulder. On Kudurru I (MDP. i, 168) there is a spear with the inscription *ilu Marduk*. On a Kudurru of Melishihu (MDP. i and ii), the same symbol is represented with some kind of horned animal. There are many seal cylinders from the time of the dynasty of Hammurabi on which this symbol may be clearly seen ; whilst on many boundary stones from the Kassite period there is a lance placed on a chest with a serpent near by, another variation of the same symbol. With reference to the serpent as a symbol of Marduk one may refer in particular to an inscription of Agum Kakrime (KB. iii, pp. 140 ff.), where we are given a full description of how Marduk's statue was brought back to Esagila, and after a detailed account of the manner in which it was adorned, we are informed that a serpent lay at the god's feet. Marduk's character as a warrior is further symbolized by the long detailed list of weapons with which he is described as arming himself on entering into the fray with Tiamat (*Enuma Elish*, col. iv, 29 ff.). In the story of the combat between Marduk and Tiamat, when the former was appointed to be the avenger against the latter, and lord of heaven and earth, his universal power was evidently symbolized by a miracle. They placed a " garment " in their midst, and spoke to him, saying :—

When thou openest thy mouth the garment shall disappear !
Command it again, so shall the garment (again) be unhurt !
Then he commanded with his mouth, and the garment
    was destroyed ;
He commanded again, and the garment was (again)
    created.
When the gods, his fathers, saw what proceeded from his
    mouth
They rejoiced, they did homage : Marduk is King.

The expression " be unhurt " can hardly be used of a cloak, and Jeremias therefore suggests [1] that it is a cosmic cloak which is referred to, symbolizing Marduk's universal power and lordship over the destinies of mankind. He thinks that the account of the High Priest's robe and the ephod with their adornments had the same symbolic thought underlying them (Exod. xxviii, 31), and mentions the fact that one of the mediaeval German Emperors had a coronation mantle made in Byzantium with representations from the apocalypse to symbolize the same idea. In the story of the combat when Marduk's work is finished, the Igigi gather round him in adoration and fifty names are bestowed on him. According to one tradition, the number fifty corresponds to the number of the Igigi, and this, therefore, symbolically represents Marduk's absorption of the qualities of all the other gods.

This can also be seen from the fact that in astronomical texts he is often described as *sharru*—the king par excellence—and even in the Gilgamesh epic we read :—

Upon the first appearance of dawn
There arose from the horizon dark clouds
Within which Ramman caused his thunder to resound ;
Nabu and Sharru marched at the front.

---

[1] *The Old Testament in the Light of the Ancient East*: Engl. Trans., vol. i, p. 177.

With the transfer of the headship of the pantheon to Marduk, he also assumed the attributes of En-lil, the storm-god, and is therefore represented as subjecting the winged monster Tiamat. The horned dragon from being the symbol of En-lil, now became the symbol of Marduk, and subsequently of Ashur, as the head of the Assyrian pantheon. In the new Babylonian Empire, there gradually arose a tendency to associate divine power with only the more important gods of the pantheon. Marduk thus absorbed the rôle of other gods, and his name actually became a generic term for deity. Thus, in a tablet published by T. G. Pinches (*Journal of the Victoria Institute*, xxviii, 8–10), Nergal is called " the Marduk of Warfare ", Nebo " the Marduk of earthly possessions ", Ninib " the Marduk of strength ", En-lil " the Marduk of sovereignty ", Nebo " the Marduk of possession ". In a lexicographical tablet there is a reference to four dogs of Marduk ; whilst on a seal cylinder representing the legend of the flight of Etana are two dogs in a crouching position. The dogs are a symbol of the solar god Marduk.[1]

BEL

The very name Bel, " Lord," par excellence, signified the wide scope of his power as Lord of the universe. As Jastrow says : " He represents as it were the unification of the various forces whose seat and sphere of action is among the inhabited parts of the globe." [2] Therefore with Anu, the god of the heavens, and Ea, the god of the watery ocean, he symbolized the eternal laws of the universe. In the Semitic pantheon Bel took the place of the Sumerian En-lil, whose manifestations, as his name designates (Lord of the Storm), was the wind or storm and all the phenomena which accompany it such as thunder, lightning, etc. The storm which is referred to as his word is his great weapon, and he is usually represented as a rushing torrent which brings terrible disaster and havoc

[1] *RBA.* 528. [2] *RBA.* p. 52.

in its train. On seal cylinders one may often see representations of a god with jars on his shoulders pouring forth streams of water. This could very well be a symbol for different gods of the Babylonian pantheon, but as Bel was believed to control the upper waters, and was regarded as the god of the atmosphere above the earth, it would most suitably symbolize his power. So long as he pours out the waters, they are for the benefit of mankind ; but once they are beyond his power the fertilizing rain is turned into a curse and becomes a deluge. Many of the terra-cotta images of Bel found at Nippur represent him as an old man with a long flowing beard, holding what is most likely a thunderbolt in his hand.[1] Bel was also described as "the great mountain". His consort was known as *Nin-harsag*, "lady of the mountain " ; whilst his temple was known as E-Kur,[2] "mountain-house." The following passage, taken from an old Babylonian hymn to Bel, is worthy of note in this connexion :—

O great mountain of Bel, imkharsag,
Whose summit rivals the heavens,
Whose foundations are laid in the bright abysmal sea,
Resting in the lands as a mighty steer,
Whose horns are gleaming like the radiant sun,
As the stars of heaven are filled with lustre.

On the relief of Maltaja he is represented with long flowing hair and a long beard. In his left hand he has a ring and staff, and his right hand is slightly raised. From his cloak projects a sword, and he is standing on an animal with a jackal's head. This would agree well with the older conception of Bel as creator of the universe, and therefore in conflict with a monster whom he conquers. On the Esarhaddon Stele the gods mentioned in the text are represented either by statues or by their symbols. The

---

[1] Hilprecht, *Explorations in Bible Lands*, p. 464.
[2] Probably connected with the word *igura* which occurs in Aramaic Papyri of the fifth century B.C. See Sachau, *Drei Aramäische Papyrusurkunden aus Elephantine.*

third figure, which is somewhat similar to the one described above, causes some difficulty in identification. Seeing, however, that Bel is referred to in the text and is not elsewhere represented either by his symbol or otherwise, it seems most plausible to suggest that he is represented by this figure. His supreme power is represented in various ways. In the myth of the storm-god Zu we are told that En-lil of Nippur holds the tablets of fate, by means of which is symbolized his controlling authority over the whole of mankind. He bears the title " lord of the lands " (*bel-matati*)—a title which was afterwards transferred to Marduk—" father of the gods," " king of all the Anunnaki," etc. Another mark by which Bel can be recognized is his cap with horns, which was apparently also intended to mark his supreme power. We are informed in some inscriptions that he is clothed with the crown of his lord-ship (*age belutishu*). As will be noted from the hymn quoted above, he is often described as a " mighty bull ", and his horns are said to shine like the brilliance of the sun. This idea, no doubt, goes back to an earlier time, when he was thought of, primarily, as the god of vegetation. In many religions of antiquity the bull symbolized the power residing in the sun, and to the Babylonians it was thus an appropriate symbol for the nature of En-lil as a solar god and lord of vegetation. We have already referred to the golden calves made by Jeroboam as symbols of the God of Israel who had brought His people out of Egypt,[1] and to the suggestion that the Israelites may have derived this symbolism from the Canaanites, to whom the bull was the symbol of Baal. Furthermore, bull symbolism, as we have also noted already, was common amongst almost all the Semitic races. And as to Assyria, one may also say fairly definitely, that the massive bulls at the entrances to the Assyrian temples are representations of En-lil; whilst the numerous figures which have been found having the

---

[1] 1 Kings xii, 28 ; see chapter on Animal Kingdom.

form of a crouching bull with a human face are also symbols
of the same god.

ANU

Originally Anu was a mere personification of the heavens,
but later he was raised to the dignity of symbolizing " the
abstract principle of which both the heavens and earth are
emanations " (Jensen, *Kosmologie*, p. 274). His position
in the pantheon was all-important, and was symbolized in
various ways. He was known as the " Father " of the
gods, and his temple as *Eadda*, " house of the father."
The Anunnaki and Igigi are designated as his offspring,
whilst the sun's ecliptic is known as " the way of Anu ".
The heavenly origin of fire was further symbolized by
designating Gibil and Nusku as the sons of Anu. He is
always represented as a powerful god, and his symbol is a
horned crown. In the building inscription of Esarhaddon
there is a reference to the crown of Anu (*anim agushu*),
whilst in the Etana myth (KB. vi, 1, 585 f.) we are informed
that a sceptre, diadem, royal crown, and staff are placed
before Anu in heaven. Ur-bau described Nannar as the
" bull of Anu ". The reference is, of course, to the
position of the moon in the heavens and to its crescent
shape, which represents a bull's horns.

ASHUR

Ashur was the great war-god of Assyria, the protector
of her armies and the embodiment of her genius. With the
establishment of Assyria as a military power it was natural,
therefore, that his influence should have increased
enormously, eventually attaining the position of supreme
god of her pantheon. In fact, the other deities really
became " diminutive Ashurs by the side of the big one,
and in proportion as they approach nearer to the character
of Ashur himself, is their hold upon the royal favour
strengthened ".[1]

---

[1] *RBA.* p. 202.

Shalmaneser II conquers his enemies with the powerful weapons of Ashur (KB. i, p. 166), the god places a powerful weapon in the hand of Tiglath Pileser I (KB. i, p. 22), whilst he also stands at the side of Ashurnasirpal I with his unconquerable weapons (KB. i, p. 54). Whenever the names of a number of deities are mentioned, his name always occurs first. The most frequent expressions are " with the help of Ashur my Lord . . . ", or " with the help of Ashur and Ishtar and the great gods my lords who walk at my side . . . I defeated my enemies ". Ashur was originally a solar deity, and the Assyrians explained his name as a contraction of An-shar, " Anu of the universe." We thus have in the combination of nshur and Ishtar a representation of the union of sun and earth standing by the Assyrian kings in their hour of need. The solar character of Ashur was symbolized by a sun disc with wavy rays extending to the circumference of the disc. This symbol was often placed by the Assyrian kings above their images which they erected on their monuments, and it lent the god a much more spiritual character than if he had been portrayed in human or animal form. Later, in order to represent the warlike character of the god, this pure symbol was despiritualized, and a figure of a warrior with an arrow was sometimes represented in the disc. A good example of these different types of symbols may be seen from some discoveries which were made some time ago at Khorsabad. One of these, which seems to have been the top of an Assyrian standard, shows bulls as symbols of the sun-god and also the rays of the sun. Another one is a more spiritual symbol, consisting merely of a sun-disc with protruding rays. Later, this was despiritualized, and the warlike character of the god was symbolized by the addition of the warrior with the arrow (Botta et Flandin, *Monument de Ninive*, ii, pl. 158).[1]

---

[1] For further symbols of this type see Ward, *Seal Cylinders of W. Asia*, pp. 224, 227, and Mansell, *British Museum Photographs*, Nos. 391, 394, etc. ; also Menant, *Recherches sur la Glyptique Orientale*, ii, 17.

The question has often been raised as to why Ashur was represented by a standard. The most obvious suggestion is that it was chosen on account of the ease with which it could be carried about from place to place and brought into the thick of the fray as an assurance that the god was present with his people as their protector and deliverer. The fact that Ashur was represented by a movable symbol would also explain why so few temples were erected in his honour. But it must not be forgotten that it was only at a later time, when the Assyrian military genius had fully developed, that his symbol was changed to a standard, and that originally he was represented by a statue. Sennacherib, in his building inscription, speaks of the images of Ashur (Meissner-Rost, *Bauinschriften Sanheribs*, p. 94) ; whilst on the Esarhaddon Stele there is a representation of the god with a long cloak and a crown. In his left hand he has a ring and staff, and in his right hand he holds some kind of weapon. He seems to be standing on two bulls, one of which has a horn projecting from its head. On the rock inscription of Nahr el Kelb, the Bavian Relief and the Sargon Stele, he seems to be wearing a crown, and in Esarhaddon's building inscription there is a reference to the artistic kingly crown made of gold and precious stones, which is a symbol of his sovereignty.

RAMMAN

Ramman or Adad was an Amoritish deity known in Syria and Palestine as Hadad, and imported into the Euphrates Valley from the west. The ideograph Im, by which the name of this god is represented, means distress, and thus symbolizes his character as a storm-god. In the myth of Zu it is Ramman—the storm-god par excellence—who is called upon to go and conquer Zu with his thunderbolt. Seeing that he manifested his power in thunder and lightning, his symbol is the thunderbolt or forked lightning. " May Adad attack his land with awful lightning," reads an inscription of Tiglath Pileser I. On the Bavian Relief his symbol is a three-pronged fork of lightning, the meaning of which is explained in the inscription attached to it (Jensen, *Hittiter*, 143, Anm. 1). On a seal cylinder dating from about the period of the first dynasty of Babylon between the determinative *ilu* and the ideogram *Im*, which stands for Ramman, there is the symbol of a lightning fork. A similar symbol occurs on the Nahr-el-kelb rock inscription and the Sargon Stele. On the Esarhaddon Stele from Zinjirli he is represented as holding a three-pronged lightning fork in his right hand ; whilst his left is slightly raised. On the relief of Shamashreshuṣur he is represented with long hair and a beard. He wears a long cloak, and holds a two-pronged lightning fork in each hand.

The inscription *ṣalam Adad* (image of Adad) shows clearly the deity whom the symbol is supposed to represent.

As the god of storms and thunder, Ramman was looked upon also as a beneficent deity whose rain-storms bring fertility to the soil and supply the inhabitants of the land with water. But as thunder and lightning might also bring destruction in their wake, for heavy rain-storms would destroy the crops and bring hunger and ruin, he came to be regarded as a war-god, and Assyrian kings constantly refer to him as the warrior-deity who helps them to destroy their enemies and achieve their conquests. To Nebuchadrezzar I, for example, he is the god of battles who helps him to destroy his enemies. This aspect of his character is symbolized by an axe. In Layard, *Monuments of Nineveh*, pl. lxv, he is represented with an axe in his right hand and the lightning fork in his left. He has a short cloak with a girdle round his loins and four horns projecting from his head. Sometimes he is also represented as holding a spear as well as a lightning fork (Menant, *Glyptique*, i, 165, fig. 103). Similarly, on another seal-cylinder, he is represented as standing on the back of a bull and holding a pair of reins and a lightning fork in his left hand, and a hatchet in his right (Blinkenberg, *The Thunder Weapon in Religion and Folklore*, p. 26, fig. 13). The hatchet as a component of the symbol by which Ramman was represented reminds one of pre-Mycenæan Crete, where we find Zeus represented with the double hammer (Sofas Muller, *Urgeschichte Europas*, 59) ; whilst in Europe we have Thor with a double hammer. Under another form Ramman was worshipped as Rimmon at Damascus (2 Kings v, 18). He was also the Teshup of the Hittites imported into Rome by Syrian traders.[1] Ramman was also a solar deity. This trait of his character he probably acquired through his association with Enlil, of whom he became a counter-part, and although he acquired later the character of storm-god, he was always, in Assyrian literature, brought into association with the sun-god. This may be due to the fact that, being known as Barku, the god of lightning, it was only natural for him to be connected with the sun, the great light of the heavens. In any case, his character as a solar deity was symbolized in various ways. He was known as the " Lord of Justice ", a term strictly applied to Shamash, and, like Shamash, he is also referred to as " Lord of Revelation ", and is consulted on questions of birth. For example, in K. 2370, we are informed that a priest consults Ramman because one of his clients has, contrary to his expectations, given birth to a girl. Again, it is of interest to note that the bull, which, as we have already seen, symbolized the power residing in the sun, formed part of his symbol, and so we sometimes meet with his symbol, consisting of a two-pronged fork of lightning on the back of a bull (Delaporte, *Catalogue des Cylindres Orientaux de la Bibliothèque Nationale*, pl. xvii, 247–9, Kudurru of Nazi Maruttash, MDP. i and ii). On the boundary stone of Melishihu there is a small pedestal on which are some lightning forks ; whilst in front there is a bull.[2] Just as Ramman was associated with Shamash, so he was also often brought into connexion with Anu, who was originally also a

---

[1] Jupiter Dolichenus is really Ramman-Teshup.
[2] See also Layard, *Monuments of Nineveh*, i, pl. 82, and C. Bezold, *Ninive und Babylon*, Abb. 45, S. 57.

solar deity. In religious writings, for example, Ramman was often symbolically represented as the son of Anu, and in the temple of Ashur which Tiglath Pileser I rebuilt, Ramman was placed by the side of Anu and permitted to share the honour with him. This partnership of sun-god and storm-god, which is a common phenomenon in the Assyrian religion, would no doubt symbolize the two great forces of nature upon which the welfare of the country depended. Sometimes Ramman is represented as holding a sceptre made from the boughs of a tree, and Prinz (*Altorientalische Symbolik*, p. 128) has suggested that this may have been intended to represent him as a god of vegetation.

EA

Like various other early races of mankind, the Babylonians had many water-deities. It is difficult for primitive man to bring water in its many forms under one divinity, and in ancient times each individual body of water was thus believed to have its own spirit. In the study of ethnography one finds that water was worshipped amongst many races in their infancy. Early man regarded water as a living force, which controlled his life and existence. It gives fish to the fisherman and crops to the husbandman. The onrushing torrent is caused merely by the anger of the spirits which the water contains—for water is in reality made up of a number of spirits which are its very soul and cause its movements. Man therefore prayed to water and propitiated it by means of sacrifices. Even to-day amongst the Kaffirs streams are worshipped as personal deities and a man will ask leave of the spirit or stream previous to crossing it. The sacredness with which the Ganges is held by the modern Hindus provides, perhaps, a better-known example of this type of worship.

The most important reason to account for the many water deities worshipped by the Babylonians is probably the fact that the country depends to a great extent upon her streams and canals for her fertility, and as each stream and canal had its own deity, the number of such gods increased considerably.

Of the many water-deities worshipped in Babylonia, Ea held supreme rank. Ur Bau, who built a temple to Ea at Girsu, calls him "king of Eridu". It was no doubt the importance of Eridu and its dependence on the Persian Gulf which was regarded by the Babylonians as an illimitable sheet of water, that caused Ea to be regarded as the great water deity of their land. The very name of the god is composed of two ideograms, meaning "house" and "water". Sargon, in naming some of the gates of his palace after the gods of the pantheon, describes Ea as "the one who unlocks fountains". In the well-known myth of Adapa the latter is described as "the Son of Ea", by which is meant that the fisherman is placed under the god's protection.

When Ea is described as the "king of the ocean"[1] it is not the salt ocean which is referred to. This was really symbolized by Tiamat, but Ea represented the ocean which flows under the earth and by means of canals irrigates the fields and gives fertility to the soil. He thus came to be regarded as a great beneficent power. In the Deluge narrative it is he who prevents En-lil from carrying out his purpose, and this may represent an ancient rivalry between the centres of the two gods, Eridu and Nippur. He also occupies an important place in the incantation texts. Water, as we have already seen, was an important means of symbolical purification and healing. Ea, as the god of humanity, thus came to be regarded as a great physician who knows all the forces from which healing can be obtained from maladies caused by sorcerers, and who can also drive away evil spirits. To protect the dead from evil spirits that may attack them in the grave it was customary for a symbolical purification ceremony to take place previous to the burial of the body. The priest who performed the ceremony sprinkled some water over it, and in order that his appearance might suggest the great water-god on whose behalf he was supposed to act and whose presence he was supposed to symbolize, he dressed himself in fish costume—the fish being a symbol of Ea. In one case

---

[1] *Shar apsi.*

when a man is afflicted with terrible disease and plague, and is overwhelmed by misery and pain, we are told that through the exorcisms of Ea " The ban is peeled like an onion, cut off like a date ". The seven evil spirits are described as being hostile to Ea, which, of course, really means that they are hostile to mankind. It is of interest to note that in many parts of the British Isles people still drop nails and rags into their wells and expect the water to cure them from all kinds of disease.

In the Assyrian pantheon Ea held the same position as in Babylonia. Shalmaneser on his famous obelisk describes him as " king of the ocean ". In the Deluge narrative he saves mankind from absolute destruction. He is the one who decides the fate of humanity. Thus we are informed that if a man does not observe the law of his land Ea, " the king of destinies," will judge his fate. As the god of civilization and of fine arts he is the great artist and architect, and the bulls which were placed at the entrances to the Assyrian temples were really made by him. When Nabu-apal-iddin makes an image of Shamash at Sippar it is through the wisdom bestowed on him by Ea. In one form of the Deluge narrative Atra-hasis, who is usually known as Ut-napishtim, says to Ea his lord, " Never have I built a ship, draw for me a sketch of it upon the earth, then I can look at the sketch and build a ship."

In this capacity as an artist and as the god who instructs mankind in the arts he has assistants, who can hardly be described as deities, and whose names show that they were really intended to represent symbolically that all wisdom and skill exercised by man has a divine origin. Thus one of these is known as Nin-igi-nangar-bur, " lord who presides over metal-workers." Another who was evidently the patron of the stone-quarrier was known as Nin-kurra, " lord of the mountains," whilst another was known as Nin-zadim, " lord of sculpture." The tradition that the Babylonians obtained their wisdom and science from a water deity like Ea was preserved amongst other peoples, and one may refer to the Oannes of Berossus, the mystic being, half-man half-fish, who came out of the waters daily to instruct the people. Eusebius, in his *Chaldean Archaeology*, informs us that in Babylonia there were many different races of people living together like wild beasts. A year after the creation there appeared from the Erythræan Sea, where it borders on Babylonia, a mystic being with the name of Oannes, part of his body being like a fish and part like a man. During the day this being lived with mankind and taught them the arts and sciences. His instruction was so valuable that since that time nothing has surpassed it. He even wrote a book about the origin of civilization, which he gave to man. As he was amphibious, however, he only used to spend the day on land, and at sunset returned to the water, where he spent his nights.

Ea is often symbolically represented by a ram's head on a stick projecting from a frame. This symbol can be seen on the Bavian Relief and the Esarhaddon Stele. On boundary stones he is usually symbolized by an animal resembling an antelope with the bowels of a fish. One may mention as an instance of this the Kudurru of Melishihu (MDP. i and ii). On the Kudurru of Nazi Marrutash, the symbol is not quite clear, but some traces of the ram's head and the antelope's horns are still recognizable. Like Marduk he is also often represented with a horned creature at his feet. M. Heuzey [1] has shown that the representation of a god with a spouting vase is very often a symbol of Ea. In MDP. i, 177 (Kudurru Fragment, no. 6) there is a representation of a god wearing a cap and a long cloak. He holds a vessel in his hands in front of his breast, from which there flow two streams of water. This is also most probably a symbolical representation of Ea. The water is *aqua vitae* and it is sometimes represented as flowing from the god's shoulders as well as from his breasts. From the time of the first dynasty of Babylon we have an interesting representation of the god. There is a male deity with a horned crown seated upon a throne. He holds a jar with *aqua vitae* in his right hand. Above this seat there seems

---

[1] *Les Origines Orientales de l'art* ;   also *Seal Cylinders of W. Asia*, chap. xxxvii, p. 213.

to be a kind of goat-fish, whilst in front are the figures of a male and female with the inscription *ilu En-Ki ilu dam-gal-nun-na* above them. We thus have a representation of Ea with his consort Damkina.

On the other hand, it must be remembered that the power of dispensing the " waters of life " and the " herbs of life " was amongst the characteristic features of other Babylonian gods, particularly the more important ones; and such symbolical representations may not necessarily therefore represent Ea. Furthermore, whilst we think of Ea as the great god of the deep, we must not forget that this conception of him only goes back to a period about the time of Hammurabi. In Ezek. xxviii, 2 ff., we read "I am a God, I sit in the seat of God in the heart of the seas." The passage obviously refers to the royal residence at Tyre, although some scholars see a mythological allusion to Ea enthroned in the ocean. Whether Dagon, the Philistine god, who is regarded by some as a divinity of fish form, is to be compared to Ea remains an open question.

ZAMAMA

Zamama was one of the minor gods of the Babylonian pantheon. He was worshipped at Kish in northern Babylonia, and was identified with Ninib as a form of the sun-god. He was also a warrior deity, and was known as the god of the battle, whilst his temple was called " the house of the warrior's glory " (*E-me-te-ur-sagga*). His warlike character was represented on boundary stones by his symbol, which consisted of a mace with the head of a vulture.

CHAPTER VI

BURIAL AND MOURNING CUSTOMS

CHAPTER VI

BURIAL AND MOURNING CUSTOMS

In attempting to trace the origins of some of the symbolical customs connected with burial and mourning amongst the Semites, we find ourselves confronted with great difficulty. It has been suggested that there may be some physical reasons to account for many mourning customs. Thus, tearing one's garment would palliate nervous irritation, beating the breast would relieve the heart oppressed with a tumultuous circulation, crying aloud would divert the attention from anguish of body or mind; whilst shaving the head would help to relieve the excited brain. Again, it has been suggested that many mourning customs have arisen from a desire on the part of the mourners not only to avoid their usual practices in daily life, but to do the very reverse. Thus many savages who usually paint themselves refrain from doing so when in mourning.[1] Amongst certain West African tribes which are very fond of overdressing, it is found that when a death occurs the men divest themselves of all clothing and the women wear as few as possible.[2] Also amongst the modern Egyptians it is customary when the master of the house or the owner of the furniture is dead to turn upside-down the carpets, mats, cushions, and coverings of the divans.

Although many non-Semitic mourning customs may perhaps be explained in one of these ways, a careful study of the origins of symbolical mourning customs amongst the Semites shows clearly that they have a much deeper significance than suggested by any of the previous explanations. For example, to quote but one instance, how are we to account for the fact that some of the signs of mourning actually coincide with those of joy? Thus, besides the wailing men and women at a funeral

[1] Charlevoix, *Histoire du Paraguay*, p. 73.
[2] Wood, *Natural History of Man*, i, p. 586.

we read of " flute-playing " as an accompaniment to the
mourning ceremonies (Jer. xlviii, 36). In Zech. xii, 11–12,
there is a reference to alternate singing between the men and
the women; whilst Meissner[1] quotes one instance at the
funeral of an Assyrian king where choral singing formed part
of the ceremony.

Again, it seems curious that so many rites connected with
religion such as self-mutilation, fasting, the removal of the
shoes, the offering of food, etc., were also symbolical mourning
ceremonies for the departed. It seems clear, therefore, that
either some of these symbolical mourning rites have a religious
origin or else religion has borrowed some of its rites from
mourning customs.

Before we attempt to trace the origin of some Semitic
mourning symbolisms we will consider briefly the Semitic
conceptions of life after death. The Hebrews and Babylonians
seem to have shared very similar views with reference to the
conditions of the dead. With the dissolution of the body the
soul passed to another world. Death was thus only a means of
passing to another life. The home of the dead was described
in Babylonia as " the land of no return ", " the dark dwelling ",
" the house of death " ; whilst the two most common names
for the underworld are " Aralu " and " Shualu " (Hebrew
שְׁאוֹל). To the Hebrews Sheol was apparently a lower world
quite distinct from the grave. Thus, Jacob who thought
Joseph had been torn in pieces said he will go down to Sheol
to his son mourning (Gen. xxxvii, 35). It seems to have been
a general receptacle for all the dead, regardless of their moral
worth.[2]

Although we have no direct statement in the literature of
the Sumerians as to their conception of life beyond the grave,

---

[1] See his article in the *Wiener Zeitschrift für die Kunde des Morgenl.*,
xii, 59 ff.
[2] The question as to whether man has any further existence once
his soul has departed from his body, which is raised in some of the
later books of the Old Testament, such as Job and Koheleth, is regarded
by many modern critical scholars as the effects produced upon the
Hebrew mind by later Greek thought.

there are very frequent references to their sacrifices to the dead
and their partaking with them of a common meal.   Death
seems to have been looked upon with very great fear, and such
expressions as " his god has gathered him " or " the fate of
his night came upon him " show the horror with which death
was regarded.   The body was either buried or cremated.   When
the body was cremated the needs of the soul were symbolically
provided for by placing ashes in an urn containing jars of
water and bread.   In cases where the body was buried, food
and drink was placed for the soul of the dead.   At Ur skeletons
were found accompanied by jars, platters of bread, and even
brushes for colouring the deceased's eyes.   These symbols
of the material needs of the dead soon rose to a more spiritual
interpretation, and the bread and drink which were placed
in the coffin gave rise to the mystery of communion with the
deified souls, and then with the deity himself.   This consisted
of the symbolical rite of " breaking the bread " for the souls
of the dead.   One of the months in the Babylonian calendar
was known as *kisig-ninazu*—the month of breaking the bread
to Ninazu, the god of the lower world.   This month was
followed by the month of the feast of Ninazu.

To the Babylonians, particularly, death was looked upon as
a terrible calamity, for once a man has been removed to the
underworld he can no longer hope to return.   The gods have
no power whatever to restore him to life in this world ; and
when some of them are described in incantations and hymns
as being able to restore the dead to life, the reference is
to their power of curing mankind from disease and saving
from the grave one who is at the brink of death rather
than to actually reviving the dead.

A clear idea of the Babylonian conception of the underworld can be obtained from the representations on a bronze
tablet from Hamath, to which Clermont-Ganneau drew
attention many years ago.[1]   On one side there is a monster
with a face and body like a lion, and with huge wings ; whilst
at its sides are the heads of other monsters.   The scenes on

[1] *Revue Archéologique*, 1879, pp. 337–49.

the reverse are divided into five divisions. First come the symbols of the leading deities of the Assyrian pantheon. Then there are symbolical representations in the forms of animals of seven evil spirits who are the messengers of the gods of the heavens represented in the first division. Next comes the funeral ceremony proper. A priest dressed in fish costume, and another in a long cloak are standing at the end of a funeral bier on which lies a dead body. The priests are apparently performing some purification ceremony and seem to be attempting to guard the body from being attacked by two demons who appear by their gestures to be trying to obtain possession of it. In the next division the terrors associated with the nether-world are symbolized by two hideous-looking monsters. One of these is, no doubt, Allatu, the goddess of this region. She is represented as kneeling on a horse in a barque. In the fifth and last division are two trees and some flowing water with fishes swimming about. A duplicate of this stele, which has been described by Scheil,[1] was found at Zurghul in Babylonia. It differs from the Hamath tablet in some slight respects. The horse on which the goddess Allatu is kneeling is not represented, nor do we see any trees near the water.

These five divisions on the tablet represent clearly the Babylonian conception of the divisions of the universe. First the heavens, then the atmosphere, then comes the earth, then the nether-world, and finally the flowing water symbolizes "apsu", the deep which flows beneath the earth.

In the nether-world everything is in a state of inactivity and even decay. The dead are too weak to attend to their requirements, and must therefore be satisfied with dust as their food. In the Gilgamesh epic we are informed that man was formed from clay and returns to clay. In the account of Ishtar's descent to Hades we are told that she goes to " a house whose inhabitants are deprived of light, the place where dust is their nourishment, their food clay ". The underworld had its own special pantheon. It was only

---

[1] *Recueil de Travaux*, xx.

natural that amidst such gloomy conditions the chief
authority should be symbolically assigned to Nergal, the
god who was the very symbol of all misery and destruction,
and who was represented by a lion. The underworld is
thus the future home of all mankind, and it is only one who
can succeed in winning the favour of the gods who can have
the good fortune of being taken to the " Island of the
Blest ". Even the great hero Gilgamesh has nothing else
to look forward to, and in his attempt to obtain immortality
he ventures on a long journey in search for Ut-napishtim,
the Babylonian Noah, who was granted eternal life, in order
to learn from him how he has obtained such good fortune.
The spirit of his friend Eabani now appears to him, and
Gilgamesh asks him to describe his experience in Aralu.
In his reply Eabani says that if he were to describe his
experience he would " sit and weep the whole day ".
It was only natural that as the place itself was looked upon
with such fear its inhabitants should also be regarded with
terror and even with distrust, for the dead may unite with
the demons of the underworld and come to plague the living.
Everything must therefore be done to secure their favour
and to prevent their returning to this world.

But we must bear in mind that the Babylonians only
developed this gloomy conception of the underworld very
gradually. This may be seen from the fact that amongst
the pantheon of Aralu is a solar deity Nin-azu [1] who is
described as " god of healing " and consort of Allatu.
That the consort of this goddess is represented as a
beneficent deity who symbolized the morning sun, suggests
that the goddess herself was not originally as terrible and
awe-inspiring as she was later represented.

Stade and many other scholars believe that ancestor
worship prevailed among the early Hebrews. These
scholars base their arguments on the fact to which we have
already referred, that certain usages practised by the
neighbours of the Hebrews in the worship of their gods were

[1] See p. 215.

also observed in mourning. Furthermore, the emphatic prohibition in the Old Testament against some of these practices as signs of mourning, suggests that they must have held quite an important place in the religious life of the other Semitic peoples. They also point out that some of the burial places of the Hebrew patriarchs were later sanctuaries (Hebron, Gen. xxv, 9; xlix, 30, etc.; Shechem, Joshua xxiv, 32).

There is certainly not sufficient evidence to show that ancestor worship ever existed among the Hebrews, although Lagrange suggests that this lack of evidence from the Old Testament is due to a desire on the part of the Hebrews to suppress all traces of it. On the other hand, we have definite evidence that hero-worship formed part of the religion of the ancient Semites, and it seems to the present writer that the rites connected with this form of worship were afterwards performed for all the dead, and then became symbolical mourning customs.

Now the word " Rephaim ", which is a Hebrew term used to denote the inhabitants of the underworld, was also employed by the Hebrews in the sense of " giants " to describe the early giant peoples of Palestine. It seems, therefore, that there must be some connexion between the two meanings of the term. Again, in Isa. xiv, 9, although mentioned in speaking of Sheol, the Rephaim appear as people of authority. It is possible therefore that the name " Rephaim " was originally only applied to distinguished dead heroes, and later became a common term for all dead.

It is also of importance to note that from the time of Shar-Gani-Shari many of the early kings of Babylonia were deified. In a tablet in the Museum at Constantinople there occurs the name Ili Urumush, " My god is Urumush," [1] whilst on the obelisk of Manishtusu there is a name Sharru-Gi-ili, " Sharru Gi is my god." Naram Sin has the determinative for deity preceding his name, and is even described as " god of Akkad ", and Gudea, Dungi, and Ur

---

[1] See *OLZ.*, 1908, col. 313 f.

Lama I were all deified. In fact, the practice seems to have been regularly adopted during the period of the later kings of Lagash, and it arose through the fact that many of these kings assumed the divine title when still alive. And therefore just as they were worshipped as gods when alive, so they continued to be worshipped in the same manner after they had passed to the next world. Dungi, who was the first king to claim such honours during his lifetime, assumed the title of divinity on the expansion of his empire ; whilst Ishmi-Dagan actually called himself " spouse of Ninni ", the goddess of Erech.

It was probably from the fact that these hero divinities were often consulted as oracles that the Hebrew term "Sheol" (Babylonian " Shualu "), which is connected with the verb " to ask " or " to inquire ", was applied to the underworld.   Sheol would therefore mean " place of inquiry " or " place where an oracle can be obtained ". With reference to this practice amongst the Hebrews one may refer to the case in 1 Sam. xxviii, 11, where we are informed that Saul brought up the spirit of Samuel to learn from him the result of a forthcoming battle.

Now, if we accept the suggestion that many symbolical mourning customs have their origin in hero-worship, we are able to explain the meanings and development of many of these practices. The Semites regarded the world as being divided into three divisions, the upper and lower regions being very similar in form, and even, in some respects, symbolical of the earth. The seven gates which surround the underworld were symbols of the seven zones which surround the earth. Similarly, in Babylonian mythology, just as the celestial " earth " culminates in a double-peaked mount above the summit of which stands the deity, so the summit of the universe was also regarded as a mountain on which was the throne of a god. There is also a similarity between the forms of life in the three worlds. Spencer in his *Principles of Sociology* (vol. iii, p. 182) informs us that amongst primitive peoples life in the other world is conceived as identical in nature with life in this world. Hence, as the living chief was supplied with his food and drink, oblations are taken to his burial-place and libations poured out. As animals were killed for him while he lived, animals are sacrificed on his grave when he is dead. If he had a large retinue, the numerous beasts which were slaughtered to maintain his court are paralleled by the animals sacrificed for the support of his ghost. The homage which was paid to him when alive by frequent visits to his residence is translated into a pilgrimage to his tomb. Just as laudations were uttered before him when he was alive, so they are repeated even to a greater degree in the presence of his spirit; whilst all kinds of music and dancing which were originally spontaneous expressions of joy in his presence, become, later, part of the ceremony connected with the worship of his ghost.

We can now understand the origins of many mourning customs, such as the wearing of sackcloth, offering sacrifices at the grave, etc. They were originally intended as symbols of respect to a dead hero, in whose honour they had also been performed during his lifetime. It is of interest to note that in Egypt there have been found in some tombs representations of men and women with their tools ready to carry out the command of the dead when called upon.[1] Again, as the importance of law in primitive society was the fact that it embodied the dictates of the dead to the living, it was presumably only from the spirits of men who in life were specially endowed with powers of insight that communications were sought,[2] so that they could continue to give their advice and counsel as they had been doing during their life in this world.

In connexion with music and dirges at a funeral, this explanation helps us considerably. The living must do their utmost to obtain the favour of the dead hero, and continue to recount his piety and good deeds in funeral dirges.

---

[1] *Recueil de Travaux*, xxii, p. 67.
[2] Cf. Tiresias, in Homer.

Those who used to sing his praises when he was alive must, therefore, continue to do so even when he is dead, if they desire him to use his influence on their behalf. In the story of Ishtar's descent to Hades the mourners are advised to commence lamenting for her ; whilst the attendants of the goddess who were devoted to her worship—the ukhati— are actually told to sing dirges which are to have flute accompaniment. Ishtar, the goddess of the underworld, has great power and influence with Allatu, and by the singing of dirges and an official mourning the mourners may succeed in obtaining the sympathy of Ishtar.

Whenever a national catastrophe occurred in Babylonia, such as defeat by an enemy, bad harvest, or destructive rains and storms, a whole series of lamentations were recited in order to appease the anger of the gods. These lamentations developed at Nippur, but after a time, when, as a result of the reforms of Hammurabi, Marduk became chief of the pantheon, they were transferred to him in the hope that as a solar and beneficent deity, he would replace their troubles and sorrows by happiness and joy. There is reference in Babylonian literature to a sister of Tammuz, the goddess Belili. This goddess was said to have broken a most valuable vessel as a symbol of her grief for Tammuz. If, therefore, mourners for a dead relative combine with their grief mourning for Tammuz also, they would secure the sympathies of Belili. At the festival of Tammuz mourners were, therefore, advised in lamenting the loss of the solar hero to sing a dirge in memory of their own dead relatives.

The importance which the Semites attached to the burial of the body can be understood by taking into account the following considerations. The Semites, as we have already noted, regarded the universe as consisting of three kingdoms—the upper regions which were confined to the gods, the earth which was the home of mankind, and the underworld which was the home of the dead. The dead who were unburied were therefore left without a home, not only for their bodies, but for their spirits also. To give to the dead proper burial and not to disturb the body once it had reached its resting-place, was a great and sacred duty. In a Phœnician inscription we meet with the following passage: "Do not uncover me or remove me, for that is an abomination to Astarte." [1]

There is a belief amongst many primitive peoples that if a man's body is mutilated his soul will arrive in a similar condition in the next world. This is another reason why the non-burial of the body was regarded as such a terrible curse. It is worthy of note also that in many of the Kudurru inscriptions reference is made to a curse against the one who should violate or destroy them, the curse being that his body may lay unburied. This belief existed amongst many non-Semitic peoples also, and of the instances referred to by Tylor [2] one may refer to the Hurons of North America, who believe that the souls of those who commit suicide or are slain in war arrive in the next world in a mutilated condition, and are not admitted to the spirit villages of their tribe. Amongst the Assyrians this belief is clearly represented on the Eannatum Stele, in which the warriors of Lagash are represented as being carefully buried; whilst vultures are flying off with the heads of the enemy in their beaks. Ashurbanipal also informs us that he scattered the bodies of those who took part in a rebellion organized by his brother Shamash-Shumukin like thorns and thistles over the battlefield, and gave them to dogs, and swine, and the birds of heaven.

Just as it was necessary to provide a home for the dead by burial, so it was of importance to leave food on the tomb or place it on the grave, otherwise the spirits of the dead would be compelled to come and disturb the living. It was probably this belief which gave rise to the practice

[1] See *Inscription of Tabnit*, ll. 5, 6. There are many references in classical literature to the sacred duty of burying the dead with proper rites so that the spirit should not wander along the banks of Acheron.

[2] *Primitive Culture*, ii.

of funeral offerings.   Amongst the Algonquins of North America, it was customary to offer all kinds of dainty foods to the dead.   In fact, they believed that the gods would severely punish them if they neglected to do so.[1]   In Madagascar the mausoleum of one of the kings was provided with a table, two chairs, and also some wine and water in order that the spirit of the departed king might come there occasionally and taste some of the things he was known to be fond of in his lifetime.   This would perhaps also explain the origin of the funeral feast referred to in the Old Testament (Jer. xvi, 8; Hos. ix, 4, etc.).   Originally it was a kind of act of communion with the dead which consoled the survivors.   The practice of offering sacrifices at a funeral seems to have existed in very early times.   On the Vulture Stele there is a representation of a bull being securely bound with ropes to two stakes, ready to be offered. Near it is a nude man pouring out a libation.   He seems to be pouring some liquid from a small vessel into a larger one.

Another explanation has been offered for the origin of the communion feast among the Hebrews which is exceedingly plausible.   According to Hebrew law, the man in whose house anyone died became unclean, and even the food which had been standing there in an open vessel at the time shared the same fate.   It was only natural, therefore, that a practice should have arisen by which the friends of the mourner should come to his house to comfort him and share his sorrows, and that they should even bring their food with them, and thus join him in eating the funeral meal.   When David lamented the death of Abner we read how all the people came to eat bread with him that day (2 Sam. iii, 35).

Robertson Smith thinks that the rending of garments in mourning was originally designed to procure a rag-offering for the dead.[2]   A person's garments are, so to speak, part of himself, and when Jonathan makes a covenant with

---

[1] Charlevoix, *Histoire et description générale de la Nouvelle France*, vol. i, p. 75.
[2] *Religion of the Semites*, p. 336.

David he invests him with his garments. Therefore to make a rag-offering from one's clothing for the dead was a symbol of attachment to them. But the tearing of one's garments and the practice of clothing oneself with sackcloth are so often referred to together that one cannot help regarding both practices as parts of one ceremony. If we also examine the passages in which these practices are referred to we will note that one was really a preliminary to the other, so that after a time either one or the other of these acts was referred to as implying two symbolisms. Schwally [1] thinks that the practice of tearing one's garments arose through the desire to put on the sack which was a girdle round the loins worn by man in his primitive stage, and also at a much later time by slaves. It was, therefore, a symbol of submission to the dead, who still had power to help or harm the living. Jensen argues that it was a kind of linen cloth put on over the head and worn by those who were extremely poor. The point which seems clear from the various explanations is that the sack was regarded as the poorest form of dress, and by tearing his clothing and putting on sackcloth a man symbolized either his submission to the dead or his readiness to give up all his pleasures and luxuries as the result of the bereavement he had sustained. After a time the putting on of sackcloth dropped out of usage, and the mere tearing of one's garments symbolized the same idea. It is of interest to note that Ashurbanipal is actually represented in a torn garment pouring out libations for the souls of the kings who had preceded him. Now it is obvious that if a person removes his garments in order to show his willingness to deprive himself of everything in life, he ought also to remove his shoes. This explains why the shoes were removed by the mourner as well as by the worshipper on approaching sacred ground.

There are a few symbolical rites observed by modern Jews which are of interest and to which we may here refer. We have already noted that water is one of the great

[1] *Das Leben nach dem Tode*, p. 13.

sources of symbolical purification. Some orthodox Jews as well as pious Moslems, therefore, wash themselves just before death in order that they may leave this world in a state of ritual purity. (See *Maabhar Yabok*, 78a, cf. also Ps. xxvi, 6.) The burial vestments in which the corpse is clothed amongst Jews must be of a very simple nature without the slightest ornaments, nor must it contain any knots. This is to symbolize that the dead is thus removed from the worries and entanglements connected with this world. The reference in the Old Testament to the angel of the Lord standing between heaven and earth with a drawn sword in his hand (1 Chron. xxi, 16) gave rise to the symbolical manner by which the angel of death is represented in Jewish tradition. He is so tall that he reaches from one end of the earth to the other and is constantly lying in wait with a drawn sword in his hand as a mark of his vocation. He stands at the bedside of the dying man with his sword drawn in his hand, and a bitter drop at the edge. As soon as the patient sees him he begins to tremble, opens wide his mouth, swallows the bitter drop which the angel pours down his throat, and dies. The passage in connexion with the death of Jacob (Gen. xlvi, 4) " Joseph shall put his hands upon thine eyes " has also been thought to refer to some symbolical practice. There are references in Rabbinic literature to the custom of closing the eyes of the dead, as soon as the soul has passed away, by a near relative—preferably, however, by the eldest son or heir (Mishna, *Shabboth*, xxiii, 4). In Jewish literature the practice is explained in the following manner. A man cannot see the great world beyond until his sight has been completely removed from this world. On the other hand, seeing that a man visualizes the *Shechina* when he is on the point of death, he should no longer direct his gaze from that sacredness to something unholy and profane (*Maabhar Yabok*, 128a).

We shall now proceed to consider some of the more important symbolical practices connected with death and

Q

mourning and the suggestions as to their origins and
development.

SELF-MUTILATION

Amongst the Hebrews the mourner showed his sorrow
for the death of his friend by cutting his body and also
part of his hair so as to leave bald patches on the head.
Amos (viii, 10) says : " I will turn your feasts into mourning, and all your songs into lamentation and I will bring
up sackcloth upon all loins and baldness upon every head."
Jeremiah (xvi, 6), prophesying the destruction that was to
fall upon Judah, describes how the people shall die and
there shall be none to bury them or mourn for them.
" They shall not be buried, neither shall men lament for
them, nor cut themselves, nor make themselves bald for
them." Similarly Ezekiel (vii, 18) says : " They shall
gird themselves with sackcloth, and horror shall cover
them, and shame shall be upon all faces, and baldness
upon all their heads " ; whilst Micah (i, 16), advising the
inhabitants of the Southern Kingdom to prepare themselves
for their coming calamities by shaving like mourners,
says : " Make thee bald and poll thee for the children of
thy delight, enlarge thy baldness as the eagle, for they
are gone into captivity from thee."

These practices were forbidden to the Israelites by the
Deuteronomic Legislation (xiv, 1) : " Ye are children unto
the Lord your God. You shall not make any cuttings in
the flesh nor baldness between your eyes for the dead."
On the death of a husband, father, or other near relation,
Arab women cut their hair and scratch their faces with
their nails. Amongst the Arabs of Moab it is customary
for the women on the death of a near relative to scratch
their faces, tear their garments, and spread tresses of
hair on the tomb. In ancient times it seems to have been
customary, also, amongst some Semitic peoples to tattoo
on the skin the symbol of the deity or his name. From

the Old Testament (Lev. xix, 28) tattooing seems to have
been associated with cuttings in the flesh made in mourning, thus suggesting that these tattoo marks were scars
made by a person who wished to draw blood from his body
and so dedicate himself to his god.   Even now it is customary for the pilgrim to Mecca to receive three cuts on his
face.[1]   The account given in 1 Kings xviii of the savage
frenzy of the prophets of Baal when they called upon their
deity to do according to their wish but all to no purpose,
and then the manner in which they cut themselves with
swords till the blood streamed down them, is merely an
example of such practices amongst the neighbours of the
Israelites.   And we can thus understand how such barbarous excesses should have been learned by the Israelites
at a very early stage in their history.

There are many customs in the East in which one person
shows his love for another by cutting his body, and allowing
his blood to flow freely in the presence of the one to whom
he is thus attached.   The more blood he allows to flow
from his body the more does he show his affection for his
friend.   The Persians at an annual festival in memory
of the death of some martyrs make gashes in their arms.
One writer,[2] describing the scenes of flesh-cutting by
mourners on the occasion of a funeral which he witnessed
amongst some barbarous tribes, states that the women made
cuttings into their flesh and allowed the blood to flow into
an apron which they wore.   When the apron was almost
saturated with blood it was dried in the sun and given to
the nearest relative of the deceased as a symbol of their
regard for the departed and of their sympathy with and
affection for the bereaved ones.

W. Robertson Smith has suggested that these lacerations
practised by the mourners amongst the ancient Semites
were intended as a symbol of a blood offering which was to
create a covenant of blood between the mourner and his

---

[1] Maltzahn's *Wallfahrt nach Mecca*, ii, S. 132, 244
[2] Ellis, *Polynesian Researches*, i, 529.

dead kinsman. By means of these mutilations a corporal union would thus be established between the living and the dead. In the Old Testament (Exod. xxiv), when Moses, as the representative of God, read the "Book of the Covenant" to the people, we are informed that sacrifices were offered, and that half of the blood of the animals was placed in some basins and half sprinkled upon the altar. Robertson Smith points out that in certain cases in Arabia a man still seeks protection by drawing his own blood and wiping his gory hands on the doorpost of the man whose favour he entreats. All these symbolical ideas may have been connected with the ancient Semitic conception of blood.

To the Hebrews the blood of men, animals, and birds seemed to contain the very soul of the living creature. In fact the blood was identical with the soul. In Lev. xvii, 11, we read, "The soul of the flesh is in the blood"; whilst in verse 14 we read, "The soul of all flesh is its blood itself." [1] It was only natural, therefore, that as the soul was considered as something sacred the blood should also be regarded as sacred. The very sight of blood filled man with feelings of mystery and divine awe. It was this which naturally brought about the feeling that blood must not be eaten but poured out on the ground like water.

This also helps to explain why, amongst many ancient peoples, the liver, which was regarded as a mass of coagulated blood, came to be synonymous with life. The liver often occurs in Semitic literatures as the seat of the emotions, and it is of interest to note that in Gen. xlix, 6, where the verse, as translated from our Massoretic text, reads, "unto their assembly mine 'honour' be not thou united," the Greek reads "liver" (suggesting כְּבֵדִי instead of כְּבֹדִי). Similarly in Lam. ii, 11, where Jerusalem,

---

[1] Bähr in his *Symbolik*, ii, 207, translates Lev. xvii, 11, כי הדם הוא בנפש יכפר, the blood atones by means of the soul. He attempts to show that בנפש, which is generally rendered as the object of the verb, must instead be the instrument.

grieving over her destruction as a mother robbed of her children, exclaims, " My liver is poured out on the ground," meaning that her very life has been destroyed.

Babylonian liver divination, which consisted of an examination and interpretation of the lines and markings of the liver, was also based upon the same belief. When an animal was selected for sacrifice it became as one with the god to whom it was to be offered. " The two souls became attuned to one another like two watches regulated to keep the same time." Therefore, by examining the liver of the animal, one could read the mind of the god. By some scholars the English word " liver " is actually connected with the verb " to live ", because of its importance to life or vitality.[1]

In early times, amongst the ancient Hebrews, when an animal was slaughtered at an altar, the blood was poured out as an offering to God. This has been regarded by many scholars as the earliest form of sacrifice. In fact, amongst the Semites, the idea of sacrifice was really based upon the idea of forming a covenant by means of blood. The outpouring of blood was thus a desire to renew one's union with one's god. In Syriac *ethakashaf*, which means " to pray ", is probably connected with a root meaning " to cut oneself ".[2] Even when the blood has been poured out on the ground it still retains its vitality, and so in Gen. iv, 10, 11, when Abel has been murdered by Cain, God says to him, " The voice of thy brother's blood crieth unto me from the ground."

The symbolism of the nose-ring, so commonly worn in India to-day, is explained by a story that when Vishnu was incarnated as Krishna, his mother bored a hole in his nose and placed a ring in it as a sign of identification. She then exchanged him for another infant, as his life was being sought for. The blood caused by the wound was really a sacrifice to prevent his being captured by his enemies. The nose-ring is thus a symbol that the child's blood has

[1] Cf. German *Leib* and *Leber*.
[2] See Oxford Hebrew Lexicon BDB., p. 506, כשׁף.

been given as a covenant to the god and an assurance that its life will be protected. Herodotus iii, 8, describes a method of making a covenant amongst the Arabs which consisted of the two parties drawing each other's blood from their thumbs, licking it, and then smearing it on seven stones. Even nowadays the Jews of Tunis regard a bleeding hand as a symbol of brotherhood. We know that the early Babylonian kings regarded their offerings to the gods as means of intercommunion with them. And it is possible that, just as in the Old Testament the words " table " and " altar " are sometimes used interchangeably,[1] so in Assyrian the word for " altar " (surkinu) was used primarily for " table ".[2]

From these outlines of the customs which have existed and still exist amongst many peoples of making use of blood in order to make a covenant, we learn that the basis of the blood covenant was the belief that blood is life itself, that its presence in the living body is in reality the very cause of the existence of the life which is in it, and that the commingling of the blood of two different persons is, therefore, equivalent to the commingling of the lives of two different individuals. By allowing some of his blood to flow freely over the dead body of his relative the mourner was really vivifying it, for he was placing in it a portion of his own living spirit, and one common life was thus established between the two friends. This symbol for the establishment of a bond of union between two friends— living as well as dead—is to be found all the world over, and in most cases, where both parties are living, the friends drink each other's blood. " A covenant of blood, a covenant made by the intercommingling of blood has been recognized as the closest, the holiest, and the most indissoluble compact conceivable. Such a covenant clearly involves an absolute surrender of one's separate self, and an irrevocable merging of one's individual nature into

---

[1] See Mal. i, 6–7.
[2] *Trans. Soc. Bib. Arch.*, vol. iv, pt. i, pp. 58 f.

the dual, or multiplied personality, included in the compact." [1]

There is one custom which was observed in Norway, and is of special interest in connexion with this possible explanation of blood-letting as being the means of covenanting in death. One of the means of establishing friendship between two persons was for them to dig out a sod of earth, place themselves underneath it, and then cut or pierce their hand and cause the blood to flow unto each other. The idea being that as the blood of one man flowed on to his neighbour, as they each lay in their graves, a union of blood and therefore an indissoluble union of the souls of these two people was created, so that after the symbolical ceremony when they raised the sods from above their heads it could be said that there was one soul in two bodies. We may quote here from Spencer's *Principles of Sociology* (vol. ii, p. 70) : " Those who give some of their blood to the ghost of a man just dead and lingering near, effect with it a union which on the one side implies submission, and on the other side friendliness. On this hypothesis we have a reason for the prevalence of self-bleeding as a funeral rite, not among existing savages only, but among ancient and partially civilized peoples—the Jews, the Greeks, the Huns, the Turks. We are shown how there arise kindred rites as permanent propitiations of those more dreaded ghosts which become gods."

The idea of " cutting " in making a covenant may have given rise to the Hebrew expression כרת ברית (to cut a covenant). On the other hand, some scholars have suggested that animals were slaughtered on the making of a covenant as a symbol of the punishment which either of the parties would deserve if they were to break the agreement. It has been pointed out that whilst the verb " to give " or " put " (נתן) is used when God makes a covenant with Abraham by means of circumcision

---

[1] Trumbull, *The Blood Covenant*, p. 204.

(Gen. xvii, 1–12),[1] the verb "to cut" is used when a sacrifice is referred to.

Amongst many ancient peoples the ceremony of establishing brother friendship includes the killing of an animal and cutting it up between two parties. Each party must eat his part of the animal.[2]   It was only natural that the religion of Israel which regarded man as having been created in the image of God should have forbidden all forms of mutilation such as have been described above.   And what is perhaps even of greater interest is that whilst amongst their neighbours such practices were regarded as being specially incumbent on the priests and prophets of the people, the command in Lev. xxi, 5, makes these customs specially prohibited to the priest.   Again, the prohibition of self-mutilation as a mourning custom may be considered in connexion with the law against any form of human castration.   In Deut. xxiii, 1, we read that any man who was mutilated in this way was excluded from the privileges of the community.

Another suggestion to explain the symbolic idea underlying self-mutilation as a mourning custom is that the mourners allowed their blood to drop over the corpse in order to provide their friend with nourishment for his life in the next world.   Human blood is often given for medical purposes.   Amongst some Australian tribes a weak person is fed by his male friends with blood from their own bodies. The Arabs believed that the blood of kings was a cure for certain kinds of nervous diseases.   The Sabeans regarded blood as food and nourishment for the gods, and amongst certain African tribes it is held as a dainty ; whilst the Mohammedans make dainty dishes from the blood of camel's veins.   It is possible that instead of the mourners mutilating themselves in order to draw blood for the nourishment of their dead relatives, there arose after a time a custom of substituting their own blood by that of a

---

[1] e.g. Gen. xvii, 2, ‏ואתנה בריתי ביני ובינך‎.
[2] Smith, *Araucanians*, p. 262.

slaughtered animal. The custom amongst the Egyptian women of visiting the tomb of a relative the third day after the funeral and slaying a lamb or goat as a sacrifice may perhaps be explained in this way, although it is now known as " el-kaffarah " (expiation), and is regarded as a sacrifice to expiate some of the minor sins of the deceased.

Perhaps we ought not to leave this subject without mentioning that in Babylonia various kinds of mutilations were inflicted by order of a judge upon a criminal, and the form of mutilation inflicted was symbolical of the offence committed. Thus, the hands were cut off to mark the sin of the hands in striking a father, in unlawful surgery or in branding. The eye was torn out as a punishment for unlawful curiosity. The ear was cut off to mark the sin of the organ of hearing and disobedience ; whilst the tongue was cut out for ingratitude evidenced in speech. These practices are, of course, entirely different from self-mutilation, although they would perhaps suggest that blood-letting may have been regarded as a means of expiating for the sins of one's soul symbolized by the blood (i.e. the soul) allowed to flow from one's body.

CUTTING OF HAIR

Hair, like blood, is a symbol of life. Therefore, just as two people form a covenant by the intermingling of their blood, so by placing the hair of the living at the tomb of the dead a perpetual bond of union is established between the mourner and his dead relative. This custom is found in various parts of the world. In New Zealand, as part of the funeral ceremony, the mourners cut off some hair and hang it on trees beside the grave. In ancient Egypt the hair of a relative who was deeply attached to the deceased was often buried with his mummy (Wilkinson, ii, 32). The Aborigines of Australia at a funeral cut off a portion of their beards and throw it upon the corpse. They also tear the skin between their eyes, perhaps in some similar fashion to the Hebrew custom of making a baldness

between the eyes.[1] The inhabitants of Virginia cut off
locks of hair and place them on the dead body. We are
informed by Syriac writers that it was customary in the
East to allow the hair to grow long for some time and then
to shave one's head at a temple. Amongst the heathen
Arabs shaving the hair was an act of worship commonly
performed when a man discharged a vow or visited a temple.
The hair was really an offering to the deity and was therefore mingled with a meal offering. It was also customary
to shave the head of a child and then daub it with the
blood of a sheep which had been slaughtered as a sacrifice.
This was done to avert evil from the child by shedding
blood on its behalf. Even in modern Egypt the first
time a child's head is shaved a religious ceremony is held.
The peasants slay a victim, generally a goat, at the tomb
of some saint in or near their village, and make a feast with
the meat, of which their friends and any other persons who
please, partake. This custom is most common in Upper
Egypt, and among the tribes not very long established on
the banks of the Nile. Their pagan ancestors in Arabia
observed this custom and usually gave, as alms to the poor,
the weight of the hair in silver or gold. The victim is
called *akeekah*, and is offered as a ransom of the child
from hell.[2] In Syria and Arabia boys sacrificed their
hair on reaching manhood (Lucian, *De Dea Syria*, 55).
In Greek literature we read of the custom of youths offering
their hair to the river-god on attaining manhood ; whilst
they also vowed their hair to the gods as an offering in
return for help during times of trouble and calamity. We
read in the Iliad (xxiii) that Achilles did not cut his hair
because his father had vowed it to the river-god if he should
return home from war. In this connexion it is of
interest to note that the Hebrew בפרע פרעות בישראל
(Judges v, 2) is translated by Robertson Smith " when

[1] J. Bonwick, *Daily Life and Origin of the Tasmanians*, London, 1870.
[2] E. W. Lane, *Manners and Customs of the Modern Egyptians*.
Wellsted, *Reise zur Stadt der Chalifen*, S. 123.

flowing locks were worn in Israel", and is regarded by
him as referring to the consecration of their hair by the
warriors. The religious importance which the neighbours
of the Hebrews attached to such practices help us to
understand the command in the Old Testament forbidding
the Hebrews to let their hair grow long and then shave it
off. We are informed by Herodotus (iii, 8) that some
Arabian tribes adopted as a special symbol of their religion
the practice of shaving the hair of their heads in a most
peculiar manner, viz. : either on the crown of the head or
towards the temples, or else of disfiguring a portion of their
beard. This explains the command in Lev. xix, 27, " Ye
shall not round the corners of your head, neither shalt thou
mar the corners of thy beard." Those who practised these
customs are described as קְצוּצֵי פֵאָה (Jer. ix, 26 ; xxv,
23), which is translated by the RV. " Those that have
the corners of their hair polled ".

The offering of the hair may really be a substitute for
the sacrifice of the individual himself. Amongst primitive
peoples it was the usual thing to give part for the whole
in sacrifice, and it was only at a later time when the part
given as a tribute to the deity decreased very considerably
in value that full sacrifice was substituted. Again, in
sacrifice in order to appease the anger of the deity, it was
necessary to offer up that which was of the utmost value
to the worshipper. The Phœnicians annually sacrificed
the eldest sons of noble families to propitiate the anger
of their gods. The king of Moab, when the battle went
against him, offered up his eldest son as a burnt offering.[1]

The hair was regarded as a most important part of
man's personality. Thus in ancient magic one of the best
means of obtaining influence over a man was to obtain
some of his hair. At a feast which the Phœnicians held
at Byblus it was customary for the virgins previous to
marriage to sacrifice either their hair or their chastity.
Shaving the hair and then offering it may, therefore, have
symbolized the sacrifice of oneself to the deity. The rule

[1] 2 Kings iii, 27.

amongst the Hebrews which prohibited the Nazarite from using a razor reflects the primitive belief that hair, on account of its rapid growth, is a special seat of life. The Nazarite was forbidden not only to shave but even to reduce the hair of his head, the luxuriant growth of which symbolized his consecration to the deity and his divine power. This idea may be seen from the passage in Num. vi, 7, where the law referring to the Nazarite states, " the consecration of his god is on his head." Similarly, the Brahmin who was a hermit was forbidden to cut his hair (*Manu,* vi, 66). When we read the story of Samson, who may be regarded as a life-long Nazarite, we find that his strength was in his hair. Although the case of Samson is the only one in the Old Testament in which physical force is associated with long hair, the symbolic idea underlying the connexion is obvious. Samson's physical strength was ascribed to the spirit of God. When his hair was cut his superior strength left him. In other words the bond of union by which he was consecrated was broken, and curiously enough when his hair grew again his strength returned. There are numerous parallels to such beliefs amongst primitive peoples. The inhabitants of the island of Zacynthus believed that the strength of the ancient Greeks lay in some hairs on their breasts and that it vanished as soon as these hairs were cut. There are many peoples amongst whom not only a person's strength but his very life is supposed to reside in his hair. The cutting off of the hair therefore means death. On the other hand, there are immortal hairs which prevent the angel of death from attacking a man. In classical literature the immortality of Pterelaus was due to the golden hair on his head given to him by Poseidon.

There are numerous legends from different parts of the world where a person accused of some crime persisted in maintaining his innocence until his hair was cut off, when, realizing that his last hope had thus disappeared as his strength and courage had now left him, he confessed his guilt.

Persons accused of witchcraft or sorcery were compelled to have their body shaved, as the power of evil was supposed to reside in their hair.

The above examples, taken from the beliefs of various peoples of antiquity to show that hair was regarded as a seat of life and a symbol of strength, suggest that the cutting of the hair of the mourner may have represented his desire to supply the dead with a portion of his own strength for use in the next world. This would then be analogous to the explanation that has been suggested for self-mutilation as a means of supplying the deceased with a portion of one's own blood, so as to provide him with nourishment in the life hereafter.

There may be another explanation of the symbolism underlying the cutting off of part of one's hair as a symbol of mourning. The Hebrews greatly admired strong and thick-set locks of hair, thus causing them to depreciate nothing so much as baldness, to which such ignominy was attached that " bald-head " actually became a general term expressing profound contempt. It also seems from certain passages of the Old Testament that a bald man was often exposed to the ridicule of the mob (2 Kings ii, 23 ; Isa. iii, 24).[1] One may refer to Absalom's long hair, which was regarded both as an ornament as well as a symbol of strength (2 Sam. xiv, 25 ff.). Furthermore, bushy black hair was regarded as the perfection of beauty in manhood, and the practice of anointing the hair of the head in order to increase its thickness thus became an essential part of the daily toilet (Ps. xxiii, 5 ; xlv, 7 ; Eccles. ix, 8). Again, the numerous terms in Hebrew for the different fashions of dressing the hair are further evidences of the importance attached to this art. Amongst the Babylonians excessive long hair was a mark of royalty. In early Sumerian times we already find that the Semitic

[1] Another reason why baldness was looked upon with such contempt in ancient Israel was perhaps because it suggested that the person may be suffering from leprosy. In Babylonia cutting short of the hair was regarded as a mark of degradation.

Babylonians were known as " black-headed ones " because
they retained the black hair of their heads and faces, in
contrast to the Sumerians who used to shave their hair.
The Greeks also regarded long hair as an attribute of beauty,
and even represented the gods as wearing long hair. If,
therefore, the wearing of thick hair and anointing it was
considered part of one's daily toilet and looked upon as a
mark of beauty, it is only natural that plucking out the
hair, cutting it off, allowing it to grow in sordid negligence
or shaving it off, should all symbolize that the wearer was
afflicted with some trouble or calamity. In connexion with
the Hebrew preference for long hair, it is of interest to
note that in mythology the beneficient rays of the sun are
spoken of as hair and the sun is described as possessing a
long beard and locks of hair. According to the astral
theory of Jeremias, long hair characterizes the summer
with all its brilliance and splendour ; whilst shorn hair
symbolizing blindness and imprisonment characterizes the
winter sun. The Greeks called Helios " the yellow-
haired ", and in an American legend the sun-god Bocsika
is represented as an old man with a long beard.[1]

Another explanation of the origin of the practice of
" cutting the hair " as a mourning custom is worthy of
note. In Deut. xxi, 12, we read that if a man wishes to
marry a woman whom he has taken captive in battle he
shall bring her to his house and she shall shave her head,
pare her nails, and remove her garment of captivity. The
reference to the change of garments in particular shows the
idea of these symbolical practices. They were all intended
to disguise the woman, to show that she had been translated
from one religion to another—" from the state of heathen
and slave to that of a wife amongst the covenant people."

The practice of shaving the hair of one's head as a means
of disguising oneself from the spirit of the deceased exists
amongst many peoples. Amongst some of the tribes of
British East Africa a person who touches a corpse must

[1] J. G. Muller, *Geschichte der Amerikanischen Urreligionen*, p. 429.

bathe his body and shave his head so as to disfigure him beyond recognition in case the ghost of the deceased should pursue him. For a similar reason the relatives, after a funeral, must return home by a different route—in order to deceive the ghost of the dead. Similarly, there are many peoples amongst whom it is customary for the mourners to assume a new name or for the widow to have her finger-joint amputated or her eyebrows shaved, so that her husband's ghost will not be able to recognize her and thus lose all attraction for her.

THE NAME

Just as it is customary amongst orthodox Jews of the present day for the surviving sons to recite annually a prayer known as *Kaddish* on the anniversary of the decease of their parents, so amongst the ancient Semites there was a ceremony at which the son called upon his dead parents by name. This was apparently considered a mark of respect to the memory of the deceased. In 2 Sam. xviii, 18, we read that Absalom reared up for himself a pillar, for he said, " I have no son to keep my name in remembrance," and he called the pillar after his own name. The passage thus suggests that as it was the practice for a son to call upon the name of his deceased parents, and as Absalom had no son to survive him and perform this ceremony, he set up a pillar which would act as a memorial to him. We also read in Isa. iv, 1, how, after a terrible period of destruction during which a considerable portion of the male population has been destroyed, seven women shall seize hold of one man saying, " we will eat our own bread and wear our own apparel : only let us be called by thy name ; take away our reproach." In other words, the women will be prepared to bear the responsibility of providing their own material needs so long as they can marry and leave children to call upon their name when they are deceased. In Syriac litera-ture, in connexion with the false report concerning the death of Ahikar, the following passage occurs : " When Nadan my son had reached my house he made no feast of bewailing for me, nor did he perform the act of invocation."[1] Amongst the Arabs there also existed a custom known as *dhikr* or *zikr*, by which the son called upon the name of his deceased parents,[2] and amongst the modern Egyptians as soon as a person dies part of the lamentation consists of calling upon his name.

Amongst various Semitic races there existed the institution known as "Levirate marriage". This, as we are informed in the Old Testament, was in order to raise up seed to one who died without issue. The aim of Semitic marriage was procreation of children. Childlessness was looked upon as a terrible evil (Gen. xvi, 4; xix, 31), for if a person left no children his name would eventually be erased from "among his brethren and the gate of his town". Furthermore, there would be no one to invoke his name when he had passed away, and thus his name would be blotted out from Israel. In order to remove this reproach from the departed it was regarded as the duty of the eldest surviving brother to marry the widow, and the first-born son resulting from such an alliance was considered as the representative and heir of the deceased.

The Egyptians believed that one bestowed a great boon upon a man by causing his name to live, and, on the other hand, nothing worse could occur than that a person's name should be allowed to perish. They therefore endeavoured to destroy the names of the people they hated. We have a tomb from the Old Empire in which the names of the two sons of the deceased have been carefully chiselled out—although the rest of the tomb is quite intact. This was probably done at the request of the father, as his sons may have caused him some displeasure. When Amenhotep IV instituted the worship of the sun's disc he very carefully erased everywhere the name of the god Amen, and

---

[1] *The Story of Ahikar*, by Conybeare, Rendel Harris, A. Smith Lewis (Cambridge, 1913).
[2] See Goldziher, *Wiener Zeitschrift für die Kunde des Morgenlandes*, xvi, p. 313.

during his reign constantly tried to strike out the name of the god from all the temples in his dominions. He informs us that his object in establishing the worship of one god was in order that " his name should endure for ever in the mouth of the living ".

" Calling upon the name " was not merely a custom used in connexion with mourning rites, but was also part of religious worship. In Isa. xxvi, 13, we read, " O Lord, our God, other lords beside Thee have had dominion over us ; but only Thy name shall we invoke." Again, in Hos. ii, 17, " I shall remove the names of the Baalim from her mouth and their names shall no more be used as an invocation." In these two passages the Hebrew verb " to invoke " is זכר, connected with the noun זֵכֶר—equivalent to the Arabic *dhikr* or *zikr*—to which we have referred. In other words, the naming of a deity or a man was equivalent to calling upon his זכר, and we actually find that the Hebrew זכר and שֵׁם are used synonymously. Thus in Exod. iii, 15, God says to Moses, " This is my name for ever and this is my זכר for all generations."

In Egypt, those performing the *zikr* are known as Zikkeers. Lane,[1] in describing a typical act of the *zikr* which he witnessed in Cairo, states that after reciting the opening portions of the Koran the performers sitting cross-legged upon some matting chanted in slow measure *La illaha illa illah* (there is no deity but God), bowing the head and body twice in each repetition. They continued thus for about a quarter of an hour, and then for about the same space of time they repeated these words to the same air, but in a quicker measure and with correspondingly quicker motions.

What is the meaning of this rite of " calling upon the name " and how is its origin to be explained ? Amongst many primitive peoples there is a belief that the soul of a deceased person animates the body of another human being,

---

[1] *Manners and Customs of the Modern Egyptians*, vol. i, p. 308, etc.

especially of an infant, and the naming of a child is actually
connected with the return of the soul of its ancestors.
This was also supposed to explain why a person so often
resembles one of his dead ancestors. Among the Tacullis
of N.W. America the medicine man is the medium by which
the soul is reincarnated. He places his hands on the breast
of the dead, then holds them over the head of a relative
and blows through them. The next child born to this relative
of the deceased will be animated with his soul and will
bear his name. Amongst the Khonds of Orissa the priest
decides on the seventh day after birth which of the child's
ancestors has appeared in his person, and the child receives
the name of that particular ancestor. Some Indians of
North America treat a child as having taken the place of
the last one who bore its name. In New Zealand the priest
repeats a long list of the names of the ancestors of the
child, and during this repetition the name at which the
child starts crying or sneezing is considered to be the one
selected for its own name.

To both the Hebrews and Babylonians the name was
identical with the object or person it represented. Already
in the early times of the Sumerians we find that it was
customary to give symbolical names to all kinds of sacred
objects and statues which were dedicated to the gods and
placed in the temples, either as a mark of gratitude for some
past favour, or in order to ensure the blessings of the deity
in the future. One may refer in particular to statues
which were dedicated by Gudea, patesi of Lagash. Thus
one statue of E-ninnu he named " The shepherd-who-
loveth-his-king-am-I-may-my-life-be-prolonged ",   whilst
to another larger statue for the same temple he gave the
long symbolical name " Ningirsu-the-king-whose-powerful-
strength - the - lands - cannot - support - hath - assigned -
a - favourable - lot - unto - Gudea - the - builder - of - the -
temple ".[1] These symbolical names were probably bestowed

---

[1] See L. W. King, *A History of Sumer and Akkad*, p. 273.

on the statues because they were supposed to symbolize the worshipper and to plead with the deity on his behalf.

" Like other nations of antiquity, the Babylonians conformed the name with the person who bore it ; it not only represented him, but in a sense was actually himself. Magical properties were ascribed to the name, and it thus became of importance to know what names were good or bad, lucky or unlucky. An unlucky name brought evil fortune to its possessor, a lucky name secured his success in life. A change of name influenced a man's career ; and the same superstitious belief which caused the Cape of Storms to become the Cape of Good Hope not unfrequently occasioned a person's name to be altered among the nations of the ancient East." [1]

If a sorcerer wished to gain control over a spirit or person he had to learn the name. Once he succeeded in that, all he needed to do was to utter that name, and he was then able to carry out his desires. Some scholars find instances of this idea in the Old Testament. In Gen. xxxii we read how Jacob after his struggle with the angel asked him his name. Again, in Judges xiii, after Manoah, the father of Samson, had listened to the admonition of the angel, he said to him : " What is thy name, that when thy words come to pass we may do thee honour ? " In other words, just as the angel is able to predict Samson's character before he is born, so Manoah would be able to exercise some magical influence over the angel once he gets to know his name. In Apocryphal literature the same idea is represented.

This belief also existed amongst the Jewish Cabbalists right through the Middle Ages, who argued that as the world is comprised in God, to invoke the Divine name meant in reality to invoke the assistance of God, and it explains why amongst the Babylonians the names of the great gods were regarded as a most powerful form of exorcism.

---

[1] A. H. Sayce, *Babylonians and Assyrians*, p. 45.

But just as the act of mentioning a name could have the effect of crippling the power of a spirit and destroying its effectiveness, so it might have an equally opposite effect. It might re-create the spirit and imbue it with fresh life and vigour. In other words, the mention or bestowal of a name was equivalent to re-creation.[1] In Isa. xliii, 1, God says to Israel: " I have called thee by thy name; thou art mine." Jeremias explains this as meaning that as God has called upon Israel by name He has gained control over its person.[2]

We can now understand the meaning of the *dhikr* as a mourning ceremony amongst the Hebrews. Every time the living called upon the dead by name he gave his spirit fresh life and vigour. To call upon the dead by name was therefore a symbolical ceremony of mutual advantage. It was an advantage to the dead, because the very fact that his name was mentioned meant that he was re-created and that death did not come as an end to his existence. But it was also an advantage to the living, for it meant that by invoking the name of his ancestors he could bestow life and force upon their dead spirits, and could thus summon them to his aid whenever necessary. In Rabbinic literature we meet with the expression מעלה המת בזכורו to bring up the spirit of the dead by calling upon it by name (Talmud, *Sanhedrin*, 65B). It is also of interest to note that amongst orthodox Jews a prayer that God may remember their deceased ancestors or other near relatives is recited on certain festivals. This is known as " the Hazkarah ", i.e. " the making mention " or " causing to remember ", and the name of the deceased is actually included in the prayer.

---

[1] The identity of a person's name and his life are so fully established amongst primitive peoples, that among the American Indians if a person calls the dead by name he must surrender his own blood or pay blood-money, in restitution of the life of the dead taken by him (First Annual Report of Bureau of Ethnol., p. 200).

[2] *The Old Testament in the light of the Ancient East*, Eng. Trans., vol. ii, p. 274.

KINDLING LIGHTS

The practice of kindling lights in connexion with burial and mourning customs is found not only amongst the Semites, but in all parts of the world. Numerous explanations have been suggested as to the exact connexions between these practices, and have given rise to considerable discussion. Amongst the Hebrews it seems to have been customary for the surviving male member of a family to kindle a lamp before the image of the deceased ancestor. The keeping up of a lamp's light was used as a symbol of enduring and unbroken succession (1 Kings xi, 36; xv, 4; Ps. cxxxii, 17), for it was really a blessing upon the person that he may leave behind children to perform this symbolical ceremony. On the other hand, such an expression as "the light of the wicked shall be quenched" was a curse meaning that the person shall leave no male descendants to perform this practice.

In the course of excavations in Palestine, numerous graves have been found containing lamps [1]; and it was customary in the times of the Mishna as it is amongst Jews to-day to light candles as soon as a person dies. How are we to account for the origin of these practices? To the ancient Semites light and darkness were looked upon as two great powerful forces which were beyond the powers of mankind, but were controlled by the great gods of the universe. Light was of value and importance to them; darkness was not only unnecessary, but also a great hindrance. It was only natural, therefore, that beneficence, joy, and pleasure came to be symbolized by light; whilst trouble, misfortune, and wickedness were symbolized by darkness. Many of the great deities amongst the Semites whose attributes were so necessary for the welfare of mankind bore names which were compounded with words

---

[1] Bliss, *Mound of Many Cities*; S. A. Cooke, *Religion of Ancient Palestine.*

signifying light,[1] and their temples also bore names of similar significance. Again, seeing that in the East light has a clearness and brilliancy and is followed in its influence by considerable advantage to the inhabitants, it is only natural that it should be looked upon as representing the highest human good. " All the more joyous emotions of the mind, all the pleasing sensations of the frame, all the happy hours of domestic intercourse were described under imagery derived from light " (1 Kings xi, 36 ; Isa. lviii, 8 ; Esther viii, 16 ; Ps. xcvii, 11). The fact that light is so often accompanied by heat, and thus indirectly acts as a purifying force, may also account for the symbolical use of the term in connexion with the human soul and true religion. Darkness is associated with cold and, therefore, with death and decay.

In ancient Egypt the crested ibis, whose name is equivalent to " light ", was used as a symbol of the soul. It has already been shown by Hehn [2] that in the later books of the Old Testament light is used as a symbol of the deity because there is no possibility of a corporal form being attached to it. " The deity as light gave transition to the deity as spirit." The practice of lighting lamps in honour of the gods is found in all religions. In the Old Testament we read that it was the duty of the minister in the temple to attend to the lamps. The Rabbis explained the light which was kindled in the sanctuary as testifying to the existence of the light of the *Shechina* in the midst of Israel (*Men.* 68B). God says : " If you preserve my light burning in your soul I shall keep your light." In the same way the perpetual lamp of the synagogue was interpreted by the Rabbis as a symbol of God's presence in Israel (*Shab.* 22b).[3]

We may note incidentally that we learn from the writings of Tertullian, which contain warnings to believers against

---

[1] Shamshi Ramman, the thunder god, was almost a god of darkness, but the darkness which he caused was relieved by the lightning.

[2] J. Hehn, *Die biblische und die babylonische Gottesidee*, Leipzig, 1913.

[3] The seven-branched candlestick in the tabernacle, which corresponded on the whole to the candlestick described in Zech. iv, 1 et seq.,

possible seducements of idolatry, that in his time images of deities were found at the doors and gates of heathens, who were in the habit of honouring them by adorning their gates with lamps. Not only the gods, but even deceased saints were also honoured by having lights kindled for them. In ancient Egypt it was customary to light lamps before the statue of the deceased on certain festivals, on the first and last days of the year, and also on certain occasions when the friends of the dead came to the temple to sing praises and recite hymns in his honour. We also read of a certain Hapdefæ who made ten contracts with the priests of his town in order to ensure certain revenues for religious services. We are informed that his statues which he placed in his tomb and in the temples of Suit were to be provided by the priests with a supply of bread, beer, and meat, and that provision was also to be made for illuminating the statues on certain festivals. In modern Egypt the distinguished dead are honoured by an anniversary birthday festival known as *moled.* On this occasion the tomb of the saint is visited, and his *zikr* is recited ; whilst the people who live in the neighbourhood of the tomb hang lamps before their doors.

The practice of placing a lamp before the image of the dead may be explained in the following manner. The lamp is a symbol of the soul ; therefore, by placing it before the image of the deceased, one helps to re-create his spirit. In other words, the belief underlying it is similar to the act of calling on the name of the dead as a means of reviving him.

The practice of placing artificial lights and lamps in tombs and also near the dead preliminary to burial may have been intended by the mourners as a means of relieving some of the gloomy darkness of the underworld to which

symbolically represented the seven planets which are regarded as " the eyes of the creator ", and see everything. Both candlesticks represented a tree with almond blossoms. This symbolism may, perhaps, be understood from the explanation in Jer. i, 11, in which God's watchfulness over His word to perform it is represented by an almond.

the body was conveyed. In this connexion one may refer
to the general illumination which took place throughout
Egypt on the night of the seventeenth of Thot, when every
family, no matter how poor, placed a lamp in front
of their door in order to facilitate the visit which the
dead were supposed to make to the family residence at
this time.

The modern Egyptians, in common with other Eastern
peoples, believe that there is a class of evil spirits who appear
in the forms of various animals and in many monstrous
shapes to haunt burial grounds and other sequestered
spots and to feed upon dead bodies. Similarly, the
Babylonians believed that evil spirits prowl around the
bodies of the dead either to make use of them in their
sorcery or to feed upon them. They therefore invited
beneficent spirits and genii to come and watch over the
dead body. Some of these invisible genii clad in fish
costumes were on guard as watchmen at the head and foot
of the bed. Others who had lions' heads and human bodies
acted as guardians in the sepulchral chambers ready to
attack any spirit which may venture to enter ; whilst
others, again, stood round the house ready to ward off any
evil spirits which might attempt to gain admission through
the roof. These evil demons, however, could only exert
their wicked influences in dark places, and once a light
penetrated their abode they were rendered absolutely
powerless. It may, therefore, have been a desire to cripple
the power of the evil spirits which gave rise to the practice
of placing lamps in the tomb.

The importance of dispelling the demons of the night
may be seen from the joy which characterized the
appearance of the moon every month, and the mourning
and lamentation which took place when it disappeared.
For, as we have already seen, darkness represented trouble
and danger, and the moon was therefore regarded as a
powerful factor which helped to disperse these evil forces
and to bring about safety and happiness.

DUST AND ASHES

As a symbol of grief or mourning the ancient Hebrews used to place dust, earth, or ashes on the head. When Joshua's warriors were defeated by the people of Ai he tore his garments and he and the elders of Israel put dust on their heads (Joshua vii, 6). We are also informed in Lam. ii, 10, that when the elders of Zion mourned for Jerusalem they girded themselves with sackcloth and placed dust upon their heads. Also when the messenger brought the news of the death of Saul and Jonathan, he had earth on his head and his garments were torn (2 Sam. xv, 32). In 2 Sam. xiii, 19, we read that Tamar, after having been outraged by Amnon, put ashes on her head, rent the long-sleeved tunic which she wore, and put her hand upon her head—all of which occur elsewhere as marks of intense grief. Similar symbolical actions occur in post-Biblical literature. In 2 Macc. x, 25, when the followers of Judas heard that Timotheus was approaching with a great army, they scattered earth on their heads and girded their loins with sackcloth.

There are also some references in the Old Testament to actual sitting in ashes. In Jonah iii, 6, we read that when the bad tidings reached the king of Nineveh he arose from his throne, covered himself with sackcloth, and sat in ashes. Also in Job (ii, 8) we are told that he took a potsherd to scrape himself withal; and he sat among the ashes. An explanation of this passage is difficult. Macalister (Hastings, DB., vol. iii, p. 329) suggests that Job sat among the ashes to mitigate the itching. Another explanation is that the character of his disease necessitated his leaving home and settling on an ash-heap outside the city with the lepers. But it seems much more likely that Job resorted to this as a mark of grief for the great loss and bereavement he had sustained.

The custom of covering oneself with ashes in mourning as a symbol of grief is almost universal.[1] Herodotus tells

---

[1] It is held by some scholars that the modern custom of wearing black in mourning may have arisen from the ancient practice of blackening the body with ashes.

us that the ancient Egyptians used to smear their faces with mud as a mark of grief. Even the modern peasant women of Egypt smear their faces and portions of their clothing with mud, in mourning. Amongst many peoples the custom is explained as having arisen through a desire on the part of the mourner to disguise himself from the dead man lest his ghost should follow him about and do him some harm. Amongst certain Australian tribes the widow must cover herself with ashes during her period of mourning. This is to prevent the ghost of her husband from continually following her about and finally killing her.[1] In California the mourner mixes the ashes of a dead man with grease and smears his face with it.

Ashes are also used by spirits as a means of recognizing the way in their attempts to return to the living. Therefore the Araucanians strew ashes in a haphazard way as the coffin is being borne to the grave so that the ghost will not know how to return. In this connexion one may refer to a passage in the Talmud where Raba says that if a person will strew some ashes near his bedside he will see the footprints of devils in the morning. Whilst this explanation of the symbolism may be quite acceptable for other races, much more plausible explanations have been offered for the use of ashes as a symbol of mourning amongst the ancient Semites.

Robertson Smith has suggested that the ashes which were strewn on the head were probably the ashes of the victim sacrificed at the grave, just as it was customary to take some dust from the grave and strew it on the head. He compares with this the draught known as *solwan* taken by Arab mourners to forget their grief. This consists of water mingled with dust from the grave. Sprinkling with ashes may thus have been regarded as the means of imparting fresh vigour and life to the mourners, and the

---

[1] Baldwin Spencer and F. J. Gillen, *The Northern Tribes of Central Australia*, 1904.

custom may have arisen through the mourners using the ashes of the animals which were sacrificed at the graveside. We know that in many primitive religions it was believed that the ashes of a sacrificed animal have the power of fertilizing the land and of giving strength and vigour to the inhabitants. Robertson Smith points out that amongst certain African tribes when a boy reaches the age of puberty he is daubed with fat and soot on being initiated into manhood—the fat being regarded as a seat of life and as possessing some special divine power which had originally belonged to the animal from which it was taken. In the ritual connected with the Red Heifer (Num. xix) the ashes of the offering are to be placed in water and then a portion of this is to be sprinkled on the unclean person. Evidently the ashes of the animal still possessed some of its sacredness in being able to purify the unclean.

But perhaps the use of ashes in mourning can be explained in a much more interesting and plausible way. The Hebrew for " ashes " אֵפֶר is almost identical with the word for " dust " עָפָר. These two words are really synonymous, and occur together for the sake of emphasis in the expression עָפָר וָאֵפֶר (dust and ashes). The words are also used interchangeably in the Old Testament, and in Rabbinic literature, synonymously. On fast days the ark of the covenant as a sign of mourning was sprinkled over with earth as a substitute for ashes (*Mishna Ta'anith*, 16a). It was also customary to sprinkle ashes upon the bridegroom during the marriage ceremony in order to remind him of the destruction of Jerusalem. In Lev. xvii, 13, where the Israelite is commanded to cover over the blood of an animal or fowl that has been slaughtered with עָפָר (dust), the Rabbis explained this as signifying dust *or* ashes. It is also of interest to note that Nöldeke,[1] in a most interesting article, " Mutter Erde und verwandtes bei den Semiten," has suggested that עָפָר is a name

[1] *Archiv für Religionswissenschaft*, viii, p. 161.

given to the matter of which the earth consists. On the basis of these facts Jastrow thinks that in many passages in the Old Testament relating to mourning the word אֵפֶר, which we translate "ashes", really means "dust" or "earth", and is used to express the idea that the mourners placed some earth on their heads. He finds support for this suggestion from Assyriology.

The Vulture Stele, which is one of the finest examples of early Sumerian art and depicts the triumph of Eannatum of Lagash over Umma, throws considerable light upon the customs of the ancient Sumerians. On one of its fragments are represented two living figures engaged in burying the dead. On another fragment are represented a collection of dead on the field of battle. The attendants are climbing up a mound near the pile of corpses. They have baskets on their heads, and it has been suggested that these are filled with offerings for the dead. It seems, however, much more likely that these baskets contained earth and were brought by the attendants to be thrown on to the mound so as to build it up. In the text we are informed that after the battle with Umma, Eannatum piled up twenty burial mounds. It seems, therefore, very likely that we have here a representation of one of the mounds being constructed, from which we can understand the desire on the part of the Babylonians to bury their dead properly. The Hebrews as well as the Babylonians also took great pains to give their dead proper burial, for they believed that the unburied dead not only bring trouble upon the living relatives, but also bring a curse and defilement upon the whole land (2 Sam. xxi, 10, 11 ; 1 Kings xiii, 22).

Jastrow thinks that this custom of carrying a basket of earth on one's head in order to build up the mound of the dead gave rise to the symbolism connected with the practice of placing dust upon one's head as a symbol of mourning or grief.[1] His explanation is that the earth was thrown

---

[1] See his article "Dust, Earth, and Ashes as Symbols of Mourning among the Ancient Hebrews" in *Journal of American Oriental Society,* xx (1899), 133–50.

on to the ground to straighten out the grave and build up
a mound over the body after it had been committed to
burial. But as the custom was found to be unnecessary,
after a time the earth was no longer thrown on to the ground
but into the air. Thus, according to this suggestion, the
earth placed by the mourners on the head was not taken
from the grave, but was rather intended for it.

The present writer would go further and suggest that
this may have given rise to the practice of "wallowing
in ashes" referred to in the Old Testament. In Jer. vi, 26,
we read : " O daughter of my people, gird thee with sackcloth and wallow thyself in ashes ; make thee mourning as
for an only son." The Heb. והתפלשׁי, translated
" wallow thyself ", is rendered by the versions " sprinkle
thyself ". In Job ii, 12, after a description of how his
friends came to comfort him on hearing of his misfortune,
we read : " and they rent everyone his mantle and sprinkled
dust upon their heads towards heaven." This verse is
usually explained as meaning that they threw some dust
upwards towards heaven which fell upon their heads, thus
symbolizing that they were laid in the dust by a calamity
from heaven. But there is another explanation. We have
already seen that when a change took place in the manner
of burial, and it was no longer customary to carry a basket
of earth on the shoulder, the earth was placed on the head
as a symbol of mourning and then sprinkled up into the
air. To sprinkle oneself with dust, therefore, became a
mark of grief and humiliation. Seeing that dust and ashes
are used interchangeably, the command to the daughter of
Zion to sprinkle herself with ashes would be equivalent to
sprinkling dust on her head.

Again, the verb פלשׁ is no doubt connected with
פלס,[1] which means " to make level or smooth ", and is
actually used of straightening or making smooth a path
(see *Oxford Heb. Lexicon BDB.*, p. 814). The fact that

---

[1] On the relationship of ס to the original values of שׂ and שׁ see
Nöldeke, *ZDMG.*, 1893, pp. 100 f., and Haupt, *ZDMG.*, 1880, pp. 762 f.

254   BIBLICAL AND SEMITIC SYMBOLISM

the same verb is used in Hebrew in the sense of " to sprinkle oneself " and also " to straighten out a path " gives further support to Jastrow's suggestion that the symbolism arose through the mourners throwing earth on to the tomb in order to straighten it out.

This practice of covering oneself with dust or ashes as a symbol of mourning caused it to become later a general mark of humiliation and submission. In certain regions of the Congo the symbols of homage to a chief are to prostrate oneself and then cover one's forehead or arms with dust. At a later time the symbolism was interpreted differently. The mourners in their state of affliction naturally looked upon the dust which is trodden under foot as symbolizing the state in which they had been placed as a result of their bereavement.

Again, sitting in dust would symbolize that man is formed from dust and returns to dust. The Babylonians represented dust as the food of the dead, and the Hebrew עָפָר may be connected with the Assyrian for food (*ipru*), so that placing dust on the head would also show that man returns to the state where dust is his food.

THE THRESHING FLOOR

In Gen. 1, 10, where the story of Jacob's burial is related, we read : " And they came to the threshing floor of Atad which is beyond the Jordan, and there they mourned with a very great and sore lamentation." It is important to note that this is only one of numerous instances in Semitic literatures where the mourning for the dead takes place at a threshing floor. On the death of a Syriac peasant his body is often taken to the threshing floor, where several symbolical mourning customs are performed.[1] Again, in Arabic literature we read that the lamentations for the dead took place at a large open square. Thus we are informed in Mohammedan tradition that the prophet held a service for the dead at a place called *al-musalla* at Medina.

[1] J. G. Wetzstein, *Die Syrische Dreschtafel.*

In the Talmud (*Moed Katan*, 5 B) we read of fields known as " fields of lamentation " where the people lamented the dead. In Jer. vii, 29, the prophet says, " take up a lamentation on bare high places." The prophet may have indirectly referred to a threshing floor, for in ancient times the threshing floor consisted of a round open space most frequently on an eminence, " where it was exposed to the free sweep of air currents."

We have already noted that to the Semites the main purpose of marriage was procreation, and as the threshing floor symbolized the fertility of the earth, it became the acknowledged centre where marriages took place and where ritual prostitution—which was an important part of Semitic religious ceremonialism—was carried out. It thus came to be regarded as a sacred place. Analogies for this can be found in other parts of the world also. In the Southern provinces of Ceylon, when the corn is being placed into the bags, the threshers behave just as though they were in a temple of the gods.[1]

There are various instances in the Old Testament where the threshing floor is referred to as a centre for religious ceremonial. In 1 Kings, xxii, when the kings of Israel and Judah were in doubt as to whether they should make war on Syria, we are informed that four hundred prophets were assembled at the threshing floor. Gad told David to build an altar in the threshing floor of Araunah. In Hos. (ix, 1) we read : " Rejoice not, O Israel, for joy, as other people, for thou hast gone a whoring from thy god, thou hast loved hire upon every cornfloor."

Amongst the Greeks at the festival of the threshing floor in connexion with the worship of Demeter certain mystic rites were performed by intoxicated women, who also baked cakes in the forms of the male and female organs of generation. These symbolical rites no doubt had as their object the fertilizing of the soil.

[1] " Customs and superstitions connected with the cultivation of rice in the S. Province of Ceylon ": *Journal of Royal Asiatic Society*, N.S., xvii, 1885.

CHAPTER VII

MISCELLANEOUS SYMBOLISMS

CHAPTER VII

MISCELLANEOUS SYMBOLISMS

Amongst every people the work of the architect, the sculptor, and the painter is to translate the religious conceptions of his people into some visible form. The architect gives expression to his ideas by the manner in which he constructs his temple; whilst the sculptor and painter symbolize their religious conceptions by the way in which various images of the gods or sacred objects in the temple are represented.

Grant Allen,[1] referring to the great influence which religion has exerted upon the æsthetic sentiment, says: " if the house of the chief receives exceptional decoration, much more does the house of that deified ghost-chief the god. Wherever we look we see that all the resources of art, infantile or full-grown, are most fully employed in the service of religion. Painting, sculpture, music, the thousand minor arts of decoration, and dress all combine to do honour to the gods of the country." Art and religion were always closely united. It is by an examination of Babylonian art that we are enabled to obtain an insight into the fundamentals of their religion, and an examination of the structure and the sacred artistic figures of the tabernacle and temple may help us, therefore, to realize the fundamental ideas on which the religion of the ancient Hebrews was based.

Although there is not the slightest reference in the Old Testament to any symbolic meaning of the tabernacle, scholars, both ancient and modern, have suggested that both in its structure and in its appurtenances it symbolized various religious truths. The Hebrew *mishkan* " dwelling "

---

[1] *Colour Sense*, p. 248.

expressed the idea that God dwelt amongst His people, *Ohel Moed* " tent of meeting " represented the idea that God met His people there ; whilst the name *Ohel ha-Eduth* " tent of the testimony " constantly called to mind that the decalogue inscribed on the Tables of the Ark bore witness to the covenant between Jehovah and His people. But there are other ideas symbolized by the tabernacle. The innermost chamber, the Holy of Holies, was the dwelling-place of the deity Himself. This could be entered by the high priest alone, and only once a year on the Day of Atonement. In this chamber everything was made of gold and decorated with beautifully made fabrics ; whilst the vestments of the high priest were conspicuous by their gorgeous finery. This gave expression to the thought that God's most holy minister and His chief abode should be adorned with becoming dignity and splendour. On the other hand, in the Holy Place, which could only be entered by the priests, the furniture was of gold ; whilst the outer pillars, which were taken, no doubt, as belonging to the court, were made of brass. The court, which was for the people, had only brass. The covering for the Holy of Holies was made of costly materials with figured cherubim, the curtain at the door of the Holy Place was without cherubim, and that at the court was simply made of white linen. We can thus see how the costliness of the adornments of the different apartments symbolized their sacredness, and the more sacred a chamber, the more sumptuously was it decorated.

Some scholars have argued that the tabernacle and temple, which were to the Hebrews the visible dwelling-places of God, were intended to symbolize in form His invisible abode. The Holy Place and Holy of Holies therefore represented the heavens and the highest heavens (1 Kings viii, 27), whilst the forecourt symbolized the earth, which was regarded as God's footstool (Isa. lxvi, 1). To Josephus the tabernacle represented the world ; whilst the Holy of Holies, being inaccessible to man, was a symbol of heaven.

One need hardly say that there is not even the remotest hint in the Old Testament that would support such suggestions.

Many ancient peoples represented their deities as a nobleman dwelling in his palace, and we have already noted that the features and routine of Egyptian temples were similar to those of large households. First came the small chamber symbolizing the mysterious dwelling of the deity himself. The larger hall in front of this can be compared to the audience-chamber where human kings receive their subjects ; whilst the large space in front of the building was primarily a meeting-place for the people. The Egyptians as well as the Babylonians and Assyrians regarded the temple as the palace of the god's representative on earth. It contained a special chamber in which the image of the god was kept, and the image was also washed and anointed and had food placed before it. To this chamber only the priests and kings were allowed on special occasions, and it therefore corresponded to the Holy of Holies of the Hebrew temple ; whilst the ordinary worshippers assembled in an outer court which was separated from this by means of an enclosure. The Hebrew for temple, " hekhal," corresponds to the Babylonian " ekallu ", which is the word for a palace or large house.

Just as other nations took with them images of their gods into battle, so the Israelites took the ark of Jehovah with them whenever going to war. Its raised position was a symbol and pledge of Jehovah's presence and help. In this connexion one is reminded of the passage in Jer. iii, 16, where the prophet looks forward to the time when no such material symbol of Jehovah's presence will be needed, and the ark having served its purpose will be neither " remembered nor missed nor made again ".

The ten curtains of which the tabernacle proper was made up, were spread over the framework in two sets of five curtains. They were of very fine linen with figures of cherubim in beautiful colours. In the words of Kennedy,

" they were designed to form the earthly and with the aid of the attendant cherubim to symbolize the heavenly dwelling-place of God."

The two pillars Jachin and Boaz which stood in front of the porch of the temple were probably symbols. The temple of Melkarth at Tyre and the temple at Hierapolis had two similar pillars in front of them which were symbols of the deity, and as Solomon's temple was constructed on the same principle it has been suggested that these two pillars were symbols of Jehovah. We are certain that they did not stand in the inside, so that they were not erected for supporting the roof as has been suggested by some scholars. Nor do they seem to have been mere ornaments, for the very fact that they had special names assigned to them suggests that they were of some specific importance. Kimchi thought that the names of the pillars (Jachin—he will establish, Boaz—in him is strength) show that they were placed there to symbolize the strength of the kingdom of God in ancient Israel.

In Solomon's temple, besides a very large vessel called the molten sea, there were lavers of brass which were very ornamental and elaborate. A minute description is given of the bases on which they stood and of their several parts and ornaments (1 Kings vii, 27–39), but they are exceedingly difficult to understand, and although we are told by the chronicler (2 Chron. iv, 6) that they were used for washing the sacrifices, scholars have suggested that they were also placed there to symbolize some religious truths. Nowack sees some connexion between the lavers and the chariot of the cherubim (Ezek. i). In Ezekiel the cherubs are the bearers of the cloud-throne, here of the collected waters. Kosters thinks that the lavers symbolized the clouds (Ps. xviii, 11). The molten sea is described as being a round copper reservoir mounted on 12 copper bulls, and as 12 is an astronomical number, H. P. Smith suggests that the bulls were symbols of the 12 constellations and that " the sea was a symbol of the great celestial reservoir from

which the earth is watered ". We have already referred
to the importance of water as a source of symbolical
purification, whilst in connexion with ancient cosmological thought one may refer to Ps. xxix, 10, where the
sea represents the water or flood upon which Jehovah as
God of the rain is enthroned. Similar " seas " have been
found amongst other Semitic peoples also. In the Babylonian temples there was a great basin known as *apsu*
which symbolically represented the domain of Ea—the
great water-god,[1] and this, together with the Zikkurat or
temple tower, which represented the face of the earth,
became symbols of their cosmological conceptions. The
ornamental figures on the smaller laver Smith also explains
as being symbolical. He says, " the bulls were sacred to
Jehovah, the lions were symbols of Astarte, the cherubs
were well-known mythological figures, and the palms were
also probably sacred," and he concludes, therefore, that the
significance of the ornamentation indicated a syncretistic
purpose in the building of the temple. This suggestion
has certainly nothing whatever in the Old Testament
to support it.

The sacrificial system of the Hebrews has also been
considered to have had a deep symbolical import. To
many scholars it symbolizes self-surrender and devotion
to the will of God, the need of forgiveness, and the blessing
of divine fellowship. Each offering has been regarded as
symbolizing in its own way some divine religious truth.
The peace offering with its communion feast showed the
idea of fellowship between God and man, the " tamid "
or continual offering is regarded as having symbolized
Israel's pledge of unbroken service to Jehovah ; whilst
the sin offering with its sprinkling of blood symbolized
the fact that one of the conditions of cleansing oneself
from sin was to place oneself submissively before God.

[1] The annual rainy season, during which there were heavy floods
producing chaos and destruction, caused the Babylonians to regard
water as the first element in existence. This was represented by
apsu, the deep that covers everything.

In the description of Solomon's temple (1 Kings vi, 29) we read that he carved all the walls of the house round about with carved figures of cherubim and palm-trees and openings of flowers. In 1 Kings vii, 29, 36, we read that on the borders of the molten sea and on the plates of the ledges, Solomon engraved lions, oxen, and cherubim, and "cherubim, lions, and palm-trees". We have already discussed the symbolic meanings of the lions and palm-trees, but how are we to interpret the cherubim ? In Exod. xxv, 22, Jehovah said that He will meet Moses and commune with him from between the cherubim. Surely this passage is clear enough to indicate how closely connected they were with the presence of the deity. The carved figures of cherubim everywhere in Solomon's temple—on the walls, doors, and vessels—as well as in Ezekiel's visionary temple, were no doubt intended to represent the nearness of God's presence.

We now proceed to consider the structure of the cherubim, and in Ezek. i the prophet sees a whirlwind out of the north, a great cloud and fire, and out of the midst of this the dim outline of four quadriform living creatures with straight legs, calves' feet, and the similitude of a human hand under their four wings. The faces were those of a man, an ox, a lion, and an eagle. In the account given in ch. x the prophet adds a few details in which he states that their wings sounded like thunder, and he refers also to their eyes.

Modern critical scholars have suggested that there are two varying accounts of the cherubim in the Old Testament based on two distinct underlying conceptions of them. On the one hand we have, for example, the account in Gen. iii, 24, in which the cherubim seem to be the guardians of the entrance to the sacred garden, and are associated with a "flaming sword" that guarded "the way of the tree of life". Their office was, therefore, to drive away anyone who would attempt to intrude into the abode of the deity. Of this type seem to be also the cherubim of Solomon's temple and of Ezekiel's visionary temple. But in Ps. xviii, 11, the cherub seems to be " a pale form of the wind-driven storm cloud " which serves as the chariot of God. Cheyne therefore suggests that when the Hebrew conception of the deity passed from an earth-god to a heaven-god, the cherub passed into a new phase and became the divine chariot.[1] Whether we accept this critical view or not we must note that all the references in the Old Testament agree in describing a close relationship between these figures and the deity. Furthermore, even the most critical scholars agree that the accounts given in the Old Testament of the structure of these figures show that they were symbolical. But it is in our attempts to discover the meanings of this symbolism that we are confronted with great difficulty, and in spite of all the efforts that have been made by scholars—ancient and modern—our knowledge of the subject is still very uncertain. According to some Rabbinic theologians the cherubim were intended to symbolize the union of the earthly with the heavenly ; whilst according to others they represented the two names of God, Jehovah and Elohim. Philo[2] regarded the cherubim over the ark as representing the two hemispheres ; whilst Josephus[3] says no one had any knowledge as to what they were like. In Jewish theology the whole account was regarded as an unfathomable mystery, and although it is exceedingly difficult to reconstruct the exact form of the cherubim, some of the details given by Ezekiel help us to gain a general idea as to the symbolical conceptions they were supposed to represent.

The number four was certainly symbolical. It may have represented the four corners of the earth, and the four heads would thus symbolically represent the four types of the most important things in the world. These united together—the lion among beasts, the ox among cattle,

[1] Article Cherub in *Encycl. Biblica.*
[2] *De Cherubim*, vii.
[3] *Ant.*, viii, 3.

the eagle among birds, and man amongst all—symbolize the quintessence of creation—all of which were placed underneath or rather in subordination to the supreme deity. Their eyes represented universal knowledge and omniscience, and their wings speed and ubiquity. The cherubim may thus be taken to have represented the subordination of the universe to God, and Bähr was perhaps correct when he described them as being intended to represent a union of the most perfect forms of created life which symbolized the most perfect revelation of God and the divine life.

Lion-headed goddesses and hawk-headed gods are found amongst the neighbours of Israel. On Phœnician monuments we have representations of griffins and sphinxes, and similar abortions are particularly common in Egyptian mythology. Some scholars have therefore suggested that the religious imagination of the Hebrews working on mythological figures which they had in common with their neighbours produced these forms. There are, however, two very strong objections to this. In the first place, Professor Flinders Petrie points out that although the Hebrew cherubim resembled in some respects Egyptian cherubic figures, they differed from them also in important features: " the Hebrew figures were male, while the Egyptian protective winged figures were always female and often specialized as Isis and Nepthys." [1] Again, it seems hardly credible that the Hebrews, whose religion forbade them to construct an image of anything in the heavens above or the earth beneath, should have borrowed from an alien source a representation of a living creature and have used it in constructing their tabernacle and temple. It is perhaps correct, therefore, to regard the form of the cherubim as an original idea of the Hebrews intended to convey the symbolic meaning we have already suggested.

Bähr thinks that the shewbread (Heb. = bread of the presence) symbolized the fact that God was ever present with His people and was the giver of their daily bread. Further,

[1] Hastings' DB., vol. i, p. 158B.

just as bread nourishes the body so His constant attachment to His people was to them a source of spiritual nourishment. Neither of these suggestions seems plausible. It was called *Lechem Tamid* " perpetual bread " because it was never absent from the table (Lev. xxiv; 1 Chron. xxiii, 29). Some scholars regard this term as a standing expression of Israel's thankfulness to God for His goodness towards them. It is interesting to note that Josephus [1] associated the twelve loaves with the twelve planets and that some modern scholars have accepted this view. Zimmern [2] has shown that twelve, or a multiple of that number, of loaves was most frequently set before the Babylonian gods, and he regards this number as symbolizing the signs of the zodiac.

How are we to explain the meaning of the incense ? Surely the interpretation of Maimonides (*More Mebuchim*, iii, 45) that it was used merely to remove the stench caused by the slaughter of so many animals in the temple is hardly plausible. The great care with which the preparation of the various aromatic compounds is explained in the Old Testament suggests that there was some symbolic meaning underlying the practice, although it was no doubt also used as a disinfectant to purify and sweeten the atmosphere of the sacred house. Incense is frequently referred to in the Babylonian-Assyrian cult. After the Deluge the " gods inhaled the sweet odour ". Herodotus tells us that one thousand tablets of frankincense were offered on the altar of Bel at his annual feast, and in Isa. lxv, 3, we read of Babylon as the land where incense is offered on bricks. On Egyptian monuments we often see a representation of the king with a censer in his hand offering incense. The incense was supposed to be a means of carrying prayer to heaven, and the Egyptians also prayed that the gods would draw the soul up to heaven on the smoke of the incense. Ps. cxli, 2, would suggest that the

[1] *Ant.*, iii, 7.
[2] *Beiträge zur Kenntniss d. Babyl. Religion.*

Hebrews regarded incense as a spiritual symbol of prayer. The Hebrew " Ketoreth ", which is translated incense, means the savoury odour or sweet smoke of a burnt sacrifice.[1] This implies that the object of burning the sacrifice was not so much to consume it by fire as to make a savoury smoke to the deity. Thus an offering made by fire (isheh) produces a sweet savour to the Lord (Lev. ii, 2; iii, 16). The most simple and plausible explanation is the following : in ancient times men regarded as acceptable and pleasing to the deity that which was also pleasing to themselves. In the East it was a common custom for fumigatories to be used after meals, and as sacrifices formed the food of the gods it would be appropriate for them to be accompanied by incense. Again, perfumes were often used in honour of guests and persons of note and distinction, and in sacrifices were, therefore, a mark of reverence to the deity. The explanations of Philo and Josephus deserve only a passing reference. To Philo the universe was represented by four elements—earth, air, fire, water. These were symbolized by the four ingredients of the incense which did honour to the deity. To Josephus the ingredients which were obtained from sea and land symbolized that God is the creator of all.

In Gen. ii we read that the Sabbath was designated to symbolize the completion of the work of creation. In post-exilic literature it is often described as a sign between Jehovah and Israel, and an additional reason for the observance of the Sabbath is given in Deut. v, 15, where we are told that it is to commemorate the deliverance of Israel from Egypt. The Israelite on ceasing work after a hard week's toil would be reminded of the slavery of his ancestors in Egypt, and would call to mind the goodness of God in delivering his forefathers from bondage. We have already dealt with the symbolism of the number seven, but we may note here how the Hebrews extended and

---

[1] Compare Assyrian *kutru*, smoke, and the verb which means " to turn into sweet smoke ".

multiplied the idea of the Sabbath as the very basis of their religious and social life.

The simple weekly Sabbath was supplemented by a Sabbath year ; whilst to the latter was added the Sabbath-Sabbath year, or year of Jubilee. In other words, just as the weekly Sabbath rest was to be a short cessation from the cares of ordinary life, so that the individual could gather fresh strength and vigour for his weekly toil, so on the greater Sabbath which extended after long intervals there was to be a universal cessation of national life as a means of restoring all the earthly constituents of the kingdom of Jehovah once again to their original and necessary purity, health, and uprightness. " The agriculturist by allowing his land to be fallow on the seventh year showed, thereby, that the land belonged to his god and not to him, and his cessation from toil thus symbolized his recognition of Jehovah's ownership of his land." The same thought was at the basis of the system of Jubilee. Ezekiel, speaking in the name of Jehovah, says : " I gave them my Sabbaths to be a sign between myself and them, that they might know that I, Jehovah, am the one who consecrates them." [1] In other words, the Sabbath was a mark that Jehovah had separated Israel from all other nations and consecrated them to Himself, and the whole social and religious system based upon the Sabbath was intended further to symbolize this belief.

Amongst many peoples who practise the rite, circumcision is performed at the age of puberty, and the youth is thus permitted to marry and take his place as a full member of the tribe. Whether this practice arose, in the first instance, on account of the sanctity which man attached to the organs of generation or for any other reason, need not be discussed here. An analysis of the beliefs of the races by whom it was practised suggests that the reasons for the rite vary very considerably. Amongst the Semites it was originally regarded as a sacrifice or as a

[1] Ezek. xx, 12.

mark of consecration.[1] It was therefore an offering of
one's flesh and blood to a god, and the loss of blood was to
be a constant reminder of consecration to a higher being.
It thus came to be regarded as a tribal badge, and its
performance symbolical of the fact that the patient had
been admitted a member of the tribe.   Those who were
circumcised regarded themselves purer than others, and
explained the custom on the grounds of propriety.
Herodotus [2] tells us that the Egyptians submitted to the
rite from a conscientious feeling of purity and propriety.
Circumcision thus came to be regarded also as a mark of
purification, and as an alien who did not have the tribal
badge was not able to partake in the common worship of
the tribe, the uncircumcised and unclean are classed together.   Its symbolic importance to the Hebrews, to
whom it was an indispensable act of national purification
and consecration, can clearly be seen from the Old Testament (Gen. xvii), where we are told it was appointed
by God as a token of the covenant between Him and
Abraham.   Abraham was commanded to perform it not
only on himself but on his descendants and slaves, as well
as on strangers who joined the Hebrew nation, in order to
symbolize that they were to accept the obligations and share
in the benefits of the race to whom they attached themselves.

The name " arelim " (uncircumcised) thus became an
opprobrious term denoting the Philistines and other non-
Israelites.   The prophets looked upon the circumcision
of the flesh as a symbol of the circumcision of the heart,
and Jeremiah draws a contrast between the Egyptian and
Edomite races which, though circumcised in the flesh, are
uncircumcised in the heart.   The symbolical significance
of circumcision can be further seen from the fact that it
was later connected with the giving of the name.   The

---

[1] Barton, *Semitic Origins*, pp. 98 ff., suggests that it was originally
regarded by the Semites as a sacrifice to the goddess of fertility, and
was intended to secure her favour in the production of offspring.
[2] ii, 37.

child was given a name when it was circumcised, and this represented its new worth as a member of the community. There was thus a private and a public symbolism connected with the rite. The disfigurement of any part of the body by tattooing a symbol of the god in a prominent position either on the arm or forehead as adopted by other peoples was forbidden to the Israelites (Deut. xiv, 1). Circumcision was thus only a private reminder to the individual ; whilst the name by which he was known by all would publicly symbolize that he was acknowledged a member of the community.

The cleansing qualities of certain unguents and their powers in preventing disease seem to have caused anointing to be regarded by the ancient Semites as a necessary part of the toilet. But the use of expensive unguents, which were also mixed with various sweet-smelling substances, was a luxury which only the wealthier classes could afford, and so anointing became a symbol of prosperity and joy (Ps. xcii, 11), and the cessation of the practice a sign of mourning and sadness. As a religious practice we read in the Old Testament of the anointing of priests and kings, and even of inanimate objects as the tabernacle and its appurtenances and the stone at Bethel. The symbolism connected with this practice has been explained in various ways. By some scholars it is regarded as the imparting of divine life or potency, seeing that fat was regarded in ancient times as a seat of life. Animal fat formed the food of the gods, and oil which took its place was thus capable of imparting divine virtue. Kamphausen thinks that the religious usage was derived from the custom of using oil for toilet purposes, and suggests that the anointing of an object therefore symbolized that it was specially selected and set apart for a sacred purpose.

It has been pointed out that in the pre-Islamic period the worshippers at the Kaaba at Mecca, in order to acquire some of the sanctity of the gods, used to rub their hands over their images, and the verb here used for rubbing (*tamassuh*) is from the same stem as the Hebrew for anointing (*mashah*). It has therefore been suggested that " rubbing " was originally a means of investing with power or sanctity, and this gave rise later to the practice of anointing with oil or wine, which were symbols of luxury accompanying a more advanced culture.[1] The word " anointed " thus came to mean invested with sacred authority, and the prophets are referred to as anointed ones (Ps. cv, 15) although the ceremony itself was not performed.

The use of salt as a condiment and the piquancy which it gives to insipid articles of diet caused it to be looked upon by many primitive peoples, including the Hebrews, as a symbol of life. The Hebrews had a copious supply of salt in their own country, and it entered to so great an extent into their food that " to eat salt " with anyone meant " to partake of his fare " or " share his hospitality ". It thus became a symbol of fidelity and friendship. Every meal which included salt had a sacred character, and this domestic sanctity of salt caused it to be regarded as symbolical of the most sacred obligations. By eating salt together the people who partook of the meal established amongst themselves a sacred bond, and the Arabic expression " there is salt between us " means that the people are united by a close bond of union. The preservative qualities of salt contributed further towards its symbolical importance, and caused it to be regarded as a symbol of permanency. We can thus understand that a " salt covenant " (Num. xviii, 19 ; Lev. ii, 13, etc.) was regarded as a very solemn and enduring bond.

The Hebrews were also acquainted with the medical properties of salt. The practice of washing a new-born child with salt water in order to cleanse and harden the skin (Ezek. xvi, 4) probably also arose from a desire to preserve the symbolical and religious uses of salt.

[1] See Jastrow's article " Anointing " in Hastings' *Encyc. of Religion and Ethics.*

Why were destroyed cities sown with salt ? Two possible explanations have been offered. An abundance of
salt has the effect of preventing the growth of vegetation,
and therefore the ploughing of a city with salt would
denote that it was condemned to eternal destruction and
desolation. A " salt land " is a sterile unproductive land
(Jer. xvii, 6 ; Job xxxix, 6). Robertson Smith suggests
that as the city was placed under a ban and was dedicated
as a sacrifice to God, it was necessary to strew it with salt,
which formed part of all meat offerings (Lev. ii, 13). The
strewing with salt, therefore, symbolized the offering of
the city as a sacrifice.

The shoe is used in the Old Testament in order to denote
something worthless or of little value (Amos ii, 6 ; viii, 6).
In the New Testament the act of unloosing the shoe, which
was usually performed by servants, is a symbol of servitude.
The Semites regarded it as a mark of reverence to cast off
the shoes in approaching a sacred person or place. On
two occasions we read the command in the Old Testament :
" Put off thy shoes from off thy feet, for the place whereon
thou standest is holy ground " (Exod. iii, 5 ; Joshua v, 15).
In the Mishna (Berachoth, ix, 5) we are told that no one was
permitted to pass through the temple with his shoes on.
The modern Muslim still observes this practice and leaves
his shoes outside the mosque. How did this symbolical
practice, which is found amongst many non-Semitic
peoples also, originate ? The most plausible explanation
is the following : washing was a symbol of consecration,
and it was necessary for the worshipper to wash his garments
previous to his taking part in any special sacred function
(Lev. xvi, etc.), but as shoes, on account of the material
from which they were made, could not be washed, they
were removed as an act of consecration.

Jastrow [1] thinks that the Old Testament command " to
take off one's shoes " was simply a euphemistic phrase for
" to strip oneself ". In early Babylonian art we meet

[1] *RBA.*, p. 667.

T

with figures of naked worshippers, and the cult of the Kaaba
at Mecca was conducted by the worshippers without their
clothing.   He suggests, therefore, that it was customary
in early times for the worshipper to remove his clothing
previous to his entering the presence of the deity.   Whilst
this practice may have existed amongst other peoples,
it certainly could not have taken place amongst the
Hebrews.   When   Saul   is   described   as   lying   down
" naked " (1 Sam. xix, 24), the passage means that he laid
aside his outer robe by which his rank was indicated, and
this is also probably the meaning of the passage in which
we are told that Isaiah went " naked " and barefoot
(Isa. xx, 2).

The removal of the shoe meant the giving up of a legal
right.   Hoffmann thinks that the shoe being part of the
seller's attire was now worn by the buyer, and would be
produced by him to prove his right.   A similar significance
was attached to the act in the case of the levirate marriage
(Deut. xxv, 9, 10).   The widow removed the shoe of her
late husband's brother to show that he had abandoned a
real duty.

Amongst the Arabs the removal of one's shoe was a sign
of the dissolution of one's marriage.   A man divorcing
his wife said : " She was my slipper and I cast her off." [1]
Similarly, when a declaration was issued stating that a
ruler had lost his throne, a shoe was cast off in the assembly.

A Hebrew slave who refused to take advantage of the
liberty open to him after seven years' service had one of
his ears bored with an awl and pinned to the door, to show
that he was in future to be devoted to the service of that
house [2] (Exod. xxi, 6).   Elevation to a position of superiority was symbolized by placing a crown on the head
(2 Sam. i, 10 ; 2 Kings xi, 12, etc.).   The hand was a symbol
of power.   By stretching out the hand towards a person
or by laying the hand upon the head, one symbolized the

---

[1] Robertson Smith, *Kinship and Marriage*, p. 105, n. 1.
[2] Nowack, *Heb. Arch.*, i, 177.

transference of power from one party to another. Similarly, blessing is conveyed and sin transferred by laying on of hands (Gen. xlviii, 14 ; Lev. xvi, 21). To pour water on another person's hands was to show submissiveness to him (2 Kings iii, 11), whilst by causing a person to sit at one's right hand one showed the willingness of sharing authority with him (1 Kings ii, 19 ; Ps. cx, 1 ; Job xxx, 12). Lifting up the hand and calling upon the authority of the deity was a symbol used in taking an oath (Gen. xiv, 22 ; Exod. vi, 8, etc.). The giving of the hand showed that a relationship was established between two persons (2 Kings x, 15 ; Jer. l, 15 ; Ezek. xvii, 18). The worshipper spread out his hands in prayer to show that he desired to obtain divine mercy and help (Exod. ix, 29 ; 1 Kings viii, 22, etc.). Washing of the hands was a symbol of innocence. In Deut. xxi, 4, the calf's neck was broken to show that the murderer deserved the punishment ; whilst the elders of the city, by washing their hands, showed that they were free from the guilt. Hostility towards a person is shown by gaping with the mouth (Ps. xxxv, 21 ; Job xvi, 10, etc.) ; ill-feeling by clapping the hands (Ezek. vi, 11 ; xxi, 17, 22 ; xxii, 13) or spitting in the face (Num. xii, 14 ; Deut. xxv, 9), and anger by gnashing of the teeth (Ps. xxxv, 16 ; Job xvi, 9 ; Lam. ii, 16, etc.). The key of the door was probably looked upon as a symbol of authority, and to place it upon a man's shoulder showed that he was appointed steward (Isa. xxii, 22). Covering a woman with one's mantle signified the intention of acting as her protector (Ezek. xvi, 8 ; Ruth iii, 9). The father of a new-born child acknowledged it as his offspring by placing it upon his knees (Job iii, 12). In a Babylonian poem describing the wickedness wrought by the evil spirits they are said to snatch the child from the knees of a man.[1] As kissing is a means by which parts of the body of different persons come into contact, it was naturally a symbol of affection and reverence. Kissing of princes was a mark of homage,

[1] Jastrow, *Aspects of RBA.*, p. 312.

and we read in Assyrian inscriptions of the practice of kissing the king's feet. The ground on which the king walked was kissed to show that the very dust had become sacred by the king's feet having trodden upon it. Kneeling is a mark of homage to a superior, and is therefore referred to as an attitude of worship (2 Chron. vi, 13; 1 Kings viii, 54). Bowing down or sinking the head also showed that a man humbled himself before his god.

In Babylonia it was customary for the suitor to present gifts to the girl's parents. According to some scholars this symbolized the purchase of the bride—a practice which existed in earlier times. Various symbolisms were connected with the marriage ceremony, but their meaning is obscure. The officiating ministers bound sandles on the feet of the newly-wedded pair, gave them a leather girdle, and fastened it to a pouch of silver and gold. The first of these ceremonies may have symbolized the marriage contract between them. We are told in the Code of Hammurabi that, if a maid behaves insolently towards her mistress, the latter may put an *abuttu* on her and reduce her to slavery. The adoptive parent may do the same with a disobedient son. What the *abuttu* was is unknown. Jensen has shown that it was some kind of incised mark which acted as a symbol of the person's position.[1] The repayment of a debt or the dissolution of a partnership was symbolized by the breaking of a tablet. Mutilation is often referred to as a punishment for crime, and the form of mutilation was symbolical of the offence itself. For striking a father the hand was cut off, for ingratitude evidenced by speech the tongue was cut out, as a punishment for unlawful curiosity the eye was torn out, and as a mark of disobedience the ear was often cut off. The city walls were regarded as symbols of shelter. Swearing by the gods and the king was a means of sanctioning an agreement. When a contract was made both parties and witnesses added their names to it, and this was authenticated by

[1] Perhaps one may compare the mark on Cain's forehead.

impressing their seals or making a nail mark. The Code states explicitly that a woman was not a wife without " bonds ". This was a marriage contract which symbolized an official acknowledgement of the union. An artisan symbolized his adoption of a child by teaching him a trade. The penalty for breaking the contract was the payment of two or more white horses to the god. The exact meaning of this symbolism is unknown, but it was no doubt connected with the fact that white suggested purification and innocence.

Colour has been described as the holiest, the most divine, and most solemn of all God's gifts to the sight of man. It appears that there was a developed sense of colour in the earliest stages of civilization, and stones remarkable for their colour have at all times attracted the attention of mankind and served as personal charms. The Babylonians and Assyrians were very fond of representing objects of nature through the medium of the brush, but the colours which they employed on their enamelled bricks or stuccoed walls are simply impossible from a purely naturalistic standpoint, and were apparently only chosen because the effect is pleasing. Bright light affects all the nervous elements of the eye at once and arouses a sense of appreciation. This explains why they were so very fond of gay colours without any regard for their fidelity to nature.

Although there are various references to colour in the Old Testament, the desire of the Hebrews to fulfil the command in Exod. xx, 4, at a time when painting was to a great extent in the service of idolatry, prevented the development of their colour sense and colour vocabulary. Professor Canney has pointed out [1] that in Hebrew there is no term to express that property of light known to us as colour, and when a Hebrew wished to compare one object to another he found it necessary to use the word " ayin " (eye) in the sense of appearance. The place which colours occupy amongst the ancient Hebrews in the symbolism of sentiment and worship is doubtful. In connexion with

[1] Article " Colour ", in *Encyc. Biblica.*

the construction of the tabernacle and Solomon's temple there is clearly a preference for certain colours, although many scholars do not agree that these were symbolical. But the symbolism of the colours in connexion with the priest's garments and in Zechariah and Daniel is much simpler and has generally been admitted. An examination of the passages in the Old Testament where there is a reference to colour suggests the following symbolism.

White symbolized purity and innocence, hence it was the dress of the high priest on the day of Atonement, and the angels, as holy, appear in white clothing. It represented light, which impressed the Hebrew mind not only by its brilliance and beauty but by its divine symbolism and profound moral connotation (Lev. xvi, 4, 32; Dan. vii, 9; Ps. civ, 2). As black absorbs all colours and thus buries the light, it represented death, humiliation, mourning (Mal. iii, 14; Lam. iv, 8). Blue, representing the colour of an unclouded sky, symbolized revelation (Exod. xxiv, 10). " In Biblical symbolism there is associated with the colour the idea of the blue sky, and with the blue sky the idea of the godhead coming forth from its mysterious dwelling in the unseen world, and graciously condescending to the creature." Delitzsch has shown that in various parts of the world blue is regarded as symbolizing loyalty and truth. In India a loyal man is described as unchangeable as the indigo flower. Blue was the first of the colours used for the curtains of the sanctuary, and the Israelites were commanded to have a ribbon of blue fringe in the edge of their garments in order to remind them of Jehovah (Num. xv, 38). Red, as the colour of blood, represented bloodshed, war, guilt (Zech. vi, 2). Purple was the distinguishing mark of royalty representing dignity and honour (Judges viii, 26; Esther viii, 15); whilst green, as the colour of plants—growths to which people look forward in winter—symbolized hope and resurrection, and was also the symbolic colour of the moon. Hammurabi tells us that he " bedecked the grave of Malkat with green ", the colour of resurrection.

INDEX

Creation, symbols of, 8, 164.
Cremation, 215.
Crescent, 159, 162–3, 192–3, 198.
Crown, 191, 200, 208, 274.
Cruelty, symbol of, 69.
Culture, Babylonian, 22.
Cuneiform script, 22.
Cup-markings, 181.
Curtains as symbols, 261 f.
Cutting one's hair, 226 f.
Cybele, 23, 35.
Cypress, 28, 32, 34 f.
Cyprus, coins of, 81.

D

Dagon, 56, 209.
Damkina, 102, 209.
Dancing (in mourning), 220.
Daphnæ, 21.
Darkness as symbol of wickedness, 172, 245 f.
Date-trees, 36–7.
David, 30, 99, 145, 153, 223, 255.
Dead, sacrifice to the, 215.
Death, colour of, 278.
Deborah, 19, 30, 44.
Debt, ceremony on payment of a, 8.
Decad, 143.
Decalogue, 65 ff., 260.
Decimal system, 140.
Deluge Narrative, 22, 123, 144, 153, 206.
Demons, 21, 37, 127, 129.
Designs (architectural) traceable to Assyrian date-tree, 37.
Desolation, symbols of, 42, 47.
Destruction, symbols of, 81, 189, 217.
Devas, the, 21.
Dhat anwat, 31.
Dhikr (zikr), 240, 241, 244, 247.
Didron, 5.
Digit, 140.
Dignity, marks of, 79, 278.
Dionysus, 35.
Disc, as a symbol, 72, 177 ; the solar, 17, 162, 174–5, 201 ; winged, 160, 177.
Disobedience, mark of, 276.
Distress, symbol of, 48.
Divination, liver, 60.
Divinity, horns as symbols of, 191.
Documents, drawing up of legal, 9.
Dog as a symbol, 79, 197.
Dove, 41, 56, 60, 80, 170.

Dragon, the, 8, 53, 74 ; as a symbol of chaos, 160 ; as a symbol of Marduk, 197.
Duhm, 64.
Dumbness of Ezekiel, 12.
Dungi, 218 f.
Dust as a symbol, 249 ff.

E

Ea, 30–1, 36, 57, 74, 93, 101, 105, 142, 161, 163, 197, 205 ff.
Eabani, 70, 124, 159, 217.
Eagle, the, 60, 69, 74, 82, 160, 184, 266.
Eannatum, 80, 222, 252.
Ear as symbol, the, 274, 276.
Earth, circumscribed by an ocean, 20, 115 ; regarded as a mountain, 180 ; symbol of mourning, 249 ff.
Egelyo, 63.
Egypt, 14, 20, 21 f., 28, 67, 71 f.
Egyptian symbols, 21.
Ekron, 56.
Elam, 60, 179.
Eliezer, 8, 93.
Elijah, 65, 78, 87, 94, 99, 100, 156.
Elisha, 100.
Emblems, sacred, 13, 17, 21, 159, 177; phallic, 8, 38.
Emotions, expressed by symbols, 3.
Emphasis, words repeated for, 104.
Energy, symbols of, 17, 76.
Entemena, vase of, 184.
Eternity, symbol of, 4.
Enannatum I, 43.
Ennead of Egyptian theological system, 103, 105.
Erech, 33.
Eridu, 30, 206.
Esarhaddon, 33, 60, 63, 168, 188, 198, 202, 208.
Esau, 145, 147.
Eschatology, Pythagorean, 111; Islamic, 153.
Eshmun, 76.
Esther, 48.
Etana, 74, 83, 160.
Etemenanki, 125.
Excavations in Palestine, 13, 22, 55, 63.
Exorcism, repetition of, 103.
Eye, the evil, 108, 117 ; sun represented as an, 172 f.
Eyes, of the dead, 225; represent

Neriglissar, 74.
Nero, 95.
Nesher, 82 ff.
Net, symbol of various Bab. deities, 184.
Ninazu, the god, 215.
Nineveh, Ishtar of, 14, 167 ff.
Ningirsu, 82 f., 183 ff.
Ninib, 116, 160, 163, 183, 185, 189 ff., 209.
Nippur, 161, 189, 198, 206.
Nisroch, 83.
Nobleman, Semitic deities represented as, 180.
Nose-ring, symbolism of, 229.
Numbers, sacred, 23 ; symbolism of, 87 ff.
Nusku, 142, 161, 162, 186 ff., 200.

O

Oak, the, 27, 29, 43 f.
Oannes, 207 f.
Oath, ceremonies connected with taking of an, 7, 8.
Ocean, the, symbolized by Tiamat, 206.
Oil, 271 f.
Olives, 27, 41.
Omens in Babylonia, 60.
Ophthalmia, exorcism for, 125.
Orbit, symbol of the universal, 74.
Ornamentation, symbolical, 5.
Orphics and Bacchics, 96.
Osiris, 35, 105, 130.
Ostrakon (Samaritan), 63.

P

Paintings, symbolical, 5, 53.
Palestine, coinage of, 28.
Palm, 27, 30, 32, 35, 36, 38, 39 ff., 264.
Papsukal, symbol of, 162.
Parables, use of, 3, 4, 12.
Paradise, 37, 38, 121.
Partnership, dissolution of, 8, 276.
Passions, goddess of, 32, 166.
Peace, ass as symbol of, 76, 78, 79 ; offering, symbolism of the, 263 ; trees as symbols of, 33, 41, 42, 44, 47 f.
Pergamum, 95.
Permanency, symbol of, 272.
Perpetuity, symbol of, 8.

Persia, emblem of, 82.
Pestilence, god of, 185.
Phallic emblems, see Emblems, phallic.
Philo, 6, 265, 268.
Philosophers, Jewish, 6.
Phœnician symbols, 34 ff.
Phtha, 105.
Phylacteries (Samaritan), 106.
Physiologus, 53.
Pigeons, 80.
Pillars, the temple, 46, 262.
Planets, 94, 121, 123, 133 ff., 267.
Plant of life, see Life, plant of.
Plants, 27 ff.
Plato, 6, 97, 111.
Pleasure, symbol of, 245.
Pleiades, the, 148, 153.
Pomegranate, 28, 35, 42.
Porphyry, 4, 54.
Poseidon, 23, 236.
Post, wooden, as a symbol, 33 f.
Potsherds, decorations on, 21 f.
Power, symbols of, 17, 69, 73, 78, 110, 188, 192, 274.
Prayers, repetition of, 104.
Prodigies in ancient art, 54.
Prosperity, symbols of, 44, 271.
Prostitution, ritual, 166, 255.
Protection, 44.
Pterelaus, immortality of, 236.
Purification, 145, 149, 156, 165, 186, 206, 270, 277.
Purity, symbols of, 80, 225, 278.
Purple, 278.
Pythagoreans, 23, 95 ff., 111, 118, 131, 143.

Q

Quarantine, 155.
Quarters, the four, 116.
Quaternary, 118.
Quetzalcoatl, 118.

R

Rag offering, 31, 224.
Rahab, 74.
Rain, connected with the serpent, 72 ; god of, 118.
Ramman, 183, 202 ff.
Raven, 80 f.
Rays of sun as symbols, 69.
Reanimation of plants, as symbols, 31 f.